The Life and Work
of an Eminent Psychologist

Richard S. Lazarus, PhD, obtained his BA in 1942 from the City College of New York. After military service in World War II, he returned to graduate school in 1946, obtained his doctorate at Pittsburgh in 1948, taught at Johns Hopkins and Clark Universities, then came to Berkeley in 1957, where he has remained.

Lazarus's research career at Johns Hopkins and Clark centered on New Look experiments on motivated individual differences in perception. Among other research topics such as perceptual defense and studies of projective methods, he did research on autonomic discrimination without awareness (which he and McCleary called "subception").

At Berkeley after forming the Berkeley stress and Coping Project, he mounted efforts to generate a comprehensive theoretical framework for psychological stress and undertook much programmatic research based on these formulations, pioneering the use of motion picture films to generate stress reactions naturalistically in the laboratory. Later he shifted to field research and a systems theoretical point of view. His theoretical and research efforts contributed substantially to what has been called the "cognitive revolution" in psychology.

Lazarus has published over 200 scientific articles and 18 books, both monographs and textbooks in personality and clinical psychology. In 1966, *Psychological Stress and the Coping* process, which is now considered a classic, appeared. In 1984, with Susan Folkman, he published *Stress, Appraisal, and Coping,* which continues to have world wide influence. In 1991, he published *Emotion and Adaptation,* which presents a cognitive-motivational-relational theory of the emotions.

He became Professor Emeritus at Berkeley in 1991, in which status he continues to write and publish research on stress, coping, and the emotions.

The
LIFE and WORK
of an
Eminent Psychologist

Autobiography of
Richard S. Lazarus

 Springer Publishing Company

Springer Publishing Company, Inc.
536 Broadway
New York, NY 10012-3955

Cover design by Nancy Lazarus Holliday
Acquisitions Editor: Bill Tucker
Production Editor: Kathleen Kelly

98 99 00 01 02 / 5 4 3 2 1

Library of Congress Cataloging-in-Publication-Data

Lazarus, Richard S.
    Autobiography of Richard S. Lazarus : scholar, teacher, and pioneer in stress, coping, and emotions / Richard S. Lazarus.
        p.   cm.
    Includes bibliographical references and index.
    ISBN 0-8261-1179-3
    1. Lazarus, Richard S.   2. Psychologists—United States—Biography.   3. Spiritual biography—United States.   I. Title.
BF109.L38A3   1998
150'.92—dc21
[B]   98-10419
                                                                       CIP

Printed in the United States of America

To My Family, with Love:
First and foremost, Bernice
Then David, Mary, Jessica, and Adam Lazarus,
and last but not least, Nancy, Rick, Maiya McKenzie,
and Ava Rose Holliday

Contents

Preface

Today it is very fashionable for celebrities to write autobiographies. People in the public eye attract readers interested in learning all sorts of juicy tidbits about familiar personages. Powerful political figures reveal the inside story of the making of important decisions, which affect us all. Not being a public celebrity—my visibility and influence extends to the relatively narrow circle of academic psychology and cognate disciplines—why should I write an autobiography? What are the objectives of a personal narrative?

If I include my first academic job in 1948, I have been teaching at universities for 45 years before retiring in 1991, 34 of those years as a Professor of Psychology at the University of California at Berkeley. So what I write about myself would, I hope, interest psychologists and students. And, because I came from rather lowly origins and circumstances, much of the struggle to get ahead could have inspirational value to younger persons regardless of their field of interest.

But there are other important objectives in writing my life history. I grew up during a momentous period of modern life, the changes in psychology itself and the public events of those times have had an enormous contemporary impact. My life and times include the Great Depression of the 1930s, World War II, the period of economic and professional expansion during the 1950s and 1960s, the Korean War, Vietnam, the cold war and the breakup of the Soviet Union; vast changes have occurred in business, industry, finance, and communications, which have moved from a national to an international focus, and I have witnessed growing racial and ethnic tension, not only in the United States but throughout the world. A major task of this autobiography is to chart some of these changes as they relate to my own particular experience.

Even more important would be to write an intellectual history of how academic and professional thought in psychology have been transformed over my lifetime. My intention is also to examine how my choice of field, and the way I have addressed it, reflect the influence of my childhood and the the way things were as I was growing up and during my adult years. I wish to tackle that most obscure of questions—namely, how life experiences and social environments can shape one's mature professional life.

Let me speak a bit here about the importance of one's personal perspective, which is a consistent theme that runs through my entire intellectual history. A life is centered on goals, beliefs, hopes, fears, resentments, strengths, and weaknesses. It follows a trajectory from birth to death, with major and minor events and transitions, some common to most people, others unique, some anticipated, others not.

Yet the most important feature of an autobiographical narrative is the unique outlook of the writer. Hundreds of autobiographical accounts may be written about the same societal events during the same time period. Each individual story, however, is different, both in what is perceived and emphasized, and the interpretations that are made about what happened. Every personal narrative is distinctive because the psychological impact of every event depends on the individual who is reacting.

The Great Depression and World War II affected me in ways that apply to no other individual and this is part of the story I have to tell. It is the small details of what happens rather than large-scale events that carry weight in shaping individual life choices—for example, where one lives, one's education, career, family, and the emotions and moods emerging from social transactions.

What is it we really remember when we write an autobiography? We are always constructing and reconstructing our past in the present; our ideas about that past change with the passage of time. What we remember is not necessarily factual events, but some distillate of them, which is given an interpretation, a meaning (e.g., Bruner, 1990; Spence, 1984). This doesn't mean that our memories are distortions of reality, though they can be. They are compromises between the need to perceive one's life realistically and the desire to put a positive complexion on it, one that fits our understanding of who and what we are.

The compromise usually retains the essence of reality and preserves what is critical to a person's view of self. No one can truly gainsay the validity of this construction. This is all the more true when, as in my case, the person who writes about his history is over 70 (I began writing it at age 74), when most of the life course has already been lived, and at the turn of the century, I will be close to 80.

But something else is important about autobiography as a source of data in psychology, especially for our understanding of personality. This is a time of considerable intellectual interest in the use of personal narratives in the study of individuality. Although many could be cited, I know of no more impressive examination of this than the recent discussions and research of McAdams (1996; McAdams, Diamond, de St. Aubin, & Mansfield, 1997).

McAdams suggests that the self develops over time. Modern men and women expect to live well into their 70s and more, so they think of themselves as growing and changing over their lives, and have a keen sense of past, present, and future. We seek coherence in our selves or identities over time, and we want to relate who we are to the conditions of the modern world.

McAdams writes that "A person's identity is not to be found in behavior, nor—important though it is—in the reaction of others, but in the capacity to keep a particular narrative going" (McAdams cited in Giddens, 1991, p. 54). McAdams is, in effect, proposing a theory of personality built around the narrative study of individual persons based on an integrated sense of self. Each person achieves this throughout what he calls selfing—that is, its active construction throughout a lifetime.

There are those who think that creating and sustaining a clear personal identity in the so-called postmodern world is difficult, if not impossible, because our assumptions about objectivity and rational discourse, belief in progress, and the coherence of political and economic systems have been so effectively challenged. One of the major critics of modern social psychology, Kenneth Gergen (1992) has questioned our ability to find unity and purpose in our lives as a result of constant change and the present-day overload of contradictory social roles and pressures.

Edward Sampson (1989) too has suggested that there is no longer any internally sensed temporal coherence to our lives. Diverse surrounds and contexts create evanescent selves, and what we call the self resides in the outside world rather than within the mind, in a crazy quilt of settings and influences. We are defined by the many and contradictory social settings in which we find ourselves today.

McAdams (1996, p. 307) defines a life story as "an internalized and evolving narrative of the self that incorporates the reconstructed past, perceived present, and anticipated future." Is the claim that one can no longer construct a coherent and committed self and life story an accurate portrayal of people today? Does it apply only to the present generation? How does an elderly man or woman deal with the past, present, and the future? The chapters that follow offer one person's answers to these questions, especially the last.

Whatever one says about this, I believe my life story coincides with McAdams's definition. In my autobiography, however, the emphasis is as much on an intellectual history—that is, my contributions to the psychology of stress, emotion, and coping and how they came about, as it is a personal history. My narrative keeps going into the present; the story has not yet ended. Despite all this postmodern talk of value confusion and its deconstructionism, I am also convinced it is still possible to pilot one's way through life in today's world.

When writing an autobiography, it usually seems best to begin at the beginning, which means one's birth and childhood. I have what might be considered a happy quality of not remembering too many of the details of my past, especially from early childhood. I regard my childhood and adolescence as dismal times, and I suspect that I never wanted to look back at what really happened.

Nevertheless, in my first chapter, I try to speak a bit about what I remember of my childhood and youth. It mainly provides a bit of chapter and verse for the emotional and coping patterns that have lasted my lifetime, and to suggest ways in which my intellectual history was influenced by them. The events I talk about stand out in my mind as important in shaping what I became. Or, perhaps more accurately, they seem emblematic of the atmosphere of my early development.

As distinguished from a memoir, a life story draws on numerous personal experiences, which are commonly presented sequentially, typically from childhood to a time in later life. To make the account interesting to more than family and friends, there need to be guiding themes and an organizing framework that pulls together the disparate strands of a life that make the events of the narrative comprehendible. One wants to know the significance of each event, and how it reveals the special qualities that make a person distinctive.

An organizing framework draws on two main forces—namely, environmental events, such as family atmosphere, social values, and economic and political forces, and how these events are construed and reacted to by the person who experienced them. Together with biological givens, all this combines to create a person who filters what happens through a mind which, somewhat like a prism, reflects and also distorts what has happened. The person, in effect, influences how the environmental events are presented and understood.

I have chosen to provide a framework in this Preface that focuses on themes of emotional conflict, which are not always flattering but have dominated my life, and how I coped with them. These themes, and my ways of coping, provide the glue that holds the stories of my life and times together. Spelling them out here briefly should make it easier for the reader to see in later chapters how events and times helped shape my personality and, in turn, how my personality influenced my professional development, attitudes, and decisions.

The themes are two contradictory but interdependent emotional outlooks that have dominated my ego-identity from childhood on. One consists of doubts about my resources and the need to be accepted by others. The opposing theme consists of efforts to be effective and in control of my life as much as possible. I have always wanted to be and look competent, if not wonderful. My self-doubts have been the main downside of my life, and my efforts to compensate for this produces the upside—that is, my sanguinity, hope, enthusiasm, and striving for achievement.

The downside, which arose from a sense of alienation, is connected in part with parental rejection. It also derives from my being a Jew, and the keen awareness that Jews have long been despised in the world. The hatred of Jews is not, of course, universal, though it was nurtured by the Catholic Church and manifested in particularly ugly historical episodes, such as the Spanish Inquisition and the Nazi genocide of European Jews. But this cannot be blamed solely on the Nazis, because the hatred was also nourished for ages throughout most of Europe, as the ugly behavior of other people during this period attests. It remains a long-standing blot on Christianity. Although these terrible events did not happen to me directly, I grew up with their images stamped indelibly on my mind.

In the United States anti-Semitism was especially virulent during the Great Depression of the 1930s when economic suffering was widespread and public figures, such as Father Coughlin, ranted and raved about Jews on American radio. This was when I grew up and my sense of self was formed.

The effects of prejudice on a child are quite unpredictable. I grew up feeling like an alien, first in my own home, and second in the social world. This taught me to believe that religion is a divisive influence in the world, supporting hatred of those who believe differently.

I was and am a nonobservant Jew who is suspicious of organized religion—especially orthodoxy—and, in the main, I view it as destructive and hypocritical. In my eyes, the formal institutional churches of the world, every one of them, constantly violate what they profess to believe about God and their own humanity. In this respect, I am a pessimist about the human species, which seems capable of the most terrible cruelty. Yet, for some obscure reason, I am a pessimist who hopes.

The other, contradictory, and more positive side of my nature, stems, in part, from my counterphobic defense against feelings of inadequacy and the fear of social rejection. Counterphobia means that one does the opposite of what one fears, refusing to permit the fear to dominate. The need to become competent was born of my childish wish to demonstrate to my parents, especially my father, that I was worthy of respect and love. I was really okay. Not just okay, but outstanding, better than others. I dreamed of being a great man, and I admired those who made important artistic, literary, and scientific contributions, often against the odds.

Another source of my sanguinity is the belief that there is a humane and decent side to humans, which can sometimes compensate for the ugliness of our species, and which has been manifest throughout history. It is this belief that powers my hope that somehow, without it being merely a utopian wish or a denial of reality, society can be improved. There is always, however, a "yes, but," and a sense of disappointment as my life comes to a close, that we have not made any real gains in the quality of life over the thousands of years during which history has recorded the human condition.

Still, it is the everlasting hope of betterment which, perhaps, might explain why I am rarely depressed. But given what psychologists think about this disorder, I really don't understand this absence of clinical depression, considering that I manifest all the ways of thinking that are associated with depression and suicide. This suggests that psychology doesn't yet fully understand the clinical problem.

In any case, in order to survive psychologically, I committed myself to intellectual pursuits. I represent a late incarnation of the Age of Reason in a time of postmodern deconstructionism and creeping nihilism. I became something of a perfectionist in my work, especially after I began to find increasing success. I polish my articles and books many times, rewriting again and again, certain that they can always be made better. Each time I experienced success, it reinforced my sense of competence. To me, knowledge is power, over the world, and over oneself. This conviction, and my own need to understand, led me to psychology.

Most of my life I have been poised between these two opposing attitudes, inner uncertainty and anger at human folly on the dour side, and contrary pride and sanguinity on the side of striving and doing. Anger directed outwardly against the world—and I have plenty of it—feels better than shame and anxiety. When you blame someone else rather than yourself, you need not feel so bad. And when you rail against someone or something, you gain at least the illusion of acting vigorously against your ills, which opposes the helplessness of anxiety.

I don't mean to suggest that these conflicting trends within me are unique or even unusual. They are to be found in many people; however, they have been important in my life and explain much about me. Because similar conflicts are widespread, especially in young people, perhaps knowing how it was with me and how I dealt with it might have value for readers, young and old, who find themselves engaged in similar struggles.

Before I proceed, I want to express my gratitude to my publisher, Dr. Ursula Springer, and Bill Tucker, Springer's managing editor, for having the temerity to publish my autobiography. Most publishers relegate autobiographies and memoirs to the Trade Department, and these days potential profit is always what determines the decision to publish such a book.

Their conviction that my book would be of sufficient interest to justify its publication makes it possible for me to gain a readership for what I have to say late in life. Together, we see this book as a document that is relevant to the history of psychology, a narrative that throws useful intellectual light on the nature of academic life, and a personal document about one particular psychologist that could encourage younger persons coming into the field. The Springer staff has been wonderful to work with. I hope the fate of this book justifies their support. And so, on to my life story.

REFERENCES

Bruner, J. (1990). *Acts of meaning.* Cambride, MA: Harvard University Press.

Gergen, K. J. (1992). *The saturated self: Dilemmas of identity in modern life.* New York: Basic Books.

Giddens, A. (1991). *Modernity and self-identity: Self and society in the late modern age* (p. 547). Stanford, CA: Stanford University Press.

McAdams, D. P. (1996). Personality, modernity, and the storied self: A contemporary framework for studying persons. *Psychological Inquiry, 7,* 295–321.

McAdams, D. P., Diamond, A., de St. Aubin, E., & Mansfield, E. (1997). Stories of commitment: The psychosocial construction of generative lives. *Journal of Personality and Social Psychology, 72,* 678–694.

Sampson, E. E. (1989). The challenge of social change for psychology: Globalization and psychology's theory of the person. *American Psychologist, 44,* 914–921.

Spence, D. (1984). *Narrative truth and historical truth: Meaning and interpretation in psychoanalysis.* New York: Norton.

CHAPTER ONE

Early Life

Though it was a year of economic recession, when I was born in 1922 the overall economy of the country was thriving and the mood expansive. My father was a silk salesman working for a Manhattan wholesaler who sold cloth to dress manufacturers. My parents lived in upper Manhattan in a flat on 177th Street and Humbolt Avenue.

Soon after I was born we moved to a better neighborhood, a beautiful, spacious upper-middle-class apartment in a brand-new building overlooking the Hudson River on Haven Avenue at 177th Street. For much of my early years we had a maid and in retrospect I realize we were affluent. This home in Washington Heights, New York City is what I remember during my public school years, until the economic pressures of the 1930s forced us to move to midtown Manhattan on a rapid slide into poverty.

One reason for the maid was that my mother, as I was told by my father many years later, had a postpartum depression after I was born. Afterward, she could never manage to care for our household. When I was old enough to sense this, she always seemed to be a person who needed to be taken care of, but who couldn't take care of anyone else, including her own children.

In 1929 when I was 7, the stock market crashed, followed by a disastrous economic depression that didn't end until World War II. Most people have heard about the soup kitchens; previously substantial men were now selling apples and pencils on street corners. Unemployment was disastrously high—I believe it was estimated at a quarter to a third of the men who wanted to work—but no safety net existed for them. Though some did well, it was a great social tragedy for too many, and any popular sanguinity about the stability and quality of our society was badly shaken.

When my father could not find work during the Depression, and we no longer had a maid, he did all the shopping, cooking, washing, and organizing of the household. He was a take-charge type of man, very organized, compulsive, and demanding of order and efficiency. In those days, there were no washing machines or dryers. I can remember my father putting our laundry into a big aluminum vat placed over two gas burners on the stove. The clothes were boiled, removed, and hand scrubbed with soap on a washboard. Then they were hung with clothespins on lines hanging from the kitchen ceiling, which could be lowered and, when loaded with wash, raised to the ceiling where they would stay until dry.

While we lived on Haven Avenue we were in very good shape, and if there were emerging economic problems, I was not aware of them. I would walk with friends or relatives to Broadway and visit the stores and theaters of the neighborhood. Many local theaters showed a movie or two followed by vaudeville with live stage acts, which included singers, comedians, acrobats, and skits. I wasn't excited by the singers, but I loved the comedians and their skits, and the acrobats.

From my street I could watch the construction of the George Washington Bridge. It began to rise in a slow, graceful curve from both the Manhattan and New Jersey sides, ultimately to meet in the center. I always wondered how they would get it to connect precisely in the middle of the river and was told only that engineers knew how to do such things. The Holland and Lincoln Tunnels to New Jersey were also constructed under the Hudson River while I lived on Haven Avenue. We had no car, but when we were driven through a tunnel, it was sobering to think that we were below the water level of the river, sunk deep into the mud. That thought always made me slightly uneasy. In case of disaster, there would be no escape.

Most distressing was the tearing down of the small park between our street and the Hudson River to accommodate the highway approaches to the bridge. This forever changed our New York City neighborhood from feeling almost like a small town to a big congested city. The bridge and its approaches made us lose snake hill, where we took our sleds when there was enough snow. In New York, and I suppose most places if you wait long enough, change is the order of the day. I remember many years later returning to this neighborhood from the West Coast only to find that my block and its buildings, including the apartment house I remembered so well, no longer existed.

As our economic situation deteriorated during the Depression, we had to leave Haven Avenue, and with each subsequent move we went to cheaper apartments in poorer neighborhoods signifying a worsening of our economic condition. The downward economic slide eventuated in our living in a dingy apartment on 87th Street between

Amsterdam and Columbus Avenues. This had once been an elegant neighborhood, but by then it was badly deteriorated, and long before my parents died, it became a crime-ridden slum. By this time I had a brother, five years my junior, and we shared a small bedroom. I must have been about 13 years old when we lived there.

My bed was by a window that looked out over a courtyard, a little like the one portrayed in the movie *Rear Window,* with James Stewart and Grace Kelly, except that it was less attractive and spacious—the courtyard was a back alley, and the neighboring apartments were very close. Here, when bored, I would look into other apartment windows or drop matches onto the cement floor of the courtyard below, which would light with a loud crack, like a firecracker. These were not the paper safety matches we use today, which can only be lit by scraping them over a chemically treated surface on the match box, but the kind used to light the gas stove merely by scratching the match head on any rough surface.

When I was a bit older, I would visit the Roxy and Paramount theaters, and Radio City Music Hall in downtown Manhattan, which was a short subway ride away. In addition to movies, the vaudeville there was of a higher caliber than in our neighborhood, and the acts in later years included big bands and the famous Rockettes, a line of beautiful, scantily clad, but always dignified, precision dancers that are still famous as a New York attraction.

After my mother's depression, she took up the Christian Science religion whose dogma viewed illness as the result of mortal error or sin. Christian Scientists would not go to a doctor when sick; they didn't need medicine, but a proper dose of the Christ ideal. You must pray to cleanse your spirit of evil thoughts, which were said to result in bodily ailments. Joining this church helped her state of mind greatly. However, the religious outlook, along with its focus on Jesus, was anathema to my father, and even more so to his mother, whose Romanian Jewish origins made her want to disown her daughter-in-law. To preserve a hostile peace, my mother had to agree to raise her two boys as Jews and, luckily for me when I had acute appendicitis, to receive medical care.

Later my mother became a Christian Science Practitioner, which provided income that was badly needed when my father was no longer able to earn a living. Christian Science has no preachers or ministers; practitioners serve that function. In those days, they were not allowed to charge fees, but clients normally made donations.

I also think being aware of my mother's esoteric religion probably enhanced my interest in psychology. The magical, shamanistic features were probably an even more important influence. They led me to emphasize facts and reason in my life—in effect, I adopted a scientific outlook in opposition to my mother's outlook, which, to me, resembled the Middle Ages, with their dark, primitive superstitions so impressively portrayed in Ingmar Bergman's classic movie, *The Seventh Seal.*

After she became skillful at it, my mother's practitioning produced considerable money, more than my parents were willing to admit, probably because not being able to support his family embarrassed and embittered my father. I suspect too they didn't want to undermine their very stingy attitude by acknowledging they had more; that might have led me to ask for too much.

During my childhood, my mother spent most of her time at the local Christian Science Reading Room and eating lunch, usually alone, at fancy local restaurants. I might be referred to as a latchkey child, except that I was not trusted to have a key, and so I wandered the streets without supervision until one of my parents came home. Rather than being—as the Jewish mother is often described—a matriarchal but nurturing tyrant, my mother played a negative role in my life.

My mother was the butt of much hostility from my father, but it was also directed at my brother and me. This led her to deeply resent her position, but she also feared my father's wrath and contempt. She was chronically angry and insensitive, and in trying to defend herself as best as she could, she took her marital problems out on her sons and was unable to show any genuine warmth.

So when I needed to be reassured and protected from my father's psychological assaults, she could give me no emotional support. She usually went along with whatever my father thought and did, often chiming in with the same contemptuous manner. Psychologists would refer to her behavior with the explanatory phrase "identifying with the aggressor"—that is, my father. And she was no slouch in that department. It is important to say that we were never physically harmed. Psychological assault is a different kettle of fish from physical assault, but it is still a terrible way to grow up.

Yet later on, in my 20s, in what was a strangely defensive twist, I considered it fortunate that my mother had not been nurturing and protective. Jewish mothers are apt to socialize their children through guilt, which traps them into guilt-ridden efforts to be good children who sacrifice their own emerging identities. I had seen other Jewish boys having a difficult time achieving independence and autonomy long after becoming adults. Had my mother been more nurturing, I suspect, it would have left me ambivalent, forever feeling guilty, and maybe unable to break away.

From my father's viewpoint, I could never do anything right. Were it not for his constant contempt and denigration of my competencies, I might have had more sympathy for his own plight. With the advent of the Depression, he could no longer get a job selling, but had nothing else to which to turn. He felt he was smarter than most others, and probably was, but had become a victim of forces beyond his control.

Left at age 10 by his father's desertion to care for his mother, younger brother, and sister, he had to end his schooling to help support them. His own father had abandoned the family, and if one thinks stereotypically about the family attitudes of Jews, this is a very un-Jewish thing to do. No one in the family ever heard from him again. On the other hand, as I considered his wife, my grandmother, to be an unpleasant and self-centered battle-axe, I never thought it odd that he had deserted.

What happened to my father in the Depression was terrible and had a profound influence on my growing up. Up to that time he had been receiving a good commission on everything he sold. Dress manufacturing had become a marginal business. Complicating all this was the fact that expensive silks were being replaced by cheaper synthetic fibers, such as rayon and acetates and, of course, Nylon and Orlon much later. Eventually, his company put him on what was called a "drawing." That is, he was given a weekly salary, but if his commissions did not equal what he was paid, it became a debt he had to repay. Eventually, the debt grew so large there was no longer any prospect that he could repay it, so he lost his job, and a succession of those that followed, and eventually was unable find any work.

My father was miscast as a salesman. A bright man with a sardonic sense of humor, angry at the world, certain that he would have done better if he had been educated, I couldn't imagine a more demeaning type of work for such an arrogant and embittered man. In order to sell, a salesman has to ingratiate himself with his potential customers—hardly the right role for someone who saw things as he did. Before the Depression, when the New York dress business was thriving, his stock-in-trade was knowing his merchandise, and though people didn't like him, they would buy from him because they trusted his judgment. Later, when the business was failing, he needed to do what he could not—namely, be the ingratiating salesman.

When I later became a college professor, to digress briefly, I initially saw myself as the antithesis of my salesman-father; I was a scholar who had something to say that students needed to hear. A professor professes. To my mind, professors were prophets who creatively but accurately interpret the world of knowledge and ideas for neophytes who, if they had sufficient drive, would want to learn what professors had to teach. And so I felt superior to my father.

It took me a decade or so of teaching and scholarly research to realize how wrong I had been. The reality is that the success of scholars depends on how well they "sell" their ideas. In effect, they must convince others that what they do is sound and important. I too was a salesman, and to think otherwise is to show some of the arrogance I spoke of in the Preface.

The Jewish attitude toward the scholar was always respectful, to say the least. A rabbi was regarded as someone who should be very knowledgeable, and who could teach that knowledge. This may be one reason so many Jewish immigrants to the United States were attracted to university life, especially when, after World War II, universities became accessible to Jews and other minorities, and why I ultimately thought favorably about being a professor.

In late adolescence through adulthood, I heartily disliked both my parents, felt rejected by them and, in turn, rejected them in a struggle to be my own person. As much as possible, I turned off my ungratified need for a nurturing parent. Nevertheless, I did imitate my father (psychologists, including me, would say identify with) in many ways, but selectively. Children do not simply absorb their parents' ways and outlooks, the word "absorb" here is used as an analogy to osmosis. Rather, they are always selective, picking up traits that are deemed useful in adaptation, or powerful in influencing the world (see Bandura, Ross, & Ross, 1963), rejecting those that are not.

Sometimes children pick up traits that are opposite of those manifested by their parents, and I did too. For example, I wanted to be what my father could not be, kind, thoughtful, sensitive to others' needs, and accepting of their faults. This was also a way to seek his approval, though I never succeeded in obtaining it. On the other hand, I admired and respected my father's intelligence and mental agility, his highly organized way of managing things, his conscientiousness, competence, and tendency to dominate and control. I also wished I could be as cool and detached as he seemed to be.

SCHOOL

I was usually bored in school. In fourth grade, I sat in the back of the room throwing spitballs. Discipline was strict, and I was brought before the principal and sent back to third grade where my shame was viewed by the teacher whom I had loved earlier on, Miss Bouton. (Isn't it remarkable that I have remembered such an obscure name for nearly 70 years, though I can generate no image of her face.) I didn't stay in third grade very long, but I was so chastened that, thereafter, I watched my p's and q's, which did nothing for my boredom.

Nevertheless, I must have respected accomplishment very much. When I graduated from sixth grade, I was awed by a fellow student, Robert Goodman (name changed), who was class valedictorian. I thought he was terrific. Oh to be so socially adept and intellectually accomplished! I was green with envy. Forty-eight years later in California, my daughter and son-in-law had a small party at which one of the guests, nearly my age and originally from New York, was named Goodman. I suddenly remembered Robert Goodman of sixth grade and asked if they were related. Imagine my amazement at learning that Robert Goodman was his younger brother. He was amazed too, and a bit appalled to hear of my Goodman worship in grade school. He told me that the Robert Goodman I admired had done poorly later in life and seemed to be something of a jerk. *Sic transit gloria mundi.*

In those days a modestly bright student could get through public school faster than average. I lost half a year in grade school because I had scarlet fever, a dangerous disease in the days before antibiotics. But I gained a year and a half by skipping grades and another year by going to junior high. Therefore, I started high school 2 years ahead of the normal schedule, which meant that I entered college at 16 rather than 18.

For a long time it seemed that skipping did me no good. I was always too young for my school placement, an immature kid without direction or interest in school, just going dutifully. However, one thing these accelerations accomplished was to allow me to finish college at the age of 20, before being drafted into the army in World War II. This meant I didn't have to go back to college after the war, but could start graduate work immediately after I was discharged.

When I finished junior high, I went to De Witt Clinton High School in the Bronx. Townsend Harris was then the top-rated school in the city, but I didn't apply there because I didn't think my grades were good enough to get in. We had already moved to 87th Street in midtown Manhattan. That meant an hour's subway ride to Mosholu Parkway in the Bronx.

Still a bored kid, something of a loner, I would take the elevated train home from the Bronx to Manhattan. I liked to look into the slum tenements as we rode by to see what was going on inside. Sometimes on warm spring or fall days, I threw small pebbles mischievously out the open window of the nearly empty train, which landed on the street below. Because I never studied unless I had to, doing this wiled the time away.

It was also in high school that I found myself unable to buy a decent lunch. There seemed to be no money for it, so I frequently ate a pretzel or a Milky Way. I can't remember a single course I took, a memorable teacher, or an impressive experience during those dismal years. I got my kicks playing pickup baseball, touch football, hockey on roller skates in the (asphalt) gutter, or tennis in Central Park. I was skinny but coordinated, and always effective in sports, though I never went out for school athletics.

Luckily, when the time came for me to go to college, my grades were good enough to make it into the City College of New York (CCNY), an outstanding local college where poor immigrant kids could get a free higher education if they were intellectually able. I didn't realize it at the time, but CCNY turned out a remarkable number of young people of that generation, who later achieved high prominence in a wide range of fields.

The youths who went there recognized that their future lay in getting the best education they could. They didn't have the means to go to costly private schools, such as New York University, Columbia, and the Ivy League colleges of the East Coast, or to live out of town. And as the faculty at CCNY was outstanding, these students received a first-rate education, which gave them an impressive start in life when they graduated. I have always felt grateful for this and it made possible my lifelong career.

As an immature 16-year-old I did no better in my first year of college than I had done in high school. I spent my lunch and study hours playing Ping-Pong in the CCNY alcoves and did little studying. The result was I received too many D's to remain in good standing. I was placed on probation, which required me to take a limited 12-unit program, and I was in danger of flunking out. That scared me so much I began to shape up.

In my last 2 years, when I was majoring in psychology and minoring in sociology, I did so well that overall, with better than a B average, I had a decent chance to get into graduate school. What is equally important is that I began to find quite a few subjects very interesting, which stimulated me to think of going to graduate school. I graduated in 1942 at 20 years of age, and because we were already in World War II, I was subject to the draft and classified as 1A.

WORK

Among the most notable events of my college days were those connected with the Depression, work, and the struggle to earn money.

There was no tuition at CCNY, but there were modest fees, and the need to buy textbooks. I lived at home (the college was often referred to as a subway school). I ate breakfast and supper at home, but had to buy my own lunches.

Textbooks were always a problem, but in those days the instructors at CCNY were cognizant of the large number of impecunious students, so they used the same books year after year. This made it possible to buy and sell used books for most courses. At the beginning of every semester, students would wander about the basement alcoves of the main building with signs indicating the books they had to sell and the prices. Five cents for this book, 15 cents for that, and so forth. Those were the days when you could get a pretty good lunch in a Chinese restaurant for 25 cents, consisting of egg-drop soup, American style chow mein with crisp noodles and rice, and dessert consisting of a slice of canned pineapple served with an almond cookie. Ice cream sundaes were 15 cents and ice cream sodas 10 cents.

There were few jobs to be had. I won't burden the reader with details of the temporary, catch-as-catch-can jobs I managed to find, such as delivering flowers after classes. One job, however, is worth special mention, because it reflected the 1940s way of doing business in large department stores before the advent of credit cards and computers. It also led to an episode that caused me deep shame.

I was employed by Franklin Simon, a high-class department store in downtown New York. My responsibility was to transfer customer invoices and cash, which were sent on a fast round trip between the salesclerk's station and a central cashier. The record of each sale was placed in a bullet-like container, which was forced by compressed air through pneumatic tubes to whatever location they were needed. I sat at the intersection of a number of criss-crossing tubes and had to reroute the paperwork to the right place. Concretely, this meant putting all the red containers into one chute, all the greens into another, and so on, after opening each one up to check on the accuracy of the color coding.

It was a primitive mode of transportation for billing and paying after a sale, but it worked. Students were often used for this kind of work, typically hired for 2 half-days a week, typically on Thursday and Saturday afternoons. With experience, the work became automatized and required little effort or attention. I was able to bring my books and study during lulls in sales activity.

I am mortified to say that I lost that job because of stealing. Whatever possessed me to remove a few dollars here and there from the projectiles without realizing I would surely be caught, I simply can't understand. But after a time, I was simply told I no longer had the job. Nothing was said about stealing, but they must have known. Shocked by my cupidity and stupidity, and deeply ashamed, from that time on I was determined to avoid any further stain on my integrity.

Sometimes I may have carried this determination a bit too far. I am, for example, the only Principal Investigator I have ever heard of who, while at Berkeley, returned nearly a million dollars of research grant money because I didn't think I could deliver the data promised by the grant application. It was a project to study coping with the discovery by patients that they have cancer as a result of a medical biopsy. Although the necessary approval was obtained from the hospital staffs, including surgeons, the surgeons were refusing to refer their patients, claiming they were too upset and vulnerable for them to be studied.

The irony is that typically surgeons give almost no attention to the psychological needs of their patients—though oncologists often do better—so their claim was a self-protective rationalization, which prevented the patients from an opportunity to be helped by our study. We would have been among the few professionals to listen to and empathize with their distress, something they couldn't get from the technically oriented surgeons who had little or no interest in them as persons.

When faced with insurmountable research problems, it is common for investigators to rapidly redesign their studies, keep the funds and, in all likelihood, fall far short of producing useable findings. Doing this seemed dishonest to me, and placed my research integrity at risk. I was struck by the fact that both the granting agency and the university administration were nonplussed at my decision, the former because the funds would not be returned to them to pursue other research programs, the latter because the overhead funds would be lost to the campus. I'm sure I gained no friends as a result of my neurotic concerns about integrity.

CAMP COUNSELING IN THE SUMMER

Before and during my college years, I was a camp counselor, and although appearing trivial (it was characterized that way by my father, who thought I should be earning more money), it was important work in preparing me for adulthood. I write about this because I would like to bring this kind of work out of the realm of pure self-indulgence and convey some of its practical value and romance. More than any other early influence except the Army, I believe it helped me grow up and feel I was competent and effective.

It all began when, at 10 years of age, I was pushed into being a camper at the Boy Scout Camp at Ten Mile River in southwestern New

York state. It took some urging by my father to get the Boy Scouts to waive their requirement that a boy be at least 12 years of age to be eligible. I was present at the discussions with my father when I was allowed to go that summer. Although really quite immature, I made a good impression when interviewed. I have no illusions about my parents' motives in sending me. I think the purpose was to get rid of me during the summer months. Nor did I know anything about the financial arrangement involved, but I believe the cost was very modest.

I went to the Boy Scout Camp each summer for several years, and soon got to love it. Naturally athletic, I learned archery, swimming, boating, and canoeing, and became more proficient in all the other summer sports. This later led to my being a camper-waiter, and eventually, I think when I was 14 to 16, to become a camp counselor at private camps in the Adirondack mountains of upper New York State. I was able to draw on my Boy Scout Camp experience when I later became a camp counselor—for example, as archery or waterfront counselor. I did this type of work every summer until the fall of 1943 when I graduated City College with a Bachelor of Arts degree shortly before I was drafted.

During the months of July and August, the water in Adirondack lakes, which is ice cold much of the year, becomes mild enough to swim in without feeling chilled. The countryside was verdant and unspoiled, and the weather warm with cool nights. When I spent my summers there, at different children's camps and lakes, I thought it was idyllic.

The children, ranging from the subteens to well into adolescence, were assigned to bunks, usually wooden structures—though less pretentious camps made use of tents raised up on wooden flooring. The kids were grouped on the basis of age, six or eight to a bunk. Boy and girl campers were segregated, each going to separate camps, sometimes with both on the same lake but at a distance from each other. Camps varied in their elegance, but in the one's I worked at, each bunk had a community shower, toilets, and sinks, and was served by one or two counselors who varied in age from 14 to 20, with responsibilities tied to experience, age, and salary.

The job of a counselor, comparable to a surrogate dad, was to keep order among the kids, get them involved in the endless schedule of activities, which included a variety of sports, waterfront (swimming, boating, canoeing), and drama, music and songs. At evening campfires I told Indian stories and was referred to as Chief Dickie-boy. The kids liked them so much they would often clamor for me to do my thing, and I enjoyed doing this immensely.

   Good counselors kept the kids well disciplined, happy, involved, eating and looking well, especially on weekends or special occasions when parents would come for a visit. At most camps, counselors had a day off each week. I used it to travel around by hitching rides, say, to Saratoga Springs, New York, to Lake Champlaign in Vermont, or wherever it seemed interesting. Given the continuous responsibility and daily din at camp, the silence and ease of the day off was very welcome.

   Where the boys' and girls' camps adjoined, the counselors and other employees could socialize, date, and explore their sexuality. In some camps, this kind of mixing was discouraged by the owners, for the obvious reason that all sorts of problems could arise from dating, drinking, and the exhaustion produced by late-night activities. If I remember right, most of us managed to overlook the restrictions, and a natural feature of counselor life was sorting out early in the season who would date whom.

   Salaries for counselors were very modest, even by depression standards, and we had to negotiate each season for the best pay we could get. We received room and board, which was a substantial financial asset. In the beginning, I made from about $50 to $150 a summer in free cash, untaxed because my total earnings did not warrant filing a tax return at the end of the year, even with tips from appreciative parents sometimes added at the end of the season. One season I was not paid the $75 my contract specified because the owner went bankrupt. I liked him and felt sorry for him, but my father thought he was a crook and I a fool.

   In my next-to-last summer, I received the munificent sum of $500 for being a waterfront counselor. I was proud of negotiating it, but even that amount did not impress my father, who considered my camp obsession to be a gross self-indulgence in a time of economic hardship. Waterfront counselors were generally well paid because of the heavy responsibilities of managing the boats, canoes, swimming times for the whole camp, and swim meets. The youngest children had to be taught to swim, and because swimming had its dangers, the whole process had to be closely supervised. My last summer as a camp counselor followed graduation from college. I knew it would be the last, because it was time for me to find a regular, year-round job and go to graduate school. I became one of the two head counselors and received $500 for the season of 10 weeks.

   Most camps, including this one, had an institution referred to as color war, which was usually scheduled a week or two before the end of the season. Many camp owners wished this tradition didn't exist, because the kids were usually exhausted by the frenetic activity, sometimes emotionally distressed, and they spent the last anticlimactic week or so before going home like zombies, waiting for the time to leave. Parents would find their kids looking bedraggled when they came to pick them up to go home. Owners worried that this was bad for the camp business, but it is a tradition that is difficult if not impossible to abandon, even today.

In color war, the kids are divided into two large, equally matched teams. The teams then spend a full week competing in all the usual activities of the camp: sports, drama, singing, and arts and crafts. At this camp, the two head counselors were the leaders of the blue and gold teams, respectively. I was leader of the blue team.

We and our counselor lieutenants chose the best kids for each sport at each age. It was a miniature version of being the commanding general of an army. The kids became heavily involved, and so concerned with winning that the younger one's would often cry when their team lost. The counselors tried their best to sustain the proper spirit of competition, eager but not overeager, and to soothe the unhappy losers who might be blamed by their teammates for their performance failures.

In the drama competition, the counselors on each team used all their resources to select an effective play for the evening of the performance. The music counselor helped organized the songs for both teams—for example, anthems, and fight songs. Because the counselors were usually well-educated college students, they drew on classical and semi-classical music, with words written or adapted for the camp context.

My team used the beautiful and stirring Soviet Russian army marching music for its fight song, and a theme from Brahms Ist symphony for its anthem. Words were written for each to suit an overall theme, which for the blue team that year was Robin Hood and his men of Sherwood forest. All our intellectual resources and knowledge were brought to bear in this competition.

At some of the camp lunches, an exciting skit might be planned as a surprise. Suddenly, near the end of the meal, lights would flash on several blue team squads perched on the dining-room rafters—as if in trees—and the teammates were drawn into the action. The frantic youngest kids of both teams could hardly eat when this was going on, and many of them didn't sleep much at night either. No wonder they were exhausted by the end of color war. And there was always a winner and a loser, and the severe disappointment of having been on the losing side.

When I think back, the intensity and complex orchestration of the week of competition was remarkable. The best features of color war were the unleashing of talent, creativity, community effort, and boundless energy, which was difficult to suppress. Color war was unlike anything I had previously known in my life.

My team won that year but, as usual, by a hair. Some of the kids in my bunk who were on the losing side were angry at me and had to be mollified. Though I was not a bunk counselor, I had to aid the counselor in working out this distress and preventing a continuance of ill feeling.

I had a marvelous time in camp that year, and was able to put aside what was then considered a substantial sum. It was the climax to all the previous years, and the last gasp of my adolescence before the Army and adult responsibilities. I believed I had done well and felt proud. It was a prelude to the adult struggles that were to follow in which I would acquire professional skills and strive for excellence and success. But in the meantime, I learned much that would stand me in good stead about organizing groups, dealing with people, planning programs, seeing the forest as well as the trees of any enterprise, persisting against defeat and disappointment, and keeping my spirits up when things didn't go well.

Just as developmental psychologists like Jean Piaget regard children's play as serious preparation for adulthood, so too I believe that these summer work experiences were more than merely fun and games. They honed many of the adaptational skills I would later need and use in my adult life. They were not just an escape from the real world, as my father claimed, but a useful preparation for it. The future would bring the growing sense that competition to advance a career was hardly a game or diversion, but a deadly serious Darwinian survival struggle in which winning and losing made a great deal of difference. Few would care if it went badly, and even fewer would give you a pat on the back if it went well.

BARBER ARTISTE OF THE CCNY HOUSE PLAN

Now we return to the less romantic aspects of my working life when college was in session, few of the jobs I managed to find provided enough work to pay my expenses. So, in my junior year, I conceived a plan to open up a barber shop for students on the CCNY campus. I knew how to cut hair as a result of having been a camp counselor. One summer, the regular barber never came and the owners were frantic, because when the parents came to visit the camp, the boys would look terrible. I took on the job of cutting their hair, and before long, was doing a credible job.

I happened to be a member of a daytime campus fraternity at CCNY, called the *House Plan,* which offered certain amenities and the potential for social activities. In those days all the students were male. Most of the boys were poor and I don't remember any charges for membership, except maybe a dollar a year. The House Plan had a very large, unused lounge, which might have once been part of a bathroom, and it had tile floors and mirrors all around. If a chair were placed in the right position, a customer could watch his hair being cut in front and back. I requested the House Plan Governing Council to permit me to use that room as my barber shop.

Much to my joy, the council approved, and we agreed that I would charge 20 cents a haircut, 5 cents less than the local barbers. The House Plan took none of my fees. One sidelight of this story is that another psychology major, Mort Applezweig, who was the president of the council and sympathized with my financial plight, played an important role in this agreement. I hadn't met him at the time and wasn't aware of his role in the council's approval until many years later when both of us met at a conference as professors of psychology. Mort ultimately became president of Clark University, where he remained until fairly recently.

I bought a good barber sheers, electric clipper, brush, powder, and gown for the customers—the only thing I didn't do was to use a razor. I put up a light-hearted sign identifying myself as Senior Ricardo Lazaro, B. A. of H. P. *(Barber Artiste of the House Plan),* Haircuts to Fit Your Personality, By Appointment Only. There was a weekly sign-up sheet with my schedule for each day, and every morning I checked the sheet for potential customers. Before each of my classes started, I advertised my new business. One day an amused professor of psychology, John Gray Peatman, walked in on my spiel, and graciously allowed me to finish before taking over the class.

Before long I had a thriving business, but it ended in disappointment, which was quickly followed by a great stroke of good luck. My naiveté in getting into the haircut business, and that of the Council of the House Plan Council, had been in not realizing that the law required a license to charge for giving haircuts. After some months, a policeman arrived at my shop and told me to stop because I didn't have a license, the cost of which would have been prohibitive.

Evidently the local barber on Amsterdam Avenue had asked one of the students whom he hadn't seen for awhile about where he had been. When told he had been getting his hair cut by a student at the House Plan, the barber sensibly protected his livelihood by getting the authorities to put an end to my illegal competition. Actually, I hated cutting hair; the dust from it got into my eyes and made them smart. But I needed the money and was now out of business, with no job in sight, which was the disappointment I alluded to previously.

PROFESSOR PEATMAN AND THE HIT PARADE

The stroke of good luck occurred when only a week after I was put out of business, Professor Peatman casually asked me how my barbering was going, and I told him the sad story. Peatman ran a research business that provided weekly reports about song popularity on the radio for Broadcast Music Incorporated (BMI), a collection of music publishing companies. BMI was the private industry giant of the recording industry, and it exploited the authors of the songs it sold by not paying continuing royalties. This abuse eventually led to the formation of ASCAP, the song writers union, which ultimately became a major competitor in the industry.

Professor Peatman's student-employees listened day and night to New York radio stations that played popular music. One of the most interesting features of this listening job was the ability of the students to monitor four radio stations at the same time, to identify accurately the song title from just a few bars of music, then quickly to switch to a different station to identify another song, and so on. It is the same skill that is later drawn on by a once popular television show called *"Name That Tune"* in which the winning contestant identifies a song with fewer notes than the loser.

Peatman's survey was supported by BMI because, up until then, song pluggers would unscrupulously claim high popularity for songs that might be heard by only a modest number of people. Actually, the size of the audience depended on the time of day it was played, the number of radio stations in the country that played it, and the day of the week. The most popular listening times during the day, say, 6 to 8 in the evening, meant a larger audience, and weekends were worth more than weekdays, because more people were at home listening.

The final report provided the music publishers with an accurate index of the "audience coverage"—in effect, they paid for and received an accurate estimate of how many people had heard the song at each playing. Peatman's report consisted of data on the 50 most popular songs played each week and was an early contribution to what would become a major industry years later, called survey research. It was also the basis of the "Hit Parade," which initially presented the top 10 songs each week on radio, and in the 1950s, on television.

After I told Peatman my sad story, right then and there, he offered me a job, which I accepted gratefully. I worked for him from my junior year until I graduated in the spring of 1942. My first job was to arrive at his place at CCNY at 5 AM five days a week, joining several other students in collating the day's report of the top 50 hit songs. The hardest part of the job was to deliver the reports to song publishers all over the downtown, east side of Manhattan. For a very slender kid, it was backbreaking to lug the large stack of reports on the subway, and walk with them, sometimes long distances, to each publisher. I remember how grateful I was when the stack was winnowed down to just a few reports. After the deliveries, I was able to make my first class at the college at 10 AM.

Not long after I started, I was promoted. My new job was to put together the statistics for each week's report. The student who had done this before me was about to graduate. I calculated the number of radio plays per song and weighted it by time of day, day of the week, and number of radio stations carrying the song. A formula was used to calculate how each song should be weighted in order to attain the most accurate estimate of the listening audience. The final data were summarized in what was called the "Audience Coverage Index."

Then a remarkable thing happened . My job was slated to be for 40 hours of work, for which I was paid 50 cents an hour, pretty good pay for then. Forty hours was how long it initially took me to produce the Audience Coverage Index. But I began to find ways of cutting the time needed for the report. Eventually I made the procedure so efficient that I was soon working only about 20 hours, but I was still being paid at the 40-hour a week rate. I began to get very uneasy, because I couldn't afford the technological improvements I had created.

After struggling with this dilemma for a week or 2 and trying to figure out what to do, I felt obliged to discuss the problem with Peatman, and I was very anxious about doing so. He saw my dilemma immediately, and told me right off that I had done a very good job and he was only interested in the final result. If it only took me 20 hours to generate the report, so be it, he would pay me as though I worked 40 hours each week. I was flabbergasted. Now I was able to give much more time to my studies without losing pay.

Professor Peatman's decision provided me with a generous gift. I worked hard to justify his faith in me and all of my academic life have been immensely grateful for his generosity. Some years ago I wrote him a letter when he was well into the 80s to once again express my gratitude. His example encouraged me in facilitating the careers of my own best students; it was a kind of payback for the help I received when I needed it.

INTELLECTUAL AND PROFESSIONAL CONSEQUENCES

One must never blame the past for problems of the present. We are all responsible for growing up and dealing as effectively as possible with what we have to face. I was lucky in that for all intents and purposes, I achieved a successful career, which has been a source of gratification and benefit for myself and my family. But my troubled childhood had an important effect on my intellectual and professional life, especially in my choice of vocation.

My interest in psychology was more than intellectual. It was powered emotionally by the desire to understand and cope with my own troubles, which is one reason for my emphasis on clinical psychology. When I have been asked to write brief autobiographical statements for undergraduates to read in introductory psychology textbooks, I have often pointed out that scientists often study issues emerging from problems in their own lives. They can have more than intellectual reasons for their interest. I became a pioneer in the field of stress, emotion, and coping, which had been of little importance when I started, but later became a significant part of four academic disciplines: psychology, sociology, anthropology, and physiology.

My troubled childhood also left me with an ambivalent sense of my intellectual capacities. I considered myself as having only modest brain power yet, paradoxically, I thought that most people I knew were not as smart as I. So my self-assessment included an odd combination of shyness and diffidence, based on self-doubts for which I tried to compensate, and an arrogance similar to that of my father.

An important antidote to the arrogance was my awe at the creativity and virtuosity of great writers, composers, artists, and scientific pioneers whom I admired greatly. One of the books that inspired me in my late childhood was Paul De Kruif's *Microbe Hunters,* published in 1926, the story of the great medical research pioneers, Pasteur, Lister, and Koch, who struggled against the prejudices of the time, discovered illness-producing microorganisms, and made possible the treatment and prevention of many diseases. All my life I have admired truly accomplished persons, which also left me somewhat wistful about my own limitations, and wishing I might do something similarly extraordinary.

I knew that to make it in the world, even modestly, from lowly beginnings, one had to be competent and persistent, and put one's best foot forward despite inner doubts. This awareness of the discrepancy between my inner mental life and my outer relationships with the world helped convince me of the value of a multilevel view of mind and behavior, and the importance of unconscious mental processes.

In my youth, psychoanalysis was the most influential public version of psychology, and it was about the inner conflicts and unconscious forces that shape our motives, thoughts, emotions, and actions. When I was about 16, I was reading the inexpensive Modern Library edition of A. A. Brill's compendium of three important monographs of Sigmund

Freud, *The Psychopathology of Everyday Life, The Interpretation of Dreams,* and *Three Contributions to the Theory of Sex.* Inspired by this material, I kept paper and pencil on the windowsill next to my bed in the apartment on 87th Street to write down my dreams at night so I would not forget them in the morning.

The solution I adopted for my own anxieties and self-doubts as an adolescent was to struggle mightily to become as competent as I could be. I was determined to know what I was doing and to use my resources effectively to succeed. I was, for example, the only member of my family, and those they descended from, who completed college. I was also convinced that one can improve the odds and take advantage of good fortune when it comes—an idea expressed in Julian Rotter's (1966) concept of internal locus of control.

Chance also plays a major role in life, however. I started my professional life after World War II, during a period lasting several decades in which there was a great expansion in academic life. Jobs began to appear all over the country. Money was available for research, and universities sought the best faculties. The way to advance was to take the best offers at the most prestigious institutions, which provided good opportunities to perform research and publish it. Timing in life, and that includes one's location too, can make a tremendous difference in one's fortunes—what, for example, if I had been born, say, in Germany, Russia, or Romania in 1922? Nevertheless, it is still useful to believe that we can sometimes overcome even the most unfavorable conditions.

I also believe that a touch of arrogance is useful in keeping research scholars, and others in creative lines of work, from being merely followers of accepted wisdom. To the extent it is possible, a scholar should be independent, aware of but resistant to the prevailing wisdom—perhaps even deviant, a maverick pursuing his or her own course when the crowd is going the other way. My sense of alienation no doubt contributed to my willingness, nay, my desire, to be a maverick.

This discussion of personal problems invites the question of whether becoming an expert in these aspects of psychology has helped me understand myself and cope with my problems better. I really don't know the answer to this question, but I have some hunches.

First, it is always much easier to understand and prescribe for others than for oneself. I am also sure that intellectual insight is not tantamount to emotional insight, which is what is needed to use one's knowledge effectively on oneself.

Second, I am convinced that personality traits are laid down early and that, although change is possible, and even dramatic change (as in conversion experiences) can occur with cataclysmic changes in a person's circumstances, radical change does not usually occur in later life, even after psychotherapy. Where does this leave us in dealing with personal dysfunctions and distress? I think we gradually learn to manage dysfunctional patterns and distress. As we grow older, the most important emotional trends are apt to remain in force, but we learn to accept and live with them, and somehow they become less distressing and dysfunctional.

In middle age, I wondered whether I would always be emotionally overreactive. I came to the conclusion I would remain an anxious person, quickly prone to anger, and one who anticipates and worries about what might happen and wants to control his fate as much as possible. I have learned how to capitalize on being a perfectionist by pursuing the highest quality I could attain in my research, teaching, and writing, which has gained me important advantages and honors. I believe that most successful people are to some extent perfectionists, always pursuing exacting standards in their work.

I am also sure that my introspectiveness led me to adopt a more phenomenological stance in my own theoretical work, which centers on the idea that all mammals are constantly evaluating what is happening in their relationships with the environment, especially with respect to the implications for well-being. Some who know my work may recognize this as a definition of "appraisal." In my approach to stress, coping, and the emotions, appraisal is the key mediator between person and environment. Appraisal shapes our emotions and the ways we cope with the conditions that bring them about. But more of this in a later chapter.

The next major event in my life, one highly relevant to my emotional and intellectual life, is World War II and my induction into the Army, which accounts for 3½ years of additional growing up on my part before going to graduate school to study for a doctorate in psychology.

REFERENCES

Bandura, A., Ross, D., & Ross, S. (1963). A comparative test of the status, envy, social power, and the secondary reinforcement theories of identification learning. *Journal of Abnormal and Social Psychology, 67,* 527–534.

De Kruif, P. (1926). *Microbe Hunters.* New York: Harcourt Brace.

Rotter, J. B. (1966). Generalized expectancies for internal versus external control of reinforcement. *Psychological Monographs* 80 (Whole No. 609).

Rotter, J. B. (1975). Some problems and misconceptions related to the construct of internal versus external control of reinforcement. *Journal of Consulting and Clinical Psychology, 43,* 56–67.

The Army and a GI's View of World War II

I n the fall of 1942, after graduating, I enrolled as a part-time graduate student at Columbia University with the intention of going to school at night and finding a job during the day. I was 20 years old. Finding a job was a nightmare. Because my draft classification was 1A, it was a reasonable expectation that I would soon be called into military service. Employers did not see much of a future in hiring me. I worked for a short while as a wrapper for FAO Schwartz, the toy store. My companions at work were doddering old men—the leavings of the draft—and the work was the ultimate in poorly paid boredom. I couldn't stand it and quit.

A JOB WHILE WAITING TO BE DRAFTED

I finally got a job with the impressive title of "production man" for a company called Accessory Fashions, Ltd. I never found out what Ltd., which ordinarily is a British business designation, signified, except perhaps as an affectation. It was a small, impecunious jobber that sold women's head coverings—that is, hats, such as chenille wraparounds and snoods, which were very fashionable in those days. Mr. Glassheim was in charge of this part of the business and his partner, Mr. Weinstein, whom I seldom saw, operated a button business. The hats were sold in department stores by attractive young women who eked out a very modest living.

I don't remember what I was paid, but I think it was around $20 a week. With the war and the draft, vigorous young men willing to work for a pittance were not in good supply. I don't think they were happy to hire me, but they had little choice, and I was available.

My job title concealed the fact that I was maid of all work in the back room where the stock was kept, the hats and the raw goods for making them. Accessory Fashions arranged with factory-based contractors, and also seamstresses who worked at home to produce the hats. I remember one of them, a little old Italian lady who travelled hours by subway from outer Brooklyn to obtain work. She carried her work in a rough-and-ready paper package that was tied by a string. Every few days or so contractors arrived to drop off packages of the products they made and to pick up more raw materials. The bookkeeper out front, a bitchy woman who was always complaining and sour, paid all bills, kept the records of sales at the stores, and issued checks to personnel. I've never met a more unpleasant person, and she could barely put up with me, though I don't know why.

I worked 5½ days each week and was in charge of all of the goods and finished products. I kept track of what we needed in raw materials and finished hats, phoned contractors to order them, wrote the invoices for these transactions, and did whatever was needed to keep things going properly.

Every so often the bookkeeper would come to the back room where I worked and angrily give me a bad time for miscalculating an invoice. "How could you do such a thing to a fine store like Bonwit Tellers?," she would shout. "What will they think of us if our production manager can't count?" She was always right, of course. But it seemed as though the whole business was a seething cauldron of anger, which exploded from time to time, usually at me.

At the outset, I knew nothing about how such a business was run. The hats were sold in the stores on consignment, which means that if they were not bought by customers, they were still owned by Accessory Fashions and could be returned with no charge. The saleswomen who worked in the department stores were not paid a salary, but received a commission on their sales. They often came by to pick up the hats they sold, and to complain to me angrily that they had run out of one or another model or color, thereby losing a sale, sometimes even bursting into tears about this. Their plight seemed real to me, and as a good young liberal, schooled in the evils of capitalism, I sympathized with their plight, and couldn't understand why our stocks of supplies and products were always so low that sales were often lost.

So I cooked up a plan to fix things which, as a result of my naiveté caused a crisis that brought Glassheim and the bookkeeper down on me and nearly lost me the job. I made a careful inventory of which products sold so well that we would quickly run out of them in the stores. I had the contractors make up a sufficient number of these items to last a few weeks so there would always be enough available. When the hats came in, I stocked them proudly on their respective shelves and figured I had done well by everyone.

A few days later, when the bills began to come in, Glassheim and the bookkeeper came storming into the back room in a rage. "What right did you have to order more stuff than we needed?," Glassheim shouted, and the bookkeeper echoed this in her own words. I explained my reasoning, which was impeccable. The business was losing lots of money by not ordering enough of the most popular hats. What's more, I had made a careful accounting of which colors and styles were safe to order on the basis of their sales rates. What could be wrong with that? I had improved the efficiency of the business.

It is hard to imagine the ruckus that ensued. What I said enraged them even more, and much of what was said was unintelligible to me. Glassheim called me a stupid college kid and, of course, he was right. The bookkeeper assaulted me verbally. I finally discovered what the real problem was, a product of my lack of knowledge and experience of how marginal businesses in the garment trade operated. Glassheim couldn't pay the bills for the stuff I ordered. This was a company that operated close to the financial edge, a hand-to-mouth operation, borrowing when necessary from factors, who charged exorbitant interest rates for loans, which could spell disaster. The business was so marginal that there was never an adequate cash flow.

It had never occurred to me that businesses were run like this, that is, so severely undercapitalized. Intending only good, I had created a real financial crisis. Poor Mr. Glassheim. My father knew this about many firms in the garment industry in those days, and never told me, but I had never been interested enough to ask. But they couldn't easily fire me, given the war and the absence of suitable employees to replace me. In any case, I was forbidden in the future to order more than just the exact replacements of the products we sold, and only when authorized to do so by Glassheim or the bookkeeper.

Meanwhile, the semester at Columbia was proceeding. I was taking two psychology courses at night, both taught by distinguished and well-known professors. Experimental psychology was taught by Robert S. Woodworth, abnormal psychology by Carney Landis. Distinguished or not, I found these the most boring courses on earth. Landis and Woodworth seemed to drone on in their lectures in an amphitheater in which it was impossible to hide because of the high pitch of the floor. Despite the potential appeal of abnormal psychology, Landis seemed preoccupied with statistics about how many of this or that type of mental patient there were and where, clearly advance warning that I would not be interested in epidemiological style research.

The reason I wanted to hide was that I would regularly fall asleep during the lecture. It was possible that Woodworth and Landis were not boring at all, but that I was simply exhausted from my day's work at Accessory Fashion, Ltd., or just was too ignorant to appreciate what they were up to. In order to stay awake, it was necessary for me to develop some coping strategy. As I got sleepy and my eyes would close, I would regularly plan to ask a question. That got the adrenaline going even before I raised my hand. The artificially generated excitement would continue during the professor's answer, and for a little while afterward. Then the whole cycle of sleepiness and the effort at arousal-generation would begin all over again. As luck would have it, I completed both courses and received Bs for my work.

The job with Accessory Fashions was a stopgap while I waited to be drafted, but I suppose I learned something from the experience; it was part of growing up. The courses at Columbia made me feel I had an academic anchor while the war was on, and I could return when the time came. What I learned in those courses seemed insubstantial, and I discovered that psychology could also be uninteresting when approached in certain ways. If I were teaching, I assumed I would give it more vitality.

DRAFTED AT LAST

I was drafted in January 1943, when I received that telltale letter from the government with the opening word "Greetings." The letter contained orders to report for further instructions at a government building in midtown Manhattan. I would be transported by bus on a certain day to the induction center at Fort Dix, New Jersey.

There were no tears when I left Accessory Fashions. I never saw Mr. Glassheim or the bookkeeper again. I had been lucky to have finished the semester's course work at Columbia. The university, cognizant of the war and the draft, had guaranteed students the right to return to its graduate school in good standing after being mustered out of the service, which gave me something to fall back on.

It is not so easy to say exactly when the war in Europe actually began, but the usual answer is when Hitler attacked Poland on September 1, 1939. This indicated to France and Great Britain that Neville Chamberlain's efforts at appeasement had failed to preserve peace, and these countries then officially declared war. We entered the war when Hawaii was attacked by Japan on December 7, 1941. By that time, much of Europe had fallen under Nazi control, and Germany was pressing the Allies hard in diverse sectors of the world, including North Africa.

In 1943, as a GI (a sarcastic term meaning "government issue," which I used in the title of this chapter), my view of the war was anything but sanguine, yet it was also inaccurate. The experts' analysis was that the Axis powers were losing the war by that time and likely to be beaten. To me, and the men I knew in uniform, the war seemed endless, however. Young soldiers, even those with a good education, are not well equipped to apply a broad historical vision. Besides, they might have to do the fighting and are inclined to ask, "Victory at what cost in human life?" When I was drafted, we were struggling in North Africa against the victorious forces of General Rommel.

My formal induction into the army and classification at Fort Dix took a few weeks of mostly idleness, boredom, and occasional testing. Most of the time was used up just hanging around, sometimes picking up cigarette butts and trash, and fighting the January cold. It was the first time I heard the expression "Hurry up and wait," which one learns is the way of military life. There was the usual KP (kitchen patrol), and I remember one unpleasant, rainy day of garbage duty, after which I showered in my GI raincoat, desperate to get rid of the smell of the filth that clung to it.

I was ultimately assigned to antiaircraft artillery (AA)—most likely because of the urgent need at that time for gunners to shoot down German planes—and the next morning I was on a troop train with hundreds of other recently drafted men who were making what turned out to be a long trip. We were not told where we were going, and it took 3 full days. As we travelled, with nothing to do except watch the scenery, eat, sleep (in our straight-up seats), talk, and play cards, the more savvy of us realized that most training bases were in the South, and we speculated that going west, we were probably headed for Texas. When we reached Chicago and turned South, we were even more confident. We ended up in a sad place none of us had heard of called Palacios, Texas, on the Gulf of Mexico between Corpus Christi and Houston—Galveston. The antiaircraft artillery base was Camp Hulen, which was where I was to spend the next 3 months in basic training, and a few more months in Officer Candidate Prep School (OCPS).

Palacios in January was mild one moment and ice cold the next, when a cold front from Canada would push down to the Gulf of Mexico. I remember playing volley ball without a shirt, then in the middle of the game, it suddenly got so cold we had to stop and put on warm clothes. With apologies to people who live there, GIs in those days would say we had been consigned to the asshole of the earth. Compared with New York City it certainly left much to be desired.

When we got off the train we were greeted by a sneering officer who made great sport of the accents of Noo Yawkas. His speech was larded with anti-Semitic allusions—though he never actually referred to Jews—and I doubt there were many Jews among us, just as there were few men with college degrees. I don't remember much about basic training. I have a better recollection of the good days a few of us spent on some local ranch, which was owned by a friendly family who gave us dinner and allowed us to visit and ride horses with their very pretty daughters and some of their friends.

BECOMING AN OFFICER

I wanted to obtain a commission as an officer, and was permitted to apply because my test scores were good, but not good enough to get me into the Army Student Training Program (ASTP), a special educational program for the brightest. I have always tested much more poorly than my academic performance would suggest. One reason is the strong test anxiety I experience. I have to read the same questions on the test over and over to get their meaning, so I never finished all the questions on any timed test I ever took. I also have long suspected that I have a mild dyslexia, though the current popularity of this diagnosis leaves me uncertain. To this day, I can't complete the reading of English subtitles on foreign films before they are turned off.

In earlier days, the graduates of Officer Candidate School (OCS) had been called 90-day wonders, which was the length of time it took to become a second lieutenant. Now, with the war going better, especially the air war against the German Luftwaffe, we no longer needed AA officers badly. So the high brass had to slow down the process of creating second lieutenants in two ways. First, you had to go to Officer Candidate Prep School to make sure you were qualified; and second, Officer Candidate School (OCS), which was a separate training program, now took 120 days to make second lieutenant, instead of 90. It was also highly competitive, with a goodly number of men failing to finish. I was glad to see basic training end. It was, by and large, a bore, and I breezed through OCPS, which was also a bore. In many respects it was a repeat of high school.

One of the things I had to learn in the Army was to live down my college education. Virtually no one in the OCPS, and only a few in OCS, had even been to college, much less had graduated. Remember, this was 1943, not today when going to college is quite common. The intellectual level was not very high, but it was not possible to have any comraderie unless my education and academic interests, which meant nothing to these men, could be suppressed. All relationships were temporary and superficial, unlike military outfits in which men lived and fought together over a long period. It was difficult not to feel lonely, though one never said so.

In OCPS, I made one good friend. I still remember his name, Edward Lending. He had been a member of the Abraham Lincoln Brigade during the civil war in Spain, and was a marked man because of the assumption that all of them were Communists. He fought to be accepted as a soldier in the U. S. Army and he believed in the war against fascism. But he was also 36 years of age, and I felt sorry for him on two counts.

First, it was a terrible struggle for him to manage the training. The difficulties of completing the physical demands, especially the long marches, were substantial. It seems strange to me as I look back that I considered a man of 36 to be too old. My son is now in his late 40's, and at that time I was a vigorous 21. Poor old timer! Lending could barely make it. A short time later, the draft age was changed dramatically, and men of his age were no longer draftable. But in 1943, he was in the Army, whatever his age.

Second, regardless of his politics, Lending was a kind and gentle man, and though he had volunteered for combat against the fascists in Spain, he seemed more of a sympathetic victim than a man who would lead others in combat. One of the tests of officer material was the ability to be a leader, which was evaluated by having each of us give commands to a squad of marching men. We were expected to shout commands loudly and crisply—for example, "to the rear harch" ("harch" sounds more like a short bark than the more lethargic "march"). We also had to count cadence, as in "hut-two-three-four," which indicated the desired tempo and helped keep the squad moving together.

For some obscure reason, Lending did not sound commanding when he gave these orders, and he often gave them on the wrong foot, so that the squad became confused and fell all over themselves, which didn't help his candidacy. If it weren't so sad it would have been comical, like a Laurel and Hardy film full of unintended screw-ups. He seemed unable to put himself into a commanding role. His verbal orders lacked force, his voice was weak, and he would get hoarse after a short time. I worked many hours trying to help him do it right. As it turned out, he never made it to OCS. I have no idea whether it was an ineptitude for military command, his age, his political beliefs, or maybe all three, which led him to fail OCPS. Poor Lending was left behind and I never saw or heard of him again.

Along with a surprisingly small number of graduates of the OCPS, I went to the Officer Candidate School at Camp Davis in Wilmington, North Carolina, where I eventually became a second lieutenant in the Army Antiaircraft Artillery Corps. There is little I find worth saying about officer-candidate training. It was physically—not intellectually—demanding, rigorous, and highly disciplined. Its intellectual contents included a dash of military theory and a few high-school academic subjects, such as mathematics and military history. Candidates also had constantly to give evidence of leadership, though the criteria seemed to me quite vague and superficial. They reflected military propaganda rather than a technical knowledge or a real theory of what leadership is all about.

With respect to physical demands, on one occasion we marched 26 miles in a single day with rifle and full field packs, and then, alternating running and fast walking for the last mile, we tried to look soldierly, without stumbling raggedly. In all this, the image was that of West Point cadets marching to a band. A number of men could not make the distance and dropped out along the way to return to the base in the "meat wagon." They and others who failed to meet the training standards were summarily dismissed from the school, their names being listed every Sunday.

I admired the first lieutenant who was assigned to our battery (like a company in the infantry) for this difficult march, though I can't remember his name. He was handsome and robust, and unlike many officers I had seen, was a genuinely decent person, firm at doing his job, but not trying just to be tough. He seemed interested in the well-being of the candidates in his charge; an ideal officer, as I saw him.

There was little rest or recreation. When we had part of a weekend to ourselves, most of us took off for the beaches of the outer banks on the coast of North Carolina, drinking and looking to shack up with a good-looking young woman. There's little point here in getting into this side of my military career, which had its ups and downs and was not very edifying.

There was much nervousness during the last week or so before OCS ended, lest we be dropped just before successfully completing the course. Then suddenly, the 120 days had passed, and those of us who remained had the heady experience of being fitted for officer uniforms, winter pinks and greens and summer chinos. We spent a day buying our uniforms with our uniform allowance and drawing on the officer's better pay scale for extras. Some of the newly commissioned officers used their own pay to deck themselves out as if every day they would be going to a military ball. I was frugal and bought only what I needed. I knew I would later have to finance my graduate degree. The largest portion of my pay regularly went home to help support my parents and brother, and I never saw a penny of what I sent them.

After being assigned to an antiaircraft battalion at Camp Edwards, Massachusetts, I, and all the other graduates too, were given a 10-day delay-on-route, as a leave of absence was called, to go wherever we wished. I returned to New York City, and stayed uncomfortably in my parents' apartment in midtown Manhattan. I took my girl friend to downtown hotels and nightclubs to eat and dance where servicemen were offered special arrangements assuring admission at reduced price. We also saw a number of Broadway plays and musicals.

My parents took me to a musical show in which there were plenty of chorus girls doing their thing—I think it was Billy Rose's Diamond Horseshoe. I didn't enjoy it, partly because of the troubled relationship with my parents, and partly because my mother kept glancing at me whenever one of the dancers showed some skin. I couldn't relax and enjoy it.

I kept away from home as much as I could on that visit, and on others too, during which I stayed in a hotel to preserve my freedom. With so many millions of New Yorkers, one would never think he would ever bump into anyone he knew. But someone who knew her had seen me, and my mother made a big fuss when she found out. She took my message for what it was, that I didn't want to spend time with them which, of course, offended both her and my father.

The girlfriend I spoke of was someone I had met at one of the summer camps where I was a counselor and whom I also had dated during the winter before being drafted. At one point I wanted to marry her, but her parents did not regard me as a good marriage prospect. So that relationship ended, much to my distress, during my Army years.

Years later, I became convinced that her parents did me a great service, because I would have been stuck with a highly dependent, inept young woman who, as I grew up and changed, would have made a very poor choice of wife for me. It is sometimes bad luck to get what you think you want, and good luck to be denied it, though it may not seem that way when it happens. I took the breakup as a major loss and was quite distressed, but at 20 years of age I had little insight into the kind of woman I truly needed.

I really began to grow up substantially in the military which, I think, was its main contribution to my ego-identity and career. Although deep down I was a very unmilitary person, with a great distrust of being under someone's command—actually, I think I would have made a poor combat soldier—I discovered I could cope with whatever I was presented and function well. And I eventually gained the insight I needed to find the right woman for me later on, when it counted.

A BAD MILITARY ACCIDENT

An event that probably saved my life and shaped the remainder of my military career occurred while I was at Camp Edwards, Massachusetts, in the dead of winter. Along with the other officers of an AA battalion, I was training troops to go to North Africa as a fighting unit. One of the standard weapons of an antiaircraft battalion, which was designed to bring down fast, low-flying planes, is an armed vehicle called a half-track. It was half tank and half truck, and had a power turret on which were mounted four air-cooled 50-caliber machine guns. The turret rotated at 70°/per second, and its power and gearing system made a whirring sound when it was turned on. When in operation, a gunner sat inside the turret and moved the handgrips to make the machine guns rotate horizontally and vertically. With no operator in the turret, the handgrips were normally fixed in the neutral position, so it wouldn't turn.

The accident occurred while I was bending down inspecting the oil level in the crankcase. Someone in the turret turned on the generator switch and the whirring started. Not expecting the turret to move, I paid no attention, but the handgrips had been stuck in the extreme right position. In an instant, the turret whirled around, clipped me in the lower back, and knocked me to the ground. I was seriously injured, scared, and in pain, barely able to move. Because I was at first partially paralyzed, I thought I had sustained a spinal-cord injury, which would have been a catastrophe. Happily, that turned out not to be the case. The damage was mostly to bone and connective tissue, and needed to be repaired by surgery.

I was rushed to the Camp Edwards hospital, then transported the next morning to Fort Devons, Massachusetts, where there was a major medical center. I was operated on without delay for, I surmised, damage done to three vertebrae and their respective intervertebral discs. I met the neurosurgeon briefly. This being the military, and 1943, there was no question of permission to operate, nor any discussion of what was wrong with me. Fortunately, the spinal cord had not been seriously injured, except for inflammation, though there was much pressure on several of the nerves, and severe pain. I spent 3 months in the hospital at Ft. Devons. When I recovered, I was assigned to limited-duty status, which meant that I would never be required to shoot at anyone in combat or be shot at in return.

I was shocked to learn later that my antiaircraft artillery battalion had been sent to North Africa, was assaulted by Rommel's tanks, and decimated. There were few survivors. I heard that the men, inexperienced in desert warfare and not adequately trained for what they had to do, had failed to dig in deeply enough in the sand to protect themselves against the heavy German tanks. When they saw they would be crushed, they panicked, ran, and were mowed down by machine guns. I was relieved about escaping the tragedy but, at the same time, I suffered guilt, believing that I should have been there with my unit. One knows, somehow, that this is not a sensible view to take, but the feeling of guilt remains.

When I was sent back to duty, I was assigned to train antiaircraft personnel at Camp Stewart, in Savannah, Georgia, but not to be a permanent member of any combat unit. Because I could not walk well—any misstep was still excruciating—I was excused from hiking or marching with the men being trained, or participating in field exercises. The assignment, therefore, was a drag, being neither interesting nor particularly useful, and I languished for awhile with very low morale.

You might wonder why I was not discharged then and there. There were four reasons. In the first place, I didn't complain about being retained on limited duty during the heart of the war. This was the "good war," against a terrible evil, and I would be ashamed not to do my part.

Second, I had no money and I didn't know what I would do if I got out before the war ended. I really had wanted to go to graduate school, but I had not made any advance preparations for doing so.

Third, and probably most important, the general policy of military hospitals was to avoid giving medical discharges lest there be a crush of disability pensions to be charged against military budgets. Hospital administrators followed this policy rigidly for all but the most egregiously impaired.

Later on in the war, this hospital policy resulted in the formation of what were called casual detachments, collections of thousands of men who could not do much and had no assignment but to pick up cigarette butts and other trash around the base. These were displaced men who were no longer of any use to the military, but who could not be separated from the service, except for medical reasons. There was no mechanism to do so except a Section Eight discharge, which was dishonorable. Imagine the cost of keeping so many men in the service without anything constructive to do. What a waste. This policy was soon to be changed by the authorization of Section Ten discharges, defined simply as "For the convenience of the government."

Fourth, I had a history of back problems, probably the result of an accident when I was about 15. Most likely, I had sustained a disc injury at 15, but in those days discs were not well known or understood. I am told that the first disc surgery was performed around 1938. Flying a kite in a small park in the city, I was moving backward to keep the kite in the air and failed to notice a high ledge from which I fell. This history was recorded in my military record because early on I had sought help for pain, though I was given only some empirin. I never had any pain when actively engaged in vigorous exercise, but only when sitting or standing for long periods in certain positions or lying down.

In the Army, I used to sleep on my left side, propped up against a head board or wall. At OCS when I did this, the OCS candidates would come in late at night and see me in this unusual posture, and they dubbed me the sleeping Jesus. In spite of some pain connected with sitting, standing, or lying down, I could do anything a fully healthy man could do until I had the accident at Camp Edwards.

Some years later when a medical board reviewed my case, I was retired with a medical disability. The official reason for the discharge was that an existing ailment had been aggravated by the half-track accident. I have usually managed well, over the years, but back problems and severe episodes of sciatica, especially later in life, have often been debilitating. I now take daily antiinflammatory drugs to help manage the problem.

The more active I am, the less pain I experience, but unfortunately a great deal of my work is done sitting down, and I must get up frequently and walk around. If I pack a bag for travel, I must place the suitcase high up on a table so as not to bend and lift, and I do the same when carving a turkey. I have learned many tricks to avoid a sciatic attack, and I've learned that some pain is bearable.

BECOMING AN ARMY PSYCHOLOGIST

Camp Stewart, Georgia, where I was stationed after the surgery, received all men for basic training who had just been inducted into the antiaircraft branch of the army. Every 4 months, a new group of inductees comprising 1,700 men were assigned to antiaircraft units to prepare for combat assignments. As in all such populations, an unknown number of men slipped through the induction-station screening who were in trouble emotionally and needed to be helped. Except for the most seriously disturbed, who were usually referred to chaplains or the hospital by their commanders, most men who needed help were never seen professionally.

While I was at Camp Stewart, I heard about a special unit that provided help to men who were having emotional problems. The unit was called a consultation service. The Consultation Service at Camp Stewart was headed by a psychiatrist, Major Manfred Guttmacher. It was basically a mental health outpatient clinic, staffed by a small group of young social workers who provided diagnostic and therapeutic services under Dr. Guttmacher's direction.

Some readers will recognize the name Guttmacher because of Dr. Alan Guttmacher, of Planned Parenthood fame, who was the twin brother of Manfred. Both were to play important roles in my professional and private life, Manfred when I sought to be moved from my unproductive antiaircraft training role, Alan when my wife and I later sought to adopt a child in Baltimore, Maryland.

I wanted to be part of this staff because of my interest in a career in psychology, and I wanted to do and learn something useful while in military service. So after I heard about the existence of the mental health unit, I made a visit to Major Guttmacher in hopes of being assigned to it. He asked me about my background in psychology, what I wanted to do later on, and I responded honestly. I told him I had been a psychology major at CCNY, was hoping to have a professional career as a psychologist after obtaining a Ph. D. when the war ended, and that I would greatly welcome a chance to learn and be of use.

As a 21-year-old, I had minimal psychology training and no professional experience. With so modest an education, to aspire to a professional role in the Army must have been offensive to those better schooled. The Army was full of young psychology professors with Ph.D.s, many with considerable education and experience, whose professional backgrounds were lying fallow while they served as plain GIs. However, my special circumstances—namely, being an Army officer on limited duty—made it possible for me to function in a professional role while they could not. It was a manifestation of the military class system. With my commission, they had to find something suitable for me to do, whether I was the most qualified or not. It was also obvious that the Consultation Service was severely understaffed and needed any help it could get.

Guttmacher was never inclined to waste words, but he was thoughtful and fair minded. He said he was interested in me and would let me know. Much to my surprise and joy, I was soon placed in the position of an "attached, unassigned" member of the Consultation Service, which is military jargon for a position that had no formal status or permanence. One could say its tenure depended on the needs of the unit and how I worked out.

I was delighted by this turn of events, and I suppose so was the anti-aircraft artillery commanding officer, who had been stuck with a temporary second lieutenant with little experience who was also limited in what he could do physically and had to be replaced when training was over before going into a battle zone. Anyway, the new position was an extraordinary stroke of good fortune.

Shortly after I arrived, the normal operation of the Consultation Service was suddenly transformed by the establishment of a new authority for granting a discharge, Section Ten, which stated—as you might remember—that any man could be honorably discharged "for the convenience of the government." In addition to its usual mental health activities, the Consultation Service was assigned the task of interviewing every man with no assignment to see if he qualified for discharge. Most were overqualified and quickly discharged at a great saving to the government.

Day after day I participated in the interviews, which were conducted by the entire staff who sat together around a conference table and discussed each man brought before us. Among the fascinating features of this experience was a recurring conflict about whether we should permit them to escape their military service obligation or punish them for their lack of commitment to the war. Many of the candidates for Section Ten were obvious goldbricks, unwilling to adjust to the military service, while the hard-working staff of the Consultation Service had to remain. It was galling to all of us at times, and seemed unfair, especially in certain egregious cases, and when we discussed the cases after the interviews, strong resentment was often expressed.

But there was nothing else to be done if we were to act sensibly. Many of these men were psychologically inadequate, functionally marginal, sick or physically impaired, frightened and lonely, or on drugs. It was Guttmacher's responsibility to keep us on track and not to allow our own envy or resentment to get in the way of acting in the country's best interests. During this period, Guttmacher and the rest of the staff got to know me and I gained their respect. I also developed a high regard for social workers, a group with which I had not previously come in contact.

MY FIRST RESEARCH PROJECT

The immensity of my good fortune in being appointed to work in the Consultation Service was soon to become even more evident. What Guttmacher really had in mind for me was to conduct a pet project he had long wanted to initiate. With 1,700 men arriving and leaving for combat every 4 months, many of them emotionally unstable, he believed that the Army should give special attention to those who needed professional diagnosis and help. That meant screening out those who should be seen at the clinic.

If a screening test could be found to identify which men were emotionally unstable, it could be a major contribution to the Army and the men in need. Such men not only impair the functioning of their units, but are often particularly vulnerable to injury or death in combat. Better to catch them now in training before they did serious damage to themselves and their combat units. Guttmacher also had his eye on the comparable problem in civilian life. Undoubtedly, he had hopes that screening would also work on civilians after the war.

Although screening tests were available, it was not clear how valid they were. Did they pick out the right men, miss too many who should be selected (false negatives), or identify too many of the wrong men (false positives)? To convince the higher brass to mount this kind of program required that the validity of the screening test first be established.

Like most psychiatrists in those days, Guttmacher assumed that anyone who was trained as a psychologist would be qualified to do test-validating research. In any case, he saw I was intelligent, responsible, and eager to learn. So, within a matter of a few months after my appointment, he broached his pet project to me. After listening to my ideas for such a study, and offering his own, I was given free reign to pursue the project; he was too busy to do more than occasionally ask me how it was going. Talk about luck! I was now about to launch my first research project, one for which there would probably never again be another such opportunity.

The brief test Guttmacher proposed using was the Cornell Selectee Index—so named because it was developed at the Cornell University Medical School (see Mittelman, Weider, Wechsler, Wolf, and Meixner, 1944). It was designed to reveal the existence of emotional problems and symptoms in any population. The test consisted of 64 questions with two types of items. One was called "stop questions," such as "Have you ever gotten into serious trouble or lost your job because of drinking?" Anyone with such symptoms should be "stopped" and given special clinical attention. The other type had less serious implications and consisted of standard questions suggesting garden variety neurotic problems, such as "Do you often have difficulty falling asleep or staying asleep?"

As I look back at the plan of the study, the extent of the resources and the authority that were placed at my juvenile command is astounding, almost hard even for me to believe. The project consisted of three basic steps:

First we planned to test the 1,700 incoming men with the Cornell Selectee Index. Early on a decision had to be made about the cut-off score on the Cornell Selectee Index, which would distinguish between those selected as emotionally troubled and those not. Second, we would administer the 550-question Minnesota Multiphasic Personality Inventory (MMPI), a well-known, standardized test developed by Hathaway and McKinnley (1943), which we planned to use in validating the Cornell Selectee Index.

Third, armed with the list of men who had been selected by the test as emotionally unstable, we would go to the officers and noncommissioned officers (sergeants and corporals) in the units to which the men had been assigned and interview them about how they were getting along. We also obtained ratings by the battery officers of the best and worst soldiers in each unit. And we also obtained more objective data—for example, about whether any of the men had been referred to the Consultation Service for emotional problems. A composite check sheet was developed on which we could record and quantify how emotionally troubled the men were on the basis of the information we obtained. I mention all this to convey the scope and complexity of the research that was being undertaken.

I was authorized to select my own staff from men still remaining in the casual detachment who had not yet been discharged under Section Ten. I had access to their military Form 20s, which provided a history of each man, in order to check their Army General Classification Test (AGCT) scores (measuring intelligence and knowledge) and their educations. A number of these men agreed to join the project, seeing it as interesting and unmilitary in outlook.

I ended up with some of the most able, albeit neurotic, men one could imagine. One such man, for example, who later became a respected professor at a prestigious eastern university, had been pulled out of basic training because he had fainting spells—not during or after some demanding exercise, but before every march or field problem. He certainly didn't belong in the Army, but he was a valuable member of the staff of the project.

For the next months, I ran around in a jeep and felt like a big shot. Mostly, we got good cooperation from everyone, perhaps because I was backed by an army major. Oddly enough, I never found out under what authority Guttmacher undertook this research, and in retrospect, I think he just did it on his own. It took many months to complete the data collection, analyze and pull it together, and write up a full report on what we had found.

There is no need to burden the reader with the details of our findings. Briefly, the Cornell Selectee Index was found to have only modest predictive value for identifying men with emotional problems, certainly not enough to rely on. Some of the right men were picked up by the test, but it also identified plenty who in testing research are called false positives, because they looked disturbed but were not. And we missed plenty of men who are called false negatives, because they looked in good shape but were not.

Perhaps it was naive of Guttmacher to have expected otherwise, and I was much too inexperienced to have a sound basis for a judgment. There had been relatively little research on this kind of problem, however, and it was eminently wise to try out the screening test before actually using it. The caution shown by Guttmacher in this regard was laudatory. Others might have gone right ahead without doing any research at all.

In any case, before the project was completed, Guttmacher was suddenly transferred and replaced by Major John J. Francis, a very pleasant man who was happy for me to continue what I was doing. One reason for his lackadaisical attitude was that everyone suspected antiaircraft artillery training would soon cease to exist. Indeed, in the spring of 1944, the Allies had gained air superiority and no longer needed antiaircraft weapons. This should have been a tip-off that the fortunes of war had shifted sharply in our favor. No longer would the Germans be able to bomb London and other cities in Europe or shoot down our bombers and fighter planes. But as unsophisticated Army troops, most of us were not paying attention to the big picture. We were busy struggling with our own small niches in the Army.

It was now rumored that soon Camp Stewart, Georgia, would be closed down and all remaining antiaircraft personnel were to be transferred to other types of units. The closing of the base became a reality after Major Francis was transferred and the Consultation Service disbanded. At this point, I had nothing to do but wait for orders stating where I was to be reassigned. One by one, everyone was leaving.

I now had the problem of what to do with the data and research report, which I had carefully put together, and there was no commanding officer to help. It seemed very valuable to me, even with its negative message about the possibilities of screening by a brief test. Someone should see it and take it seriously. But to whom should it be given? I made an appointment with the Adjutant General on the base to tell him the story.

Instead of embracing the study and its report, which is what I assumed he would do, then probably file it away never to be seen again, the Adjutant General was quite annoyed by what I told him. He said that the Consultation Service had no business doing research, which was not its mission. That was the turf of the Adjutant General's office. When I asked him what to do with the material, he said he couldn't care less; it was a bootleg project that shouldn't have been done, so it didn't exist. Impressed with the supreme foolishness of the military bureaucracy—bootleg or not, the report should have value for someone—I left crestfallen. After some thought, I decided to ship the data and the report home to New York City for safekeeping with the idea that after the war it might serve a useful function, though what I didn't have any idea.

No one, neither Major Guttmacher nor Major Francis, ever contacted me later about the report. I suppose that the end of the war closed the book on what we had done, and made it pale in importance compared with the task of reintegrating oneself into civilian life. But the book was not closed for me, as you will soon see.

BECOMING AN INDUCTION STATION PSYCHOLOGIST

When I received my orders to leave, I was sent to the Eighth Service Command in Dallas, Texas, and managed successfully to arrange an assignment as an induction station psychologist, first in Dallas where I was trained, then in Little Rock, Arkansas. Paul Fields, then a captain (and later a psychology professor in Seattle), was the psychologist in charge. He seemed impressed with the story of my work at the Consultation Service at Camp Stewart. By arranging my appointment, he protected me from being reassigned as an officer in some prisoner-of-war camp in southwestern United States.

In this job, I had the responsibility for assuring that those being inducted met the minimal intellectual standards for military service, which were appallingly low. I had a small staff of two noncommissioned officers who administered a very simple test, which, if passed, ushered the man into the Army. What happened when a man failed this simple test is interesting, sad, funny, and well worth describing.

The problem was to decide whether or not a failure on the test was a result of malingering—that is, a willful decision to look mentally deficient in order to avoid military service. A standard responsibility of the induction station psychologist was to decide this by means of interviewing each man who failed before signing officially that he did not meet the minimal qualifications for induction.

There was only one way to induct a man who failed the test. He had to be sent back to take it a second time. Only if he passed could he be inducted. The psychologist was not allowed to use his clinical judgment. So, when such a man was led to my desk by my staff, a cat-and-mouse game began. First came the interview to obtain evidence on which to infer whether the man was mentally deficient or had refused to make a proper effort.

I usually began the interview by asking some trick questions to gauge the man's brain power, based on items taken from the Similarities sub-scale of the Wechsler-Bellevue Intelligence Test for Adults (Wechsler, 1944). I would ask, for example, "How are an orange and a banana alike?" I knew that uneducated men, even when bright, consider a question like this to be very easy. Therefore, they can be fooled into giving the right answer even if they want to appear inadequate. They will usually answer that an orange and a banana are fruit.

However simple this question and answer might look to the malingerer, it requires being able to use an abstract concept, which persons of limited intellect cannot do. Therefore, to do so easily is a dead giveaway. Mentally deficient men will typically think hard, struggle for a few minutes, scratch their heads, and give very concrete, functional answers, such as "You eats 'em," "They got seeds," or "They taste sweet." When I would hear this kind of answer, I could be reasonably confident that the man had failed the test because he had a very limited intellectual ability, and would routinely sign the paper to reject him from military service.

What to do, however, about the man who answered "fruit," suggesting he probably had at least normal intellectual ability, yet had purposely flunked the simplest of tests? I worked out a charade that would often trap the phony. I would call in Sergeant Watson (name changed), a tall, imposing, and somewhat severe-looking man, and asked him whether the FBI agent was still around. Watson always responded by saying he was, but was getting ready to leave, on which I would say "Tell him not to leave yet, I may have another man for him."

In those days, young men being inducted believed J. Edgar Hoover's FBI propaganda slogan, "We always get our man." They were usually intimidated when, speaking coldly, I would tell them that it was a federal crime to falsify a performance on a test, and that I knew they had done so. Then I would tell the man standing before me to go back and take the test again, chastening him this time to make a proper effort.

The game worked countless numbers of times. All the men I ever sent back to repeat the test passed with flying colors. I probably missed some malingerers, but there was no way of knowing for sure. My staff and I, including sergeant Watson, were often bored with our repetitious routines, but we enjoyed playing the game.

I have no idea how the malingerers I tricked into the Army did in their military assignments. Perhaps many of them wound up in casual detachments, which would mean that our cleverness and self-righteousness in spotting them did not help the war effort in the long run. In retrospect I think what we did was short-sighted. Anyone who would try to deceive the induction station staff would probably continue to goldbrick and cause no end of problems for his commanders and their battle units. An effective unit could not be built with men who did not accept the discipline and were not loyal to its combat cause. This was also the reasoning behind Section 10 discharges, for the convenience of the government.

Being an induction station psychologist was not my last job in the military. When the time came for demobilization of large numbers of men much later on, I served as a Separation Counselor, and I also sold GI insurance as part of my job, lecturing with broad humor about the advantages of being covered by such insurance. Humor was necessary because the men, understandably, just wanted to get home as soon as possible, and all this rigmarole of being discharged meant unnecessary delay. I had fun doing this, and had to be an entertainer to argue effectively for GI insurance as a good deal.

As the war came to an end, it was getting time for me to be mustered out too. I was retired from the Army in the spring of 1946, in time to try to gain admission to the fall semester of graduate school. You will recall that I was automatically eligible for readmission to Columbia where I had studied evenings during the 6 months I waited to be drafted. But I was doubtful that I could obtain an education in clinical psychology there in 1946. I consulted with Gardner Murphy, an undergraduate professor who was highly regarded by students who took courses with him at CCNY, and he confirmed this impression.

On Murphy's suggestion, I applied to Clark University, but was rejected. My academic record at CCNY had not been stellar, except for the last 2 years. My rejection by Clark is a noteworthy part of this story because much later, in 1953, I became an Associate Professor and Director of Clinical Training there. I have learned since about many distinguished colleagues who failed to gain admission to graduate programs at which they later became professors. You might be surprised at how many such cases there are.

One example is Paul Ekman who, ironically, was turned down at Clark, but who for many years has been a full professor at the medical school of the University of California at San Francisco, and is one of the most visible and distinguished researchers—nationally and internationally—in the field of emotion. I was on the two-person committee that interviewed him at Clark and turned him down. We obviously made a mistake. The other member was Tamara Dembo. Paul and I, good friends for many years, have laughed together about this formative experience in our careers which we share in common.

In retrospect, I doubt that I would have fought hard to admit him because I never believed—and still don't—that we use the most accurate bases for accepting or rejecting students. Although there are many prejudices about what creates success, we really know little about who will make it in school and in a career, and who will not. Brains alone are not enough. Many departments—I think most—use test scores and grades as the primary and sometimes sole criterion but fail to take into account even more important qualities that influence success, such as strength of commitment, self-discipline, resiliency in the face of disappointment, imagination, and the capacity to adopt a broad, integrative perspective. Many of the brightest applicants commonly waste their talents, so clearly more than brains is involved in success.

Murphy had also suggested the University of Pittsburgh, which had a solid, up-and-coming psychology department, with a few academic stars. I applied to Pitt and was accepted. Soon the research I did at Camp Stewart would surface again when I sought a master's degree on my way to attaining the Ph. D. degree.

THE IMPACT OF THE ARMY EXPERIENCE ON MY LATER CAREER

Of all the things that happened to me in the Army, the years as a quasi-psychologist had the most profound influence on my career. It is, of course, difficult to separate the effects on my intellectual and professional life of my Army experience from the mere fact of 3½ years of growing up.

My sense is that I gained confidence during those years, especially the time I served as a psychologist in the Consultation Service in Georgia, then in Texas and Arkansas as part of the Eighth Service Command, from which I also gained increasing sophistication. The fact that I had succeeded in shaping my own military career after I was placed on limited duty confirmed to me the useful principle that one should always try, even against the odds, and that persistence often pays off.

There was also the extraordinary episode of the screening research under psychiatrist Manfred Guttmacher, which whetted my appetite for doing research. This made it easier to do a master's thesis later when I was in graduate school, and provided me with a knowledge and appreciation of research design and the skills involved in writing up complex research. Above all, my military experience reinforced the idea that I should try to make a career of psychology, though I had not yet learned much about what such a career would entail.

Nevertheless, my military experience occurred outside the culture of psychology into which I would be thrust in graduate school, and in my first academic job. That culture, with its special ontological and epistemological characteristics, would later interact with my own growing convictions about the issues worth studying and how best to study them. Just out of college, even the most committed young person still has much to learn about a discipline's history, what is important and unimportant, and how that discipline actually works. The beginnings of such knowledge must await formal education in a graduate doctoral program of study and beyond. In my case, that was to begin at the University of Pittsburgh in the summer of 1946.

REFERENCES

Hathaway, S. R., & McKinley, J. C. (1943). *The Minnesota Multiphasic Personality Inventory.* New York: Psychological Corporation.

Mittelman, B. (1944). With Weider, A., Wechsler, D., Wolfe, H. G., and Meixner, M. The Cornell Selectee Index: Short Form N to be used at induction, at reception, and during hospitalization. *War Psychiatry,* January, 1944.

Wechsler, D. (1944). *The measurement of adult intelligence* (3rd ed.). Baltimore: Williams and Wilkins.

CHAPTER THREE

Marriage and Graduate School

My wife and I have had an outstanding and loving partnership throughout our married life, and this is worth celebrating—without being too self-congratulatory—at a time when marital relationships are somewhat in the doghouse. In 1994 we collaborated on a trade book (Lazarus & Lazarus, 1994) about emotion. We also wrote a novel that was not published; both of us agree that it was not adequate. In 1995, we celebrated our 50th anniversary at a party of friends and family given by our two children and their spouses—both of whom have remained married for over 25 years. Our four grandchildren participated too.

We were married after World War II ended on the official VJ Day (Victory over Japan), September 2, 1945, which was marked by the signing of Japan's surrender to the Allies. Actually, our relationship began much earlier. It is a romantic story, which my wife and I both enjoy telling, fashioned at a time when the social outlook about such matters was far different than today. Let me tell you about how we got together.

Bernice and I (her given name was Bernice Newman, and I will use Bernice throughout this chapter and book, but I call her Bunny) first met through the U. S. mail. I knew her sister and her sister's husband, who was stationed in Savannah, Georgia. On occasion the three of us would have a meal together in that city. I told them about the breakup of a long-standing relationship back home and Bunny's sister suggested I write Bernice because she had also just ended a relationship.

There began a correspondence that became increasingly important to both of us. We wrote lengthy letters often, and I always looked forward to her next installment. The letters were personal—that is, they were about ourselves—but there was no love talk, and we never allowed them to get maudlin. We wrote about ongoing events, experiences, problems, plays we had seen, books we read, and sometimes presented self-analyses.

It was obvious to both of us that we both had brains, and a similar outlook on many things, suggesting compatibility and that we liked each other. I would write brief short stories, usually funny ones, and Bernice drew cartoons. There were subtle hints about what we wanted to know about each other, and we both usually caught the drift and obliged lightheartedly. Her mother and father would receive my fat letters while she was at work, and after she got home they would tell her that another book had arrived from Dick.

Our correspondence continued for about 10 months before we actually met. It took place during the time I was doing the research project at Camp Stewart, Georgia, while I was in Dallas, Texas, and at Camp Robinson in Little Rock, Arkansas. Very late in our correspondence we included photos.

While I was in Little Rock, we arranged an appointment to talk on the telephone, to put our voices where before there had only been written words. We both got dressed up for the occasion. During our conversation, she unexpectedly broached the possibility of her coming to Little Rock for a visit, which pleased me, and we began planning it.

Bernice's mother was not too sanguine about her traveling 1,700 miles to visit a man she and her family had never met. Her father, trusting her judgment and me from the letters he saw, thought she should go if she wanted to. Bernice wrote me about her mother's uncertainty, and I responded by writing her parents a lighthearted letter intending to reassure them. Although I did not know what condition she was in, I said I would make sure to return her in the same condition. They understood and laughed, and that settled it. In early August 1945, she was on a train to Little Rock. I had arranged a hotel room for her in town and another for myself at the same hotel.

I was at the Little Rock train station before its scheduled 2 AM arrival, waiting nervously. The train was hours late. By the time most of the passengers had gotten off, I spotted what must be her coming across the overpass toward where I was waiting. She spotted me too. I can still remember what she looked like, good-looking, slender but full feminine, dressed in a smart suit, with a firm, erect, and graceful walk. When we met, I thought I should refrain from kissing her right off; I worried it might seem too pushy, especially in light of her mother's concern. Later she told me she was disappointed, but my excessive gallantry did not last long.

From that time until her departure 10 days later, there wasn't a sour note when we were together, which was as often as possible. Except for weekends, during the day I did my job at the induction station and would meet her at the hotel in the late afternoon. We had the full weekend together.

We attended a party at the base at which the induction station staff responded to us warmly. We rented old jalopies and, on one occasion had to drive home without brakes late at night. Fortunately, there were no major hills. I suppose only young kids would have thought of this as romantic. We walked, swam, watched spiders spinning their webs, and danced at supper clubs at which I drank martinis and she manhattans.

The original plan was a visit of 1 week, and as that time approached, our money was about to run out. Bernice wired home for more cash, and extended the visit to 10 days. Although we were in love, we agreed we should be sensible. This sort of thing should be considered carefully. Right? No.

Bernice had been working full time as an office manager in New York City, and had to get back when the 10 days were up. I put her on the train and, throwing caution to the winds, promptly sent her a letter that would be waiting on her arrival. "Unconditional surrender," it read, "I want to get married." The reply, forecasting a lifetime of wifely frugality, was keyed to the number of words permitted for the minimum cost, consisting of 10 words and the signature: "Yes, yes, yes, yes, yes, yes, yes, yes, yes. Love, Bunny."

Now to obtain a leave of absence to get married from my commanding officer, Major Butler (name changed). Although World War II was *de facto* over after the atomic bomb had been dropped on Hiroshima and Nagasaki, it had not yet ended officially. The major agreed to a 10-day leave. Bernice and her parents set about organizing the wedding, and I arranged my train trip. My blood test was done in Arkansas, but it would take 3 days to obtain a marriage license in New York. We also had to talk with the rabbi and make other arrangements, all of which would leave us only a week for a honeymoon trip.

We were married at the Riverside Plaza Hotel in downtown Manhattan. Our wedding picture, somewhat worse for age, is shown in Figure 3.1. Bernice and I had urged her mother to have only a small wedding because we needed the money to get started, but we didn't get our wish. It was a big, beautiful affair, but I can't say I much enjoyed it. I didn't get along with my own parents—not many people did—and their presence made Bernice and me uncomfortable, especially me. I was glad when we were finally off by ourselves by late afternoon.

There followed a delightful week, financed by Bernice's father. We rented a car for $200 to drive to Montreal and back, and carried $200 in cash, $50 each in my two shirt pockets and $100 in Bernice's

FIGURE 3.1   Wedding photo September 2, 1945.

pocketbook. Our plan had been to remain fairly close to New York City in order not to have a long drive after the wedding. That had been a good idea, but the hotel room in Kingston, New York, was a disappointment. It was small, dingy, and on a noisy street, hardly romantic fare. We were a bit uptight and never finished the champagne we opened. So we shoved the cork back in the bottle and put it in a valise. You know what happened. You can't put a champaign cork back in the bottle. It opened and spilled in the trunk of the car, and my clothes smelled from stale champagne until we could wash them. The second night, at an expensive resort in the Adirondacks at Schroon Manor on a lake of the same name—a surefire provocation for later honeymoon jokers— was relaxing and we felt very close.

Although the standard public view portrays honeymoons as romantic, as the word implies, they're often disappointments. In those days, and in the old-fashioned tradition, the honeymoon is apt to be the first time that a boy and girl had to face living intimately together, learning about each other, dressing and undressing, brushing their teeth, using the toilet, making separate living styles fit a common daily schedule, deciding what to do and, in general, accommodating another person's tastes and idiosyncrasies. It was not so in our case. We already knew and trusted each other and our's was lovely. We were again reassured about how truly compatible we were in the many ways that count in building a life together.

While in Montreal, we regretfully saw the imminent end of our holiday, so we cooked up a telegram for Major Butler. The first draft said "Unexpected emergency, need five more days, but the word emergency seemed too strong, so the telegram we actually sent said "Unexpected developments, need five more days." The major was asked to send the answer to Bernice's mother in New York, and she would wire us at a hotel in Pittsfield, Massachusetts, on our way back.

When we got to Pittsfield on the appointed evening, there was no message. The next morning we checked again and there were two telegrams, one saying there was no word yet, the other saying "Five days leave granted." So we had 5 additional wonderful days in a great stretch of mid-September late summer.

On the way back to New York, knowing that we had only 1 more night, we tried to register at what looked like a fine resort in Darien, Connecticut. When we inquired at the registration desk, we were told the resort was closed for the season. However, there was no evidence that the hotel was closed and we became suspicious. At a nearby gas station where we asked, we were told that they were still open. How naive of us not to have known that in those days Darien was infamous for restrictions against Jews. It did not spoil our last night away, but how naive of us not to have known! The problem of prejudice and restrictions like this was effectively portrayed later in a film about anti-Semitism, *Gentlemen's Agreement,* starring Gregory Peck.

When I got back to Camp Robinson, Major Butler casually asked me what had happened. One would have thought I would be ready for this, but I was caught unprepared and, without thinking, blurted out the truth that we were having such a good time we wanted to stay longer. He was very annoyed, and I suppose I don't blame him. He realized he had been manipulated and I should have known he had no sense of humor. But the War was over and there was no sense in being concerned with trivialities. Bernice continued working in New York for another month to add to our financial resources and to ease her departure from a firm she had been with for a long time. Then we started married life together in Little Rock, Arkansas.

The period after World War II had brought a social revolution in thinking about marriage, at least among the middle class. Prior to the war, it had been generally assumed that couples should wait to marry until the husband-to-be was reasonably settled in a job and career. Wise women took more than romance into account, being concerned that the single breadwinner would have good prospects, compatible with her notion of the good life. World War II changed this. Many years had been lost, with long separations, and tragic deaths. Suddenly, young people were marrying without having achieved the economic stability once considered essential for a good marriage.

Bernice must have surely wondered about my prospects. Friends thought she was foolish to marry someone who intended to go back to school to obtain an advanced degree. Yet she and her parents believed I would get ahead. There had also been doubts about how I would turn out on the basis of negative opinions about my father. Bernice's father was also in the dress business and he knew my father's reputation as an unpleasant man, and he too had found him contemptible.

When Bernice once asked me if I were like my father, I said yes, which was true in some ways, but not all. She believed she knew me well enough to feel reassured about my character. There are always risks in committing oneself to a life together and, in those days, divorce was not easy to obtain. Risks must be taken in life, but in our courtship, we had both been thoughtful and not foolish. Nevertheless, we were also lucky in our decision about marriage.

During the 10 months I remained in the Army after our marriage, we lived in Little Rock and Fort Smith, Arkansas, and Springfield, Missouri. It was a period so rich with marital beginnings that, though the actual time was short, in our mind's eye it always seemed a very significant period. Figure 3.2 provides a bit of photographic documentation. I don't think the details would be of interest to most readers, so I skip directly to graduate school.

THE UNIVERSITY OF PITTSBURGH

I applied to the University of Pittsburgh in hopes of beginning graduate study in the fall of 1946. Luckily, I was accepted and released from the Army in time for us to get to school in the late summer and still have time to travel by car through the southeast to New York, thence to Pittsburgh. In Knoxville, Tennessee, on the way, we had a car break-down. The man who fixed our car was a moonshiner. Isn't it odd that we still remember his name: Art Fisher? We had our first taste of Tennessee whiskey, distilled illegally. It seemed pretty good, though strong tasting, but as city people we were thrilled by this new experience.

A   B

FIGURE 3.2   Married and in the Army. (A) Dick in uniform; (B) Bernice in uniform).

When we registered at a local motel, we didn't dare take our clothes off, but lay on the bed watching huge cockroaches climbing up and down the motel walls and betting on which would get to the ceiling first. From New York, where we stayed a few days with Bernice's parents, we drove to Pittsburgh in time for me to begin graduate work in the psychology department of the university.

Bernice found a job and the streetcar near our house could get her to her job and me to the university. Every morning, I saw her off to work while I remained at home to study. Bernice didn't allow me to do any of the work around the house, neither dishes, nor garbage, and so on. I was counted on to do as well as I could in my studies. Having no other significant resources, we were supported by the GI Bill and her job. Later on I was able to get a part-time job at the university, which also provided some useful experience in counseling. However, our idealistic rule was that, if possible, I should not work merely for money, but to learn what I could to advance myself in my field.

During and right after the war, many of the things one needed to get along, for example, gas for the car, meat, butter, soap, and so on, were restricted by the government, and some required ration points to buy when available. New cars could not yet be found. Although food rationing had ended by the time I started graduate school, the local butcher had very little meat to sell, especially good cuts, which he saved for his regular customers. Sometimes he would take pity on us and would give Bernice a package with the advice to use a pressure cooker to tenderize it.

When new cars began to appear, we hounded the local Chevrolet auto agency for close to a year. Finally, much to our joy, they offered us a Fleetline (top of the line) Chevrolet demonstrator, a 1946 car in 1947 with 400 miles on the odometer, which was sold as new. They loaded it with every extra anyone could imagine, $300 worth, such as silk seat covers, fog lights, a radio operated by a solenoid unit on the steering wheel, and so on. The car cost us $1,550, a fortune then if you realize that before the war the same car had sold for $600. But we considered ourselves lucky to get it. Comparable cars today cost more than ten times what they did then.

Anyway, once again we had wheels. We had arrived in Pittsburgh in an old Studebaker President, which was so dilapidated and dangerous that it could not pass the State of Pennsylvania safety inspection. It was the car we drove from Missouri when I was discharged from the Army. We were lucky it hadn't killed us.

I discovered that the graduate program at Pit was a bit like an extension of high school and college. We had to take a given number of lecture courses in each subject to meet the doctoral requirements. I had spent 3½ years in the Army and I wanted to make up for lost time. So, like the other students who had returned from the war, I raced through all the courses and other obstacles as quickly as I could. There was no time to waste.

In the postwar period, we all thought of ourselves as general psychologists. At the finish of a doctoral education, the premise was we could take a job in any subfield of psychology with just a little boning up on the details of an unfamiliar discipline. Even if our main interest was clinical psychology, we had to learn the psychological "basics," which meant running rats in mazes in the experimental laboratory. In those days it was assumed that rats and people were fundamentally alike in the way they learned; we could learn about people by studying the Norway white rat.

It is very different today. Nowadays, students apply for particular kinds of graduate programs, such as clinical, personality, social, physiological, cognition, or industrial psychology, each student having becoming a specialist in an increasingly narrow field. General psychology does not exist.

In spite of specialization, I still like to think of myself as a generalist. I resist calling myself this or that, and when asked, I answer that I am a clinical, personality, social, cognitive, and developmental psychologist—actually, I have published research in all these fields, and more. Today, students are in danger of falling between the cracks if they do not specify a single area of expertise when looking for a job. It is the same for doctors and dentists. If we need to have a tooth pulled, we see an oral surgeon; if we need a root canal we see an endodontist; if we need to cope with bone loss as a result of aging, we see a periodontist.

I was hopeful but uncertain about successfully completing the doctorate, and so I sought a master's degree on the way to the Ph.D. to insure that, if I ultimately failed, I would have something to show for the effort. The master's degree required a research thesis. It was then that the Army data and report that was gathering dust in New York became salient. I thought it might be accepted as my thesis.

I sought out John Flanagan, who was a distinguished specialist in tests and measurements on the psychology department faculty. Flanagan was highly visible for his work during the War on the assessment of men. He read my report and, instead of congratulating me as I thought he would, was less than flattering about its flaws.

For example, by not having a proper control group, the men selected in the study were, in a sense, marked as emotionally unstable, which could have biased the results we obtained. And without a control group, it was not possible to argue that the men selected by the Cornell Selectee Index were different from other Army samples. But he agreed that if I would rewrite the report to take into account the defects in the research design, he would chair my masters thesis committee. Within a few months, in 1947, I produced a spare and more sophisticated report, which became my master's thesis. I never published it, but I still keep it in my home library.

I have no photograph of me when I received my doctors degree, because I did not attend Pitt's graduation. We had already moved to my first job in Baltimore. However, I do have a photo when I received my Master of Science (MS) degree, which is shown in Figure 3. 3.

What I did at Camp Stewart, Georgia, had given me a strong taste for research. I had found the process of planning the study, collecting the data, organizing it, and writing up the results a heady experience. But what really turned me on was the future opportunity to address even more interesting questions about how the mind worked. I was really primed to obtain a doctorate and build a career in psychology.

Bernice and I worked together on my dissertation. She was much quicker in math than I, and she computed the statistics for the research on an old-fashioned calculator, which had to be hand-cranked. Its bell kept ringing while it was being operated and we both can still hear that bell: ping, ping, ping. We only stopped working on the dissertation to eat, sleep, make love, and go to the bathroom, and for Bernice's job, now only 1 day a week.

FIGURE 3.3   M.S. degree from Pittsburgh in 1947.

The data and manuscript were kept in a carton sitting on the floor of our bedroom. One night I had an anxiety dream that the building was on fire, and I had barely enough time to save one possession. As I described it to Bernice the next morning, I got her out the window then went back for my other valuable, the almost-completed dissertation. As I stooped down to pick it up, I found it too heavy to lift, and I woke up in a panic. The symbolism of the dream was, of course, that I had produced a tome so weighty that it couldn't be moved even to save it from the flames.

But Bernice knew a little Freud, and teased me by suggesting that I first saved the dissertation, the most important thing in my life, not her in the fire. I really wasn't sure I tried to save her first, rather than the dissertation, and might have cooked up the story to save face. The Freudian concept of secondary elaboration of a dream suggests the dreamer confabulates certain details when remembering and reporting it in order to make the actions more rational and socially acceptable. Bernice was teasing me about which was more important to me, she or the dissertation.

Our summers in Pittsburgh were spent trying to find a place to swim. We found Gorley's lake, a 2-hour drive from town, and often visited it on Sunday with other student couples. One such couple was Dick Evans and his wife, with whom we would study for exams on the lawn next to the lake or just relax. We entertained each other in our homes, and were also very friendly with Dave Lazovik and his wife, whose father owned a department store near Pittsburgh. Len Abramson, a single student from New York was also part of our social group.

I mention them because they all became professional psychologists of note. Dick Evans is a highly visible psychologist at the University of Houston, and we have visited together and gone to some of the same conferences over the years. Dick didn't finish his studies at Pitt, but later went to Michigan State for his doctorate. Len went back to the New York area as a clinical psychologist. Dave finished a year ahead of me and was appointed an assistant professor at Pitt, an appointment I remember being envious about. He has been retired for a number of years following a severe health problem. Except for Len, we maintained friendships and contact with the others, new wives and all.

HOW GRADUATE SCHOOL INFLUENCED MY CAREER

When I arrived at Pitt as a graduate student, my knowledge of academic psychology, as distinguished, for example, from psychoanalytic writings, which were often treated critically in universities, was quite limited. So I tended to accept what I was taught, most of which was new to me, including the prejudices of the field as represented by the professors in different subfields. Above all, I accepted the idea that the laboratory was the best place to test budding ideas about psychodynamics.

There was also a great emphasis on the psychology of learning. It made perfectly good sense to me that, to understand how animals evolved, we should examine how they learned about and adapted to their environments. In those days, as I said, it was assumed that all animals, regardless of species, learned in more or less the same way, mainly through classical and operant conditioning, and that all stimuli and all responses were functionally alike in the learning process. From this standpoint, it even seemed to make sense that the study of rats could help us also understand human personality.

Much later, however, cognitive psychologists, such as Robert Bolles (1990) took vigorous exception to the simplifying generalization that when it comes to learning all animals are alike, and by that time I also knew better about this. Bolles (1990, pp. 112–113) wrote:

> Reinforcement people say things like "pick an arbitrary operant such as bar pressing" or "choose a representative animal, such as a rat." So we did a lot of paradigmatic experiments, but then when we varied things a

little we did not find generalities, we found a lot of specificities. It seems it *does* make a difference what the animal is, what the cue is, what the reinforcer is, and what response is being required. Learning has a vastly richer texture than the old-timers ever dreamed of.

Early on, however, given my sophomoric grasp of the field and its dominant academic ideology, I didn't doubt that the psychology of learning in 1946 might not be adequate, especially in the case of people. I vividly remember a major textbook that we used at Pitt, McGeoch's (1942) text on the subject of human learning. It was terribly dull and dense, with chapter headings like "Conditions Of Which Massed Versus Distributed Practice Are A Function."

There was no real theory of mind in this massive, detailed text, only empirical generalizations. What I learned about the book's treatment of rote learning, such as the differences in the effects of distributed and massed practice (which referred to the spacing of learning trials), still seems to apply today under certain limited conditions. But it didn't provide much insight into more complex processes of learning and thinking, and it was a far cry from the cognitive psychology of today, despite that field's aversion to meaning. The graduate students made up a rhyme to express their pain, set to the tune of a popular song, "Am I blue, from reading McGeoch?" (It rhymes better when correctly pronounced M'Gyew.)

I also discovered there was a hierarchy of status and power within academic psychology, with hard-nosed, experimental psychology, learning, and physiological psychology at the top, and clinical, personality, and social psychology—that is, soft psychology—at the bottom. I suppose the metaphor here is to "soft headed," but the common expression, "tender minded," seems a bit kinder. I was clearly interested in soft psychology, which seemed to me to include the most important puzzles of the mind—namely, thinking, wanting, feeling, and conflicts among these fundamental processes.

This hierarchy of status and power seems to arise from an arrogant self-righteousness about what science is all about. However, this was the way the power structure of psychology operated, and other social sciences too. This has not changed much through the years, though in these days of postmodern thought, with its criticisms of traditional epistemology, it is less evident now than earlier in my professional life.

Nevertheless, both groups are arrogant in their own ways, with clinicians putting down hard-nosed psychology as irrelevant, and portraying themselves as the only ones on the right track to knowledge and understanding. I would like to see much more sophistication about and discussion across subfields of the epistemological and meta-theoretical disputes, many of them hidden, which divide psychologists and the subfields within which they work.

In addition to the academic hierarchy of status and power, I also discovered that soft psychologists learn more about hard psychology than the other way around. I am confident I know more physiological psychology, for example, than my physiological colleagues know about my fields of expertise—namely, clinical, personality, social, and developmental psychology. Social hierarchies tend to work this way.

In any event, in graduate school I dutifully learned physiological psychology, including anatomy and what was known about the functioning of the brain. In those days I had not yet come to the radical conclusion that mind cannot be fruitfully reduced to or understood in terms of the brain and, ironically, that despite the traditional dogma, we cannot understand brain function without having sound principles of mind and behavior.

I did not have these thoughts questioning the standard wisdom of academic psychology when I was in graduate school, or even at the start of my academic career. I was sometimes mindful of contradictions and biases, but did not yet challenge much of the substance of what I was learning. That would take more sophistication than I had yet attained.

Nor had I yet become clear about the distinction between structure and process in science. Later I was to recognize that psychology and psychometrics were unwisely focused mostly on structure and stability and that process and change was underemphasized. And I still accepted the ruling gospel that what was subjective could not be trusted.

The science of psychology—being positivist and operational in doctrine—required that we deal only with observables, and looked at making theoretical inferences from observables with suspicion. In accord with the outlook of the times, and Edwin Boring's (1950) influential epistemological prejudices, the enemy of psychological science was armchair reasoning. Hadn't we recently broken away from philosophy to become a true empirical science? I hadn't yet become uneasy about a psychology that had become so rigid and simplistic in its effort to be a science and its search for empirically based generalizations about the human condition.

At Pitt there were clinicians who also influenced me, including Victor Raimy who taught Rogerian therapy. In Raimy's course I read Carl Rogers' (1942) book from cover to cover. It seemed quite reasonable to me as an approach to treatment; it also seemed humanistic and open-minded. I did not see it so much as an attack on psychoanalytic thought as a way of doing shorter term therapy. Nor did it seem to be an adequate theory of the mind, but rather was a concrete, action-centered, and practical set of therapeutic and interpersonal guidelines.

What I missed most in graduate school was an effort to pull together all these diverse strands of thinking and research into some kind of coherent whole. I found such an effort only in personality theory, which I studied with earnestness, and if I had to make a choice of subdisciplines, I identified myself as mostly interested in personality and clinical psychology, in fact, mostly psychodynamics. Efforts at integration usually come much later in one's education, after one has learned enough to erect a scaffolding on which diverse psychological issues and details can be fitted within a larger conceptual framework, including the physical and social world. It takes time to reach this phase and many people never reach it at all.

In any case, it would be later, when I was doing research and teaching at Johns Hopkins, and beyond, that I would adopt the attitudes of a maverick, and attempt to make my own distinctive sense out of the contradictory facts and ideas I was learning.

I NEED A JOB

I completed work on my doctorate in 2 years and a summer, a speed that is not possible today, when the average time in graduate school has become inflated to 6, 7, or more years, especially in clinical psychology. I was considered to be one of the top students in the department, and toward the end of my studies in the spring and summer of 1948, it became necessary to think about the kind of job I wanted and could obtain. But I had no clear idea about the type of job I should seek.

The last thing I had in my mind was a professorship. I thought of working in industry, but I was really quite vague about this. The burgeoning field of psychology was not yet fully organized after the war and there were few guidelines. I had always been interested in clinical work, but had misgivings about whether I would want to spend my life seeing patients.

In those days too, there was no such thing as formal clinical training. Nowadays special training programs, with extensive time spent gaining experience as an intern, are mandatory for certification in clinical practice, which also lengthens the period needed to complete the doctorate. While I was studying at Pitt, the Veterans Administration (VA) initiated a training program to increase the available number and quality of clinical psychology practitioners for needy veterans. I was offered a well-funded traineeship, which required spending considerable time in mental hospitals. It was financially attractive and held the promise of a job later. But working with severely disturbed patients did not appeal to me—I thought it was too limiting—and I resisted it. Outpatient work seemed more attractive, but I was doubtful that even this would be good for me.

I waited somewhat passively for word about jobs. My chairperson, Wayne Dennis, who had substantially upgraded the quality of the Psychology Department after the war, would regularly receive information about job offers and pass them on to students of whom he thought well. One such job was a temporary one at the City College of New York—my undergraduate alma mater—which, they said, was expected to be made permanent. The job, which involved clinical work and teaching, seemed interesting, so I applied and arranged to be interviewed at a psychological convention held somewhere on the East Coast—I don't remember in which city.

Although I got the offer, the interview made me uneasy. Perhaps sensing a rank beginner, they had pulled back from the original salary terms and other important job features, and I felt I was not being treated fairly. But I had no immediate alternative. All the way back home I obsessed about the job and by the time Wayne Dennis saw me and asked about the result of the trip, I said I was reluctant to accept it. This was the first time I had realized that clinical work might be combined with teaching and research in a college or university, but I didn't like the attitude that had been projected by those I met there.

When Dennis heard what I told him, he mentioned three more job possibilities that had come to his attention while I was away. Would I be interested in any of them? One, an assistant professorship at The Johns Hopkins University, sounded tempting. Although becoming a professor had not been in the forefront of my thoughts, it now began to look more attractive, and I told him I would like to try for it.

Why wasn't it obvious to me that I should be a professor? Those who knew me in high school and college considered it a foregone conclusion that I would end up teaching somewhere, perhaps as a college professor, and I should have known it myself. But I assumed professors must be intellectually brilliant, and as you know, I regarded my own abilities with ambivalence. Still, as a youth I was highly intellectual, read a great deal, and was interested in all kinds of ideas. I had an intense curiosity about how things worked, especially people. My high-school graduation book identified me as "too intellectual," which probably was the judgment of some female students in my class, and though probably accurate, I was annoyed by the word "too." I wanted to be regarded as a regular guy, which I really was not.

I seemed to fit the concept of a scholar and teacher very well. Even in the military service I took pleasure in explaining how things worked, for example, the mechanism of the complicated M-5 fire-control apparatus that had been designed for antiaircraft artillery. The fast-flying attack plane had to be spotted and then centered in the cross hairs of a scope through which it was sighted by the coordinated efforts of three men. When the plane was correctly centered, the fire-control apparatus accurately calculated the lead in front of the plane that was necessary to shoot it down. The enlisted men seemed genuinely appreciative and felt I made difficult things clear.

When I was offered a VA clinical traineeship in graduate school, I sensed something about myself that made me doubt that it was for me. When I did psychotherapy with students later as a major part of my first academic job, it was mainly for the purpose of having a hands-on opportunity to learn about people in trouble. I regarded working with patients—at least for a time—as the best route for learning about how people got into emotional difficulties and how they might avoid dysfunction.

But I could never have spent my whole life seeing patients day in and day out. I was too interested in figuring out how the mind worked to remain constantly in practice. The best clinicians, with a strong interest in general principles, have always written influential books about the implications of their clinical experience, developing schools of thought about the causes of dysfunctional life patterns and the best approaches to psychotherapy.

Many of the most outstanding social and personality psychologists I know have also had clinical experience. It pays to keep one's mind on individuals and their problems, but not necessarily a career doing psychodiagnosis and psychotherapy. A clinically focused job in academe, however, that might be another story. It might be just what I wanted.

How I Got the Hopkins Job

When I said to Wayne Dennis I was interested in the job at Johns Hopkins, he got on the phone and talked to the chairperson there, Clifford Morgan. I didn't hear the conversation but learned later that Dennis spoke of me with great praise. Indirectly, I also learned that my being Jewish was a topic of conversation in the discussion and Dennis was asked how my wife and I would fit in. Evidently, he gave the right answers—probably that I was not one of those clannish or activist Jews—and that night I was on the train to Baltimore.

Pursuing the Jewish problem a bit further, when I became an assistant professor at Hopkins in 1948, a Jewish student quota of 10% was university policy. I tried to discuss this prejudicial policy with the top dean of the Homewood Campus, G. Wilson Shaffer, whom I liked and respected. When I asked him about its justification, he said he didn't make the policy but it was based on the fact that Jews constituted 10% of the population of Baltimore. I said this was a nonsequitur, but the matter had to be dropped—he wouldn't discuss it further, and it seemed futile to pursue it unless he were willing. Now there is the scandal at Dartmouth at the discovery that this private university also had a quota for Jews.

Incidentally, it was not possible for Bernice and me to live near the University, because that part of the city was restricted, to use the action-centered euphemism for prejudice. This was done quietly rather than overtly, but everyone was aware of it. We even saw large public signs on some of the quarries used for swimming in hot and muggy Baltimore summers that announced that swimming was for "Gentiles Only." Imagine that, overt religious discrimination in 1948, with no shame; shades of Jim Crow! Prejudice and discrimination work the same regardless of their targets. Most of us know that attitudinal patterns like this existed widely in the United States, as well as Europe, and still do.

It is also noteworthy that following World War II, religious-, ethnic- and race-based restrictions in our great halls of knowledge—I state this with some consciously intended irony—began to disappear, especially in the great state universities of the Midwest and the Far West. But the racial and ethnic attitudes that fueled them seem once again to be growing stronger again in the United States and all over the world.

But to get back to my job situation at Hopkins, the next morning I was interviewed by the chairperson and the dean. We had lunch in a lovely faculty club, which served good food at modest cost, because it was partly endowed by the University. It employed uniformed Black waiters which, along with the physical and social setting, created a feeling of the antebellum South, an atmosphere that might not be appreciated so easily today. I talked about my interests, particularly in research and teaching, and they talked about the department and what would be expected of me. The job was defined as one third teaching, one third research, and one third doing psychotherapy in the University clinic. It seemed ideal.

I was offered the job on the spot. I accepted it, also on the spot, and travelled home that night as a new assistant professor at Johns Hopkins, my first real career job. I was paid the munificent sum of $3,000 for the 9-month academic year. Bernice and I didn't question the amount. We had assumed that professors didn't become affluent, but suffered what has been sardonically referred to as "genteel poverty," with leather patches sewn onto the elbows of one's corduroy jacket.

We were to be proved wrong about this later, having become modestly affluent. The truth is always more complicated than the aphorisms by which we live.

Anyone familiar with the way jobs are obtained today might marvel at how my first job came about. Although there are many minor variations, now professorial appointments follow a pattern that is largely a product of attempts to open education and the job market to some minorities. The procedures of hiring—which I favor, though I am opposed to what is called affirmative action, which unfairly restricts rather than opens education and employment to everyone qualified— are designed to eliminate the private way in which people used to be hired, as I was at Johns Hopkins, in favor of open, public competition.

Here is a fairly typical scenario: A university department wanting to hire faculty these days publishes word of the job in several places to be read widely by potential applicants, including minority publications. Candidates send their vitae to the departmental search committee, which, after surveying them, makes up a short list of the most promising people who might be invited for a visit. On this visit, the applicant gives a major talk about his or her work, usually open to all interested faculty and students, and has an interview with as many as possible.

The search committee then struggles to choose one of the applicants, or may even decide that none of them is suitable. If the committee decides to recommend someone, a detailed letter is written to the faculty about the candidate's qualifications, departmental needs, and any other reasons for the choice. Then, at a meeting reviewing the case, the faculty (sometimes only the senior faculty) votes the candidate up or down, decides to reject all the candidates, or chooses a different candidate than the one preferred by the search committee. The department, armed with a favorable faculty vote, must convince an interdepartmental committee, or the university administration, about the merits of its choice.

This is a complex, sometimes lengthy procedure, with most of the issues—except the private thoughts and lobbying efforts of the faculty—dealt with openly. But it is a sound way of going about the selection process, and though it often results in mistakes, it is as democratic, fair, and open as any procedure involving people can be.

For the candidates, this can be a harrowing experience. They submit their credentials, including three or four confidential letters of recommendation, sent by each mentor privately to the search committee. Sometimes candidates never hear from institutions to which they have applied, and if they hear negatively, there may not be much in the way of information provided about the reasons.

Sophisticated candidates are aware that all sorts of political intangibles are involved in the decision, such as different faculty views of the department's needs. For example, when I was a candidate for the job at Hopkins, the prejudice held by Morgan against clinical practice, and other biases about the theoretical or methodological outlook reflected in an applicant's work, were important considerations in my appointment, including how I reacted to them.

The stated view of the appointment decision process is that the uppermost value being maintained is to hire the candidate with the highest scholarly and personal qualities. More frequently than not, I think this is true, with quality, of course, being variously defined by each actor in the complex hiring drama. More than once, however, at Berkeley, I had the suspicion that some of the faculty didn't really want the best person for the job, because it could be professionally embarrassing to mediocre professors or lead to more competition for scarce resources.

There are also prejudices about the institution from which the applicant comes. Distinguished universities want to hire faculty from other distinguished universities, such as the Ivy League, or the Big Ten in the Midwest. Having been educated at CCNY and Pittsburgh, I came from the other side of the tracks—that is, these were not upper-tier institutions. My credentials would have been more impressive had I studied at Harvard, Yale, Princeton, or Stanford—probably Hopkins too—or Chicago, Michigan, Minnesota, the Berkeley campus of the University of California, and undoubtedly others too numerous to mention.

However, the postwar growth of universities was so rapid that these prejudices were often tempered or abandoned. They still exist, but the wonderful thing about the American scene is the diversity of institutions and the belief—though often honored in the breach—that the quality of individuals transcends their origins. When I later came to Berkeley, questions about my background had probably ceased to be important in light of my accomplishments, Berkeley's needs, and my stints at Johns Hopkins and Clark, which were generally well respected.

When I got my first job, some of the same intangibles were undoubtedly involved, but the decision was a very private one, based on unrecorded conversations between the two chairpersons, Wayne Dennis and Clifford Morgan, and Dean Shaffer. Morgan's department was not a democracy, and decisions were often made dictatorially. I had talked with *the* two people at Johns Hopkins who had the authority to make the decision. No one else had to be consulted. That the decision could be made in less than a day, and could be made by only two people, is simply unheard of today, but was not uncommon then.

Private institutions, of course, have always been freer to do this than public ones.

So, now I am poised on the first rung of the academic ladder, starting out as an assistant professor at a prestigious institution. I take up my personal and intellectual life there in Chapter 4.

REFERENCES

Bolles, R. C. (1990). Where did everybody go? *Psychological Science, 1,* 107–113.

Boring, E. G. (1950). *A history of experimental psychology* (2nd Ed.). New York: Appleton-Century-Crofts.

Lazarus, R. S. (1947). A study of the validity of the Cornell Selectee Index in the prediction of military adjustment. Master of Science Thesis, University of Pittsburgh.

Lazarus, R. S., & Lazarus, B. N. (1994). *Passion and reason: Making sense of our emotions.* New York: Oxford University Press.

McGeoch, J. A. (1942). *The psychology of human learning.* New York: Longmans, Green.

Rogers, C. R. (1942). *Counseling and psychotherapy; newer concepts in practice.* Boston: Houghton.

CHAPTER FOUR

First Academic Job, The John Hopkins University

When I arrived at the Psychology Department at Johns Hopkins University, I had no academic experience except as a graduate student. The first order of business was preparing my courses, getting a sense of the faculty, department, and institution, and planning my research. This is always a tall order for beginning academics.

The sense of the faculty would come best from departmental meetings where curriculum and student problems were being considered, and from social activity, of which there would be plenty. Cliff Morgan, the Psychology Department Chairman, was a bright and effective fellow with very strong opinions. He was a young physiological psychologist with a substantial reputation, who had single handedly expanded the department after the war. He had a remarkable ability to select faculty members who were dedicated scholar-researchers, and who would become distinguished in their respective fields. In addition to Cliff and myself, the immediate faculty members included Alphonse Chapanis, James Dese, Charles Eriksen, Wendell (Tex) Garner, Eliot Stellar, and a few others whose names no longer come readily to my mind. The oldest member of the Department, Al Chapanis, was 36 years of age. I was 26.

The dean, G. Wilson Shaffer (whose age I didn't know, but whom I assume was somewhat older), with whom I later wrote a textbook on clinical psychology (Shaffer & Lazarus, 1952), was one of the most powerful men at the university, and he also directed the small but busy psychological clinic on campus. Though there was supposed to be another clinician, Shaffer and I were the only faculty psychotherapists who practiced there during the 5 years I was at Hopkins.

In hiring me, two more unlikely allies could hardly be imagined, Morgan, who denigrated clinical practice and theory, and Shaffer, who wanted some faculty members to do psychotherapy at the clinic. They had agreed on hiring two people with a clinical bent, myself and Charles Eriksen. Early on, however, Eriksen announced he did not want to do psychotherapy—I'm convinced he never felt any enthusiasm for clinical work. Morgan was willing to accept a few clinicians as a compromise, but they would have to be clinical research scholars, which fitted my own predilections to a T.

These two strong-willed men, Morgan and Shaffer, were later to be overtly at odds, leading Morgan eventually to leave Hopkins. After I left, he confronted the administration with an ultimatum and had no choice but to leave when it was turned down. I learned from Cliff's experience never to give an ultimatum unless I was willing to accept the consequences.

I learned much of value from the therapeutic experience I gained at Hopkins, but one incident with a clinic patient proved to be very disturbing. One day an Iranian student came to the clinic distressed and seemingly depressed. He was lonely and confused in a foreign country. The diagnostic problem was to separate his cultural style from evidence that he might be dangerously depressed. Given my ignorance of Iran, this was not easy to do. I consulted Shaffer about my unease, and we discussed how the therapy might proceed and whether or not he was a suicide risk.

We decided to wait a little longer—at least until after his next appointment—before pushing the panic button and seeking hospitalization. Normally it is best not to foreclose a patient's freedom to choose his own course of action. Although putting him in a hospital would protect his life for the present, he might lose the ability to manage life outside an institution. Hospitalization, especially if prolonged, infantilizes a person. Besides, you can't watch him closely enough after he leaves the hospital to be confident he won't try to kill himself. This is often a touch-and-go situation for the therapist.

Unfortunately, a few days later we learned that he had shot and killed himself. I felt responsible. That night I kept thinking about my first interview with him, mulling it over and over in my mind, wondering what I might have missed and why I had not urged his hospitalization. Shaffer tried to reassure me, and though I knew intellectually that he was right, the experience nevertheless troubled me greatly.

One of my more interesting patients was a young male obsessive-compulsive student who was extremely intellectualized, making his treatment a great challenge. His troubles were nebulous, including feeling isolated, confusion about what he wanted to do in life, recurrent anxiety, and the need constantly to engage in compulsive rituals in which he followed rigid action sequences when going to bed, bathing, and eating. If he failed to follow them correctly, he would feel extremely anxious, sometimes to the point of panic.

In the course of our sessions, I learned that his widowed mother had committed suicide when he was 14. She had closely controlled him and depended on him excessively as the only meaningful relationship in her life, though this also included considerable hostility toward him. One day, after an argument in which she said he would be the death of her, he left for school and on his return, found her dead, hanging in the closet, a suicide. The suicide note implied he was to blame.

He felt responsible for what had happened. Although he understood that his hostile and controlling mother had set him up for blame, he could never get beyond this. The problem was that he had elaborate intellectual insight into what was happening, but not emotional insight, which required him to connect what he knew to how he felt—he was too tightly controlled—which greatly limited any benefit from the under-standing he achieved. He was well read in psychoanalytic theory, and could interpret himself skillfully.

But he was so well-defended it seemed impossible to help him. Mainly we sparred, playing intellectual games that neither he nor I could get beyond in the treatment. I stopped seeing him when I left Hopkins, and have no idea what happened to him. I don't know what he got out of the therapy, which went on for quite a long time.

Returning now to my experience in the Psychology Department, Cliff seemed to have a high regard for me, and he liked and respected Bernice. One thing that appealed to him about me was the clever piece of experimental research I had done for my dissertation at Pittsburgh with the Rorschach Inkblot Test (Rorschach, 1921).

The person being tested is asked to identify what the blots look like or might be, for example, a bat, two people dancing, an icecream cone, or menstrual blood. It is called a projective test because, in construct-ing percepts from ambiguous inkblots, some of which are as vague as clouds in the sky, people project themselves into the task, revealing something of their distinctive personalities. The perceptual products of this projection are the basis of clinical inferences about the emo-tional status of people who are tested—for example, their inner con-flicts and ways of coping with them.

My experiment dealt what should have been a fatal blow to one of the sacred cows of Rorshach psychology, a reaction referred to as "color shock." Rorschach theory says that color generates distressing emotions in such persons and disorganizes their test performance. Supposedly, the effort to integrate color with the shapes and textures of the blots can produce evidence of cognitive disturbance in persons with neurotic conflicts. The signs of such disorganization are delays in giving a response in the presence of the color, low productivity (too few percepts are constructed), and poorly crafted percepts. These three effects were said to be signs of color shock.

There are five inkblots that contain color and five with no color. I created a black-and-white version of the test photographically to compare with the standard colored version. My findings showed clearly that the signs of color shock were just as frequent and strong in the noncolored version as in the colored one. Therefore, they couldn't be the result of the presence of color, as Rorschach theory had maintained. The theory was obviously wrong (Lazarus, 1949), though my experiment did not address the possibility that these signs were still associated with neuroticism, even if they had nothing to do with color.

I had used a classic type of research design based on one of John Stuart Mill's (1806–1873) canons of experimentation, the method of difference, to test a fuzzy clinical concept, and found it wanting. It was assumed that psychodynamic concepts, such as defense mechanisms and unconscious mental processes—very widely accepted in those early heady days of Freudian influence—could be evaluated scientifically by careful laboratory experimentation.

Hard-headed academicians, including Cliff Morgan, loved this research, because it showed clinical lore to be false. It was an application of the methods of science to notions about how the mind worked. In those days, as I noted in chapter 3, most young psychologists, including me, believed the way to distinguish fact from fancy was by means of laboratory experimentation. Only many years later did I come to see this as a simplistic half-truth.

In any case, this experiment caused quite a bit of fuss and controversy whenever I spoke in public about it. So my early research career was born in controversy, which I loved then and still do. I believe we learn to think more clearly when issues are sharply drawn and brought out into the open for debate.

My findings were ignored by clinical psychologists who used the Rorschach Test. Despite the wish to believe what we were taught— that research observations are used to evaluate and change our views—I began to learn the hard lesson that research findings do not usually unseat theories, even in the physical sciences (Kuhn, 1962). There are too many ways to protect an existing theory by explaining away inconvenient findings. Theories change only when influential scientists find what they consider better ways of understanding phenomena of interest which, for a while, then become the new dogma. This experience was for me a kind of academic growing up.

Within a decade or so, projective tests, which even the lay public had become familiar with, began to lose ground as an approach to clinical diagnosis and personality assessment, though not because of my experiment, but because of increasing general doubts about the validity and utility of the inferences being made about them. There is some indication they may be making a comeback (Exner, 1995).

FAMILY AND SOCIAL LIFE AT HOPKINS

The years in Baltimore, which began in the fall of 1948, were momentous because though we lived in an apartment we furnished it as our first home, produced a family, and for the first time since the War and graduate school, lived like a normal couple trying to establish ourselves in the community.

We divided our social life between Hopkins faculty parties and young neighbors like ourselves, many of whom lived in the same group of apartments. Often we played bridge. In Pittsburgh, we hardly ever ate out except in fast-food restaurants, which were not as common as today. In Baltimore, we occasionally splurged by having a Maine lobster or lasagna in a fashionable downtown restaurant.

In those days, Baltimore was not a great town for eating out, but we found some very pleasant restaurants. On one occasion, most of the psychology faculty couples made a visit to the infamous red-light district in the city to see a strip show at The Oasis, a rough nightclub catering to sailors just off their ships. We were all very young then.

The faculty was a small, closely knit group that entertained often— frequently serving raw oysters, clams, and steamed shrimp. We all drank heavily. The men talked shop, the women family matters. Bernice and I were said to be party poopers because we usually left for home much earlier than the others. We were early risers and still are. I can remember one time when we stayed the full length of the party, which did not end until near daybreak, with all of us pretty sloshed and still needing to drive home. One professor who was normally a severe and austere man—a sign in his office read "If you don't think, don't talk"—climbed onto the hood of his car and invited his wife to drive home with him sitting there. Fortunately, he was dissuaded from that insanity, and we all managed to get home in one piece.

The major issue in our young lives was the growing realization, after a few years of trying, that Bernice did not become pregnant. When occasionally she did, she would lose the baby within the first few months, and since we were still in our 20's we knew there was a problem. We went to see a urologist. The problem, as is so often the case, lay at the man's doorstep and in those days the alternatives were limited. We took steps to adopt a baby.

At the beginning of the 1950s, Baltimore did not have a modern adoption law. Our next-door neighbor was a respected, elderly attorney, however, who was instrumental in getting such a law passed. The new law required that at least one of the child's biological parents be of the same religion as the adopting parents—as if a newborn baby has a religion by inheritance. The adopting couple was also required to pay the medical costs of the pregnancy and delivery. For its time, the adoption law, one of the first of its type in the country, was well written and provided a set of firm procedures that were not exploitative, and would stand up in court.

The law also stated that one is not allowed to know the woman who bore the child, or its biological father, and she could not know the adopting couple. This had the purpose of preventing any contact between the adopting family and the biological mother and father. It also required the biological mother, who was offering her child for adoption, to have a year to change her mind before the adoption could be regarded as irrevocable. She indicated her willingness to give up the child by signing a paper before a city magistrate.

The dominant view in those days was that preventing contact between adopting parents and the mother was the best way to insure that the child would grow up without constant ambiguity and potential conflict, and the new parenthood could never be threatened. Bernice and I still think that this is the best way, though the dominant view has changed and now encourages the child to seek the identity of the biological parents and make contact with them. It's a difficult psychological issue to resolve and disagreement about it seems inevitable, especially without evidence about the effects of either policy.

Because adoptable babies were not in good supply, the best way to obtain a healthy baby was to work through an obstetrician, who would know the mother's intention and could certify the baby's health. Because of my connection with Manfred Guttmacher, who had been so helpful to me in my Army days at Camp Stewart, Georgia, we sought the help of Dr. Alan Guttmacher, Manfred's twin brother. Fortunately for us, he practiced in Baltimore. He promised to let us know when a suitable baby was about to become available, and our lawyer-neighbor offered to handle the legal aspects of the adoption. He recognized our impecunious state and gave us a generous gift by not charging us for his services.

In our first opportunity to adopt, the biological mother reached the 7th month of her pregnancy, only to have her parents take her to another state to deliver the baby, where she gave the child away to someone else. The day we received word of another adoptable baby that had just been born was a very exciting one. I was scheduled to give a lecture at the University, so Bernice and I met afterward and proceeded to the hospital where we saw the boy who was to become our son David. He was a calm, cheerful, and beautiful baby. We were able to take him home when he was 11 days old after all the papers had been signed.

I am hazy about exactly what happened with the adoption process afterward, but I do remember two things. One was a very threatening experience, the visit from the social worker who was charged with checking out the adopting couple and their home. We got through that okay. The other was a period of growing uneasiness as the end of the first year approached when the biological mother had to sign papers that she would have no further claim on the baby. That too passed without a hitch, and David, who is photographed in Figure 4.1 was now legally ours, our first child. As anyone who has had children well knows, having a baby changes your life drastically.

As our parental, social, and professional life waxed in Baltimore, we continued to try what we could to facilitate a pregnancy, but since our experience with David had been so positive, we remained receptive to another adoption should it become possible. A little over a year after David's adoption, Bernice became pregnant and it seemed to be holding.

Many people think that adopting a child increases the likelihood of a natural pregnancy on the theory that after an adoption a couple becomes more relaxed, increasing fertility. We have heard many stories similar to ours. I remain skeptical about this theory, however. When you are still young, the passage of time increases the statistical likelihood of pregnancy, so it only seems as though adoption has a facilitative effect. A comparison group who didn't adopt would be necessary to test this theory adequately. I am not aware of any good research evidence about this although, despite my skepticism, the common wisdom could still be valid.

When Bernice was about 4 months' pregnant, we learned of another baby, and the poignant issue arose about whether to accept it or wait until the pregnancy came closer to term and the fetus viable. We worried that she would lose this baby too. After much soul searching, we decided to do nothing about the second adoption and see what would happen. Happily for everyone, it all went well, and Nancy, our first daughter, became our second and last child. She was a bit funny looking at birth because of a temporarily misshapen head, which resulted from a rough delivery, but was lovely and a ball of fire by the end of

FIGURE 4.1   Bernice, Dick, and David, October, 1952.

her first year. We now had a boy and a girl, which fitted well into our idea of an ideal family.

After David and Nancy were born, I took the night feedings and diaperings. This was especially important after Nancy, because as a new mother who had just given birth, Bernice needed adequate rest. On Sunday mornings, when he was old enough, I would walk David in the stroller, take him to the zoo or other places that might amuse a young child. As Nancy matured, I did the same, with both children in strollers.

Young readers will recognize that in our generation, married couples with children arranged their life pattern very differently from what is the case today. Although couples usually follow the social norms of their day, each also produces its own distinctive culture, its own ways of adapting to the circumstances of their lives. Our couple culture, common for our generation, was that each partner in the marriage would have his or her own areas of responsibility, with one breadwinner and one homemaker. Nowadays this is rare. One could say today that we are a vanishing cohort, but it worked for us.

Let me try to characterize our pattern. Both of us were keen to control our lives. Bernice did not want to be managed, as my father managed my mother, and Bernice's mother managed her father. When we were first married, I knew how to cook a little, but she didn't. Being naturally bossy, I would tell her to do this or that, and when and how to do it. Finally, exasperated, she told me to get out of her kitchen. I would have to eat what she made even if it were burned. She would learn to cook herself, and she did. She is a real expert from whom everyone wants recipes.

Just as I had my work domain, she had hers. After that, my main household role was to carve the meat, serve the drinks, and take out the garbage. I was happy to have her in control of her domain, and do my own career-oriented thing. Most career women I have known since would say I had been spoiled, though Bernice was happy to spoil me, and that they needed a wife such as Bernice.

To this day, Bernice manages the household and finances as chancellor of the exchequer, and I manage job and career. As the only breadwinner in the family, freed of other competing demands on my time, doing my job as well as I could benefitted us all, socially and financially. With respect to household work, I do more today as we have gotten older, and I can say this without fear of contradiction, because I invited Bernice to edit out whatever in my story she thought was inaccurate or offensive. We have always done things this way, and recently collaborated harmoniously in writing a successful trade book about emotion (see Lazarus & Lazarus, 1994). Although we are both highly controlling, neither is allowed to override the other's will, which may be why two willful people are still married.

When the children were young, and I was struggling to make it in the world, Bunny protected my workspace at home, as well as our time together. When we had cocktails before dinner, the children played by themselves and left us alone. Both of us believed in firm discipline. We were not constantly engaged with our children as they got older, but I think we were reasonably attentive for our generation.

Nowadays, children are taken everywhere, sometimes even to work, especially when the mother is a single working parent and cannot find the best child care. Children enter into every adult social activity, at parties, in restaurants, almost anywhere. Sometimes Bernice and I wonder how parents can ever talk to each other without the children being around and involved in the conversation. It is a very different pattern from the one we remember during our own parenting years.

In this connection, in the 108 or so years between 1890 and the present, the social history of attitudes toward child rearing reveals very interesting fluctuations, sometimes from one generation to another. During these years, there was frequent oscillation between two positions about child rearing, one emphasizing strict discipline, the other permissiveness. The history of this, written by Stendler (1950), is fascinating, and it's worth digressing a bit to tell some of it.

From 1890 to 1900, a tender-minded view prevailed. The growing child was seen as a delicate flower needing to be cultivated with love and gentleness. One editor of a magazine of the day devoted to child rearing wrote as follows: "Love, petting and indulgence will not hurt a child if at the same time he is taught to be unselfish and obedient. Love is the mighty solvent." Another editor outlined a plan for dealing with a boy who was labeled lazy, careless, and good-for-nothing. He wrote in exhortation: "I thought I would try to win him with love alone, and never strike him. Mothers who have trouble with their children, bring them up the Christian way . . . with a loving and tender heart, and you will surely succeed." From this tender-minded perspective, the child must be led not driven, persuaded not commanded. Consistency and firmness should be tempered with understanding and justice. And corporal punishment is undesirable.

However, from 1910 to 1930, when Bernice and I were children, the predominant attitude toward child rearing was tough-minded and rigid. If a child refused to obey a parental command, the parent was expected to demand complete obedience lest it be "doomed to depravity" or spoiled. Disciplining the child was a contest of wills that the child must be made to lose, much as one tames or "breaks" a horse.

A child was raised on a rigid schedule, with times fixed for when it was to eat and even for its other body functions. If a baby cried or was hungry before the scheduled feeding time, it had to wait until the right time arrived. It must have a bowel movement every day, and strong purgatives, such as castor oil, were used if the child's intestines didn't cooperate with the desired household rhythm.

When I was a counselor at boys camps in the 1930s, I remember the camp physician making rounds of the cabins every night and asking each boy whether he had a bowel movement that day. If not, castor oil. That happened to me as a child too, and eventually, just the odor of the stuff was enough to make me vomit. To counteract this, I was given the caster oil mixed with orange juice, a common practice. After a time, however, I couldn't even drink plain orange juice without getting nauseous, though I eventually got over this.

This is the way Bernice and I grew up, and it was not just us, but most middle-class families followed the pattern. This doesn't mean parents treated their children with hostility, but only that strictness and control were the expressed values, which, depending on the family, may or may not have been followed diligently. The generation that grew up in the Depression years of the 1930s also had certain attitudes toward work and study, toward borrowing and spending, toward success and failure and how they were achieved. These attitudes were probably never completely lost in these adults, including us.

The pattern shifted again after the 1930s toward a more liberal, tender-minded, child-centered outlook, emphasizing spontaneity, individuality, and creativity. A child-centered outlook continues today, greatly reinforced in the 1960s for today's Baby Boomers. I think it is an effort to compensate for the pattern that dominates these days of having two hard-working parents.

It is quite possible that in the future further changes will occur, or are even occurring now, and perhaps we shall have an eventual return to a more discipline-centered pattern, as the pendulum swings once again. Indeed, I believe I see the signs of such a swing in the concept of "tough love," the "three strikes and you're out" laws for criminals, and in the Republican "Contract with America," in which a harsher "shape up or ship out" attitude is being fostered. We shall see whether the oscillation will continue.

But to return to our family life in Baltimore, to be able to commit myself to my job as a university professor meant not being available to my children and my students all the time. Rather than working mainly in my office at the university, I would spend most mornings working at home reading, writing, and planning my research, and go to my office only at scheduled intervals, for example, for classes, office hours, departmental meetings, and meetings with my research staff to deal with data or personnel problems. With two very young children at home all the time, it was necessary to get them to respect my work time and space.

To have time together without the children present, Bernice and I arranged to take every Tuesday off. We had a woman stay with the children, and spent the day by ourselves, coming home only after dinner. What we did was not particularly extraordinary—for example, sight-seeing, shopping, going to a movie, theater, or bowling, and eating lunch and dinner at a restaurant by ourselves. If something would come up at the university, it came to be known that if it was Tuesday, I would not be available, and eventually any grumbling about this gave way to quiet admiration.

Many found our solution to intrusive stresses at least reasonable, if not charming, as evidenced by the fact that they tried to emulate it, but not always successfully. We followed this pattern for roughly 20 years of our married life. When the kids eventually left home, the pattern no longer made sense. Over the years, many people have reminded us about it when we would meet them years later. Thirty-five years after we left Clark University, when by chance we met Seymour Wapner in Japan, he asked us if we still took Tuesdays off.

Whatever one says about child rearing, I have absolutely no doubt that a couple's decision to have children constitutes the most demanding commitment that can be made, and our lives were changed greatly. As we approach 80, the positive value of having done so becomes increasingly apparent at a time when, due to loss of physical and mental resources, we are apt to need our children more than they need us. And we hope they will graciously accept that commitment in return, though we would prefer not to require it, and to avoid adding too much stress to their already heavily burdened lives.

How to Get Ahead in Academe

What was it like to be a beginner at a university with high prestige and scholarly standards? What does a junior professor have to do to make it? What are the criteria for success? What compromises does one have to make between external demands and personal wishes about how to do one's job?

A striking feature of professorial life at Hopkins was the in-group atmosphere and the tendency of its young faculty to think of themselves as God's gift to psychology. This attitude permeated the atmosphere of the department. Any doubts had to be suppressed to maintain the illusion.

That the Hopkins faculty considered itself to be a group of brilliant young men who were going to shake the foundations of the field was actually a useful bit of self-aggrandizing, which tended to act as a self-fulfilling prophecy. It stimulated bold productivity and motivated each of us to attempt what we might not have dared in a different setting. I, for one, published a respected book at age 30 a modest number of years after my appointment, which I might not have done if I hadn't believed that, although a beginner, I had the knowledge and skill to produce an influential book.

But this attitude was self-defensive too. One of my most amusing experiences at Hopkins highlights the difference between a surface presentation of self and the hidden, and sometimes deeper lying uncertainties about that self. To illustrate, every year we would have a meeting to produce what was called a preliminary exam (prior to the doctoral orals) to make an assessment of the graduate students' knowledge. Each faculty member would bring a few questions from his own special field of expertise to the meeting.

First a question would be read aloud, and then a conversation about it would follow. Endemic to this ritual were some tentative queries put to the author of the question, which sounded something like this: "Uh, tell us about the criteria you would employ in grading the students' answers?" The faculty member then explained what a student had to write to get a good grade.

It was obvious that no one knew enough about each other's fields to know how to answer the questions to be put to students, yet they didn't want to admit their ignorance. By phrasing their queries in this manner, everyone could learn without embarrassment. I remember being told at my own orals that at that moment in my life, having studied diligently, I would know more about general psychology than I would ever know again as I focused in on more narrow themes. In any case, this group of ambitious young professors had created a mutually supported fiction of omniscience, which none wished to challenge. The posturing of these smart young lions was amusing because it's motivation could be seen through so easily.

Be that as it may, chairman Morgan was seeking to promote the Department of Psychology into a vigorous, visible unit that would have an important impact on the field. For most of the newcomers to this Department, success meant to remain on the faculty for about 5 years, after which it would be necessary to move somewhere else. Tenure was an unlikely prospect, because there were too few permanent positions available.

I paraphrase below the message given out by Morgan to his young faculty:

> Your most important task is to do creditable research, which will add to the reputation of the Department. You need to meet your teaching and administrative responsibilities (in my case doing psychotherapy in the clinic as well as teaching). It's good if you do these things effectively, and with aplomb—that is, you are expected to be a good academic citizen. But it's suicide to devote too much of your time to any of these activities at the expense of your research. If you fail to publish impressive research that will gain favorable professional attention, don't come crying to the Chair claiming you were too busy being beloved by students or being a magnificent therapist. The primary criterion of your performance is the research you publish and present at professional meetings.

I was always grateful to Cliff for the honesty and clarity with which he defined the job of professor to his faculty. In later years I have found much hypocrisy about this elsewhere, and often little help is given to new faculty in defining their roles and routes to academic success. But at high-status universities, one would have to be intellectually deficient not to realize that national and international acclaim is the gold standard for tenure, promotion, high salary, and job offers. At most such institutions, evidence of international influence is the main ticket to the higher ranks. Other criteria also apply, but seldom are they as powerful in the definition of success as is research influence, which is why science citation indexes are taken so seriously today.

Despite much criticism of this value system, I believe an emphasis on productive scholarship is a sound way of selecting faculty for universities that define their mission as including, in addition to teaching, advancing public knowledge, understanding, and the creative arts and literature. In psychology and most other scientific fields, it is scholarly research and writing, which others in the field read and cite, that counts most in upscale universities, and less illustrious institutions follow the same value system.

One reason for my support for this value is that I have found that the most dedicated scholars often make the most outstanding teachers, simply because they are enthusiastic about the subject, operate at the forefront of knowledge in their fields, and want others to understand why what they do is important. This means that their students are exposed to the most advanced ideas rather than stale regurgitations of standard, often out-of-date doctrines and facts. It takes an energetic commitment to one's subject matter to turn out the best students.

One must also ask what kind of students a colleague or university is trying to educate, the average, bottom third, or the upper 10% to 15% in ability and commitment. It is difficult to reach all three levels in the same class with the same material, which is one of the problems with teaching students of diverse talent and motivation. Which group to emphasize is a difficult social decision, but it defines the caliber of the institution.

There should be schools for all three student types, which was the way higher education in California was once organized, the highest level being the university, next the state colleges, then the junior colleges. There were important opportunities to move from one to another on the basis of the quality of a student's performance, which lent needed flexibility to the educational hierarchy. This pattern, once widely thought to be ideal, has gotten diluted since the politicians got their self-serving hands on our educational system.

It should also be said that there is much public ignorance about how students learn, and we will never solve our higher educational problems by arguing for change on the basis of ignorance of these problems. We do not teach students, literally, especially in higher education. We provide as much inspiration as possible, do a certain amount of guiding and explaining, make available the best source materials, encourage critical and sophisticated thinking, and offer ideas about how to study effectively.

It is self-motivation, diligence, and ability, however, that makes the biggest difference. Students usually struggle to learn what they need to, and the best of them take what they can from the available resources. Teachers make a big difference, but not in the way most people think. At CCNY, when I was at college, conditions were terribly unfavorable for learning because of the economic Depression, crowding, and shortage of space in required courses, but the best teachers helped motivate students by their example and their devotion to excellence. Even economically deprived students, many of them from immigrant families, managed to work hard and learned so well there that a large proportion of them became successful, even distinguished.

I have found that the two most important factors advancing my own understanding of my field are writing and teaching. Students, and the public too, think that scholars write what they have in their heads, and that their writing flows from their typewriters or word processors more or less as it appears in its final form. This is false, because writing is a dynamic process that feeds and expands what one knows.

When scholars write, at first they usually lay out what they know about a subject. Reading it back to themselves, however, makes it evident they are unclear about certain issues or they have not read or remembered enough. So they must reconsider what they have written, go back to the drawing board, as it were, and the library to construct a creditable manuscript step by step. In this way, they are learning from writing, not merely writing what they have already learned. They are extending themselves to the limits of what they know, and pushing it still further.

The same applies to teaching. When you lecture and present ideas to others, you must organize what you know so that it will make sense to yourself and others. For a first-rate teacher, the process of lecturing reveals, sometimes painfully, in what ways you have not adequately digested and organized the ideas. And so, after a poor lecture—and the teacher may be one of the few who realize it was poor—it becomes necessary to rethink the problem and study it further.

Feedback from students is also an important source of input to the scholar. For example, confusion about what you are trying to say and their reaction to your arguments is instructive. You learn as you teach, and teaching provides the occasion of being able to evaluate and advance the way you think about a subject matter. What I am saying has been said many times before, namely, that there is a natural affinity between scholarship, which can include original research intending to advance knowledge, and teaching.

Nevertheless, when it comes to academic research, the doctrine of publish or perish can easily be overextended and impair the quality of university research, which many, including me, think has happened. When faculty are pushed to publish quickly and in quantity in order to be promoted, there is a strong tendency to rush into print with half-baked work.

A reason psychology professors stay committed to laboratory experiments in spite of the limitations is that such research can be completed and published quickly, compared with doing extended, in-depth, longitudinal research, which the field badly needs. There is also a disincentive to replicate findings—journals usually won't accept such studies for publication—and to spend time carefully developing good observational and measurement procedures is apt to be a costly luxury.

To counter this, it should be possible to work for many years without publishing much, and such work can be judged by promotion and appointment committees as to its brilliance, usefulness, and methodology. There has been talk at the University of California at Berkeley campus of restricting how many articles can be offered as documentation for appointments and promotion, in order to disavow the common impression that quantity is everything. Although nothing actually seems to have been done to reform the system, such a policy might help restore programmatic research in our field and reduce the surfeit of publications, which are read by too few and add little to the accumulation of reliable knowledge.

MY OUTLOOK ON EMPIRICAL
RESEARCH AND THEORY

There was a great deal of ferment and excitement in the 1940s and 1950s because, although psychologists might not have foreseen it then, a way of thinking that had dominated American academic psychology was beginning to be abandoned in favor of a new one. There had been three ruling views about what psychology was all about. First, in the process of evolution, animals (humans included) were said to learn to act in ways that made it possible for them to survive and flourish. So psychology in those days was mainly centered on *how we learned.*

Second, psychology was said to be about *behavior* rather than mind, which was regarded as private and subjective. Mind could not be studied directly and, therefore, scientifically. There was a time you would be laughed off the stage if you even spoke of the mind, and if you were to be considered a scientist, you had to avoid reference to it. Instead you must be concerned only with what is directly observable, such as environmental stimuli and actions. All else was armchair speculation, not science.

Third, behavior and the way it is influenced were said to be best studied experimentally, in the *laboratory,* where one could control all extraneous influences and manipulate the variables whose influence on behavior could then be reliably observed. Today, we are more aware that the laboratory experiment is not well suited to many psychological issues—especially, in my opinion, the most important and difficult ones needed to understand the human mind and individuals with whom we share our world.

One reason for concern about the limits of laboratory research is that participating subjects differ in goal patterns and beliefs, leading them to interpret what is happening differently and, therefore, misleading the researcher about what is really going on. Even though the experimenter may have followed standardized procedures, his personality, whether likeable, supportive, unpleasant, or demanding, and the demand characteristics of the experimental procedures, are usually communicated to the participating subject and influence the relational meaning of what is happening in the experiment. Variable and unspecified social influences typically exist in the way the research subject responds to the experience of being a research subject, contaminating the results.

Experiments in psychology should be viewed as complex transactions between two people, rather than making possible controlled input and output with nothing going on in between. These transactions often overshadow the influence of the main variables of interest. In laboratory research, especially on psychodynamic or sociodynamic processes, it is a common affectation to claim that the extraneous or confounding variables are really controlled or eliminated. Too often they are not.

Although the three traditional premises I pointed out previously dominated academic psychology when I was just starting out, I took them to heart. There were also minority voices, such as psychoanalytic theorists, concerned with our inner mental lives, who viewed psychology and the mind in their own special way. Psychoanalysis, which had its origins in Europe, came on the scene at the turn of the century and became quite influential in American universities in the 1930s and 1940s, especially in clinical circles. There were also the European existentialists and phenomenologists who viewed subjective mental processes, such as perception and thought, as the causes of our actions.

Too many so-called pied pipers (Including me now, I suppose) have been telling us how psychology should be studied or conceptualized,

whether they were prominent psychologists or out-of-date philosophers of science, whose epistemological dogmas have regularly changed
with the tides. The genius of American universities has been that there
is plenty of room for divergent outlooks, which, though not necessarily
dominant at any particular time, find a place somewhere. Even unpop-
ular ways of thinking at the fringe of academic respectability often lie
in wait for awhile, only later to gain ascendancy.

In the late 1940s when I became an assistant professor at Johns
Hopkins, the three outlooks I have just described began to lose stature
in the United States because they led to oversimple formulations. They
had served as straightjackets preventing the development of creative
theories about the way we are. And by the 1970s, the earlier constraints
on how research should be done lost favor in light of the evident complexity of the human mind. We began once again to speak of psychology as the search for understanding about how our *minds* worked,
rather than as the study of behavior. In contrast with the experimental
tradition of creating events to study in the laboratory, *naturalistic
research* began to be taken more seriously and, though not ascendant,
has been increasingly gaining credibility (e.g., Willems & Raush, 1969).
Yet laboratory research, even in personality and social psychology
where it is most suspect, still dominates our psychology journals.

La Rochefoucauld, (Maxims, 1665, see The Oxford Book of Aphorisms,
p. 20) wrote that "It is easier to know man in general than to understand one man in particular." Yet if you deal with people clinically, it is
the individual you have to be concerned with. Psychology has always
been ambivalent about *individual differences.* The task of science is
usually defined as the search for general laws, which apply to everyone. There has been a growing realization, however, that we need to
know about and understand these individual differences at the same
time that we develop normative principles.

A vigorous minority movement has been emerging in the social sciences that is highly critical of the progress that has been made using
the methodological shibboleths that have dominated our field in
recent decades. Allow me to quote from Richard Jessor's (1996, p. 3)
optimistic foreword in a recent book on ethnography and human
development:

> Although still emerging from the thrall of positivism, social inquiry has for
> some time been undergoing a profound and searching reexamination of
> its purpose and its methods. Canonical prescriptions about the proper
> way of making science are increasingly being challenged, and a more
> catholic perspective on the quest for knowledge and understanding is

gaining wider acceptance. The honorific status accorded particular research methods—the laboratory experiment, the large-sample survey— has less influence on working social scientists than before, and there is a growing commitment to methodological pluralism and more frequent reliance on the convergence of findings from multiple and diverse research procedures. The openness of the postpositivist climate in the final decades of the twentieth century has presented the social disciplines with the opportunity to think anew about what it is they are really after and how best to achieve those objectives.

Having expressed some of my own present biases about research and theory in psychology, allow me now to proceed to some of my research at Johns Hopkins. I was involved in a number of interesting experiments. There were three main themes: Projective test theory; individual differences in perception (especially the role of a person's motives and ego-defenses); and psychological stress and coping. Projective tests are no longer in the forefront of psychodiagnosis, and my work in stress and coping will be extensively covered in several later chapters, beginning with chapter 7, which covers my early Berkeley years, and my cross-cultural research in Japan.

In what follows I describe only my research on individual differences in perception and unconscious processes. This work was influenced by the New Look movement in perception that came into prominence in the late 1940s and 1950s at the time of my first academic job. So I should first discuss the New Look movement from which my research sprang.

THE NEW LOOK MOVEMENT

When I arrived on the scene, there was already a strong minority dissent to traditional psychology, a point of view that sought to supplant radical behaviorism as a guiding philosophy. This new outlook, centered on a nontraditional way of characterizing human perception, took root right after World War II had ended.

The exploration of how we perceive the world has always been an important topic, as is the way we interpret ourselves and the events in our lives. But before the late 1940s, the ideological outlook underlying the study of perception consisted of three main themes, consistent with radical behaviorism and its positivist doctrine of operationism.

First, perception was studied *normatively*—that is, as the way *people in general* perceive the environment. Variations around the norm were regarded as either a nuisance, obscuring the general laws we are seeking to formulate, or as an example of psychopathology.

Second, when we respond to what is going on in the world, our perception was said to be *veridical*—that is, we perceive things *accurately,* which allows us to adapt successfully.

Third, perception is a cold process, and those who studied it had little or *no interest in ego-involvement or threat.*

The new outlook that came into being in the United States was reflected in the teachings and writings of my distinguished undergraduate teacher at CCNY, Gardner Murphy, and a number of others, especially Jerome Bruner. Each of the three themes of traditional perception research was rejected as the best or only way to understand how people perceive the world. The alternative New Look positions were as follows.

First, what we perceive depends on what we desire or need. New Look psychologists wanted to examine how this worked.

Second, the new emphasis turned away from strictly normative concerns, that is, the way people in general view and interpret the world, toward *individual differences*—that is, the unique ways people have of perceiving and thinking about the world, which is the essence of the subfield of personality psychology. Psychologists began to view deviations from the norm as healthy, rather than being necessarily pathological.

Third, research attention should be directed to the hot or emotional aspects of mind. Many New Look psychologists, me included, began to examine what happens when an individual, struggling to survive and flourish, has a high stake in the outcome of transactions with the environment, and engages in ego-defenses and collective illusions.

These two divergent outlooks, the traditional and New Look, were, of course, both correct, though they approached the question of how we perceive quite differently. They must be reconciled and integrated in a full treatment of human perception and adaptation. Among the clearest writers about the need for such a reconciliation was Kurt Lewin (1946, p. 9), who wrote:

> Problems of individual differences, of age levels, of personality, of specific situations, and of general laws are closely interwoven. A [scientific] law is expressed in an equation which relates certain variables. Individual differences have to be conceived of as various specific values which these variables have in a particular case. In other words, general laws and individual differences are merely two aspects of one problem; they are mutually dependent on each other and the study of the one cannot proceed without the study of the other. This implies that the data about the various age levels provided by child psychology have practical value for the understanding and guiding of individual children only if these data are linked with the concrete situation which is dominating the behavior of a given child at a given time.

The person whom I consider the most important progenitor of New Look thinking was Jerome Bruner. I first met him when he came to Hopkins in the early 1950s to give a colloquium. He influenced me in important ways. His early work on motivational factors in perception was, in my view, exciting. Though now in his 80's, he is still taking distinctive and creative positions on modern-day psychological issues. He argues, for example, that the study of the mind should be mainly about how we achieve meaning (Bruner, 1990), a topic that has been mostly avoided by traditional psychology, even by cognitive psychology.

Bruner reported a number of experiments, which demonstrated that needs influence what we see and how we see it. In one early study, Bruner and Goodman (1947) had 10-year-old children estimate the sizes of coins. The coins varied in monetary value, from 1 cent, to 5, 10, 25, and 50 cents. As a control condition, the children also estimated the sizes of gray cardboard discs, which were the same dimensions as the coins.

The children overestimated the size of every coin compared with the valueless cardboard discs, but the degree of overestimation increased with the value of the coins up to 25 cents. A comparison was also made of children from affluent homes and children who were poor. Every coin size was overestimated more by the poor children than the well-to-do.

This study was repeated by others and improved in design, with comparable results. In one instance, the sizes of metal slugs were estimated rather than coins. The children were also told that the slugs were made of substances of different intrinsic value—for example, lead, silver, white gold, or platinum. The results were that the more valuable slugs were overestimated, with the degree of overestimation of the poor children being greater than that of the rich children (see F. Allport, 1955 for a detailed review of this type of research).

Just think of what this means. Our perceptions are influenced not only by the actual physical conditions of the environment, but also by subjective values and needs, which vary greatly from individual to individual. To some extent, the person doing the perceiving constructs his own world. This means that to understand human variation requires that we take into account differences in what people want and believe.

This outlook became a central feature of my own later work on stress and coping, and the emotions. In the 1950s, I did studies showing that people are much more likely to attend to and perceive food objects when they are hungry than when satiated (Lazarus, Yousem, & Arenberg, 1953). It would take too much space to review all this work. However, I would like to illustrate one or two of what I regard as my most interesting, representative, and provocative studies of that period, which center on the way people deal with what threatens them—that is, by ego-defenses, which operate unconsciously and, therefore, silently.

PERCEPTUAL DEFENSE AND VIGILANCE

In addition to the idea that values and motives affect our perceptions of objects and people, New Look thinking also absorbed the Freudian idea that we often fail to perceive the way things are because they threaten us. Bruner referred to this as "perceptual defense," which is a variant of the concept of defense mechanism. But there is an opposite side to this process—namely, "perceptual vigilance."

The theory says that, just as some people fail to see what is there when reality threatens them, others become more attentive and acute in perceiving what is threatening. In other words, defense and vigilance are two very different ways of protecting ourselves against threat, each of which are preferred by different kinds of people. Defenders want not to see; vigilant persons want to identify the threat as quickly as possible in order to neutralize or overcome it.

What is it about people that leads them either to avoid (or deny) threats or confront them? Based on psychoanalytic thought, clinical patients who fail to perceive threats are referred to as conversion hysterics (I like the term *conversion reaction* better), and are said to use the defense mechanism of *repression*. They are in trouble because, unlike most of us, they experience paralyses, anesthesias and numbness in parts of the body, which are dramatic symptoms of dysfunction.

In contrast, those who are prone to see threat very readily, perhaps too readily, are referred to as *obsessive-compulsive* neurotics, and are said to use the defense mechanisms of *intellectualization and undoing.* They suffer from obsessive thoughts and compulsions, for example, difficult-to-resist impulses to engage in some ritual, such as repeated hand washing which, if not acted out properly, results in great anxiety. People without serious emotional troubles engage in these defenses too, but are less dependent on them and operate closer to reality.

Based on these premises, my Hopkins colleague, Charles Eriksen and I, with the help of a graduate student, Charles Fonda, did an unusual study (Lazarus, Eriksen, & Fonda, 1951). At a Veterans Administration outpatient clinic, we identified one group of patients that had been diagnosed as suffering from conversion reaction and another group that had been diagnosed as obsessive-compulsive.

We also constructed an audiotape on which sentences of three types were played, one with sexual themes, another with aggressive themes, and a third with neutral, nonemotional themes. One of the sexual sentences was "You have secretly wanted the sexual love of your mother." One of the aggressive sentences was "You have wanted to kill your father." These are obvious references to the Oedipus Complex. Freud considered sexual and aggressive impulses to be the most important sources of threat with which neurotic patients cope.

We then made the sentences on the audiotape somewhat difficult to hear, based on the sound engineer's concept of the signal-to-noise ratio. A weak background noise makes the signal—that is, the recorded message—more difficult to hear. Holding the signal constant in volume, the louder the background noise, the more obscure the message becomes.

We masked the sentences spoken on the tape with a white noise. From pilot observations in which we varied the relative loudness of the sentences and the noise, we achieved an average of about 50% intelligibility, which means that the patients we tested could recognize about half the contents of what was played on the tape. The study consisted of playing the audiotape to each of the men individually and keeping track of what they heard.

We found that patients diagnosed as having a conversion reaction heard far less of the contents of the emotional or "hot" sexual and aggressive sentences, as predicted from the theory, but did better on the neutral sentences. In contrast, the obsessive-compulsive patients heard much more of the contents of the sexual and aggressive sentences than they did of the neutral ones.

The evidence from this study can readily be interpreted to suggest that some people do indeed defend against threat by preferring not to hear it, whereas others vigilantly struggle to hear the self-same material. What is more, the direction of the difference could be predicted by knowing their clinical symptoms, which presumably reflected their preferred ego-defense. It's not the patients hearing that can account for this perceptual difference—that was comparable for both groups— but their way of coping with threat.

SUBCEPTION—EVIDENCE OF UNCONSCIOUS PROCESSING OF THREAT

One implication of these findings, and of the underlying New Look principle of perceptual selectivity, is that to protect ourselves from seeing or hearing what threatens us, we must somehow be able to sense the threat, yet shut it out of our minds. Shutting something out of our awareness is a form of unconscious mental activity, usually referred to as the dynamic unconscious. Here was a really challenging idea to tax the ingenuity of the researcher. So, Robert McCleary and I set out to test whether we can be unaware of threatening materials while nevertheless reacting to them emotionally.

Previous research by Elliot McGinnies (1949) seemed to demonstrate that people could distinguish threat from nonthreat without being conscious of what they were perceiving. A laboratory instrument, called a tachistoscope, was used in which emotional and neutral words could be presented on a screen at various speeds, some of them too fast to recognize dependably. McGinnies's data showed that if the speed of exposure is decreased gradually in a series of trials, the subjects react physiologically to the emotional words with a galvanic skin response (GSR), an electrical change in skin conductance that is associated with emotional arousal, but not neutral words, even before the words are consciously recognized.

McGinnies research suffered from a potential flaw, which is expressed in my use of the qualifying word "seemed." The flaw is that we cannot trust the subject's report of the emotional words, such as, whore, bitch, raped, and the like, because they can be embarrassing to say—especially in those more inhibited days. Even more important, these words could also be a source of surprise and uncertainty. After all, professors don't usually use them, at least publicly—it isn't professional. Therefore, subjects may have withheld reports about them until they were sure of what had been presented on the tachistoscopic screen. This would mean that the subjects were not necessarily unaware of the word to which they responded with physiological evidence of emotion. They might have merely been wary about responding with that word lest they appear foolish or be proved wrong.

So McCleary and I set about trying to do a foolproof experiment that would eliminate this objection (Lazarus & McCleary, 1951). The experiment was lengthy and complicated. To prevent the tendency on the part of subjects to withhold their reports of what was on the screen, we used a set of 10 five-letter nonsense syllables, which would have minimal emotional connotations. The syllables were as follows: YILIM, ZIFIL, GAHIW, GEXAX, JEJIC, JIVID, YUVUF, ZEWUH, VAVUK, and VECYD. There would be no reason to withhold reporting these meaningless syllables. Then we exposed subjects to three experimental procedures, each conducted on a different day.

The first procedure consisted of presenting the nonsense syllables on the screen tachistoscopically 100 times at various speeds, some too fast to be consciously recognized. Five different exposure speeds were used so that at the slowest speed subjects would get them mostly correct, but at the fastest speed they would see only a blur or nothing at all. This allowed us to create two groups of five syllables, both equal in how readily they could be recognized.

In the second procedure, which was a training session, we gave the subjects electric shocks when the five syllables we had designated as shock syllables were flashed on the screen at a speed slow enough to be readily recognized consciously. In this way, the shock syllables were made emotionally threatening because they were often followed by electric shock. Likewise, the other group of syllables were made emotionally neutral because they were never followed by shock. Subjects did not report what they saw in this procedure, but they were instructed to note the syllables presented.

We had, in effect, "conditioned" five syllables to an electric shock, leading subjects to expect shock about 2 or 3 seconds after they were presented on the screen. The other five syllables were "conditioned" as nonshock syllables, leading subjects to expect no shock when they appeared.

As in McGinnies' research, because subjects were hooked up to a galvanometer that measured the electrical conductivity of their skin, we could confirm at the end of this training session that they had really learned to react emotionally whenever a shock syllable was presented, but not when a nonshock syllable was presented. As emotion increases, the flow of electricity through the skin, called skin conductance, reliably increases, or to put it differently, the resistance of the skin to a current, which is the reciprocal of conductance, is reduced by whatever arouses an emotion. This change in skin conductivity to an electrical current (the GSR) was the same measure McGinnies had used.

The final procedure allowed us to test what would happen when we returned to the original procedure and exposed each syllable a number of times at varying speeds on the tachistoscope. The syllable was flashed, the subject said which syllable had been presented, guessing when he did not know, and we measured the emotional response on the basis of a change in the electrical conductance of the subjects' skin. We could then tell whether the subject showed an emotional response to some presentations and not to others by looking at the GSR's given to the syllables presented.

In a nutshell, we found that when a shock syllable had been presented, even if it was incorrectly identified, subjects gave a greater skin conductance reaction than when a nonshock syllable had been presented, suggesting the threat of shock had been unconsciously sensed. In other words, though they were not aware of what they had seen, as evidenced by having reported an incorrect syllable, the skin-conductance change showed they somehow knew unconsciously that it had been a shock syllable, and this tacit knowledge made them anxious. If the syllable presented was a nonshock syllable they did not correctly report, they showed little change in skin conductance, indicating that somehow they knew unconsciously that there would be no shock, and this tacit knowledge allowed them to remain relaxed.

On the basis of these findings, we claimed to have demonstrated *autonomic discrimination without awareness,* an unconscious process we called "subception" to distinguish it from a conscious perception. In effect, we are capable of sensing what is threatening without necessarily being conscious of the threatening stimulus. And sensing the presence of the threat, we are enabled to mobilize a defensive effort against consciously recognizing it. In effect, ego-defense and the unconscious recognition of threat are interdependent.

As a neophyte in the way social science operates, I was not prepared for the reaction of traditional behaviorists to what I believed we had demonstrated. What happened is instructive about how difficult it is to change dominant ways of thinking, even in the face of strong empirical evidence.

With one exception (Chun & Sarbin, 1968), all of the critiques of the subception experiment were about the interpretation that it had demonstrated an unconscious process, not about flaws in the experiment or its findings. The main critiques were by Bricker and Chapanis (1953); Eriksen (1956); and Howes (1954). The writers of these critiques found some way, other than a process of discrimination without awareness, to explain the findings. I replied to the one I considered theoretically most challenging and important (see Lazarus, 1956), and the issue was left with some psychologists having been convinced, others not, that an unconscious mental process had been the underlying basis of our findings.

What I have always found most fascinating about this entire episode is that in those days few academic psychologists were willing to take unconscious processes seriously in their formal theories about the mind, though they often referred to them in their private lives. Thus, the same psychologists who eschewed the concept had no compunction against speaking of their friends and others privately as engaging in unconscious defenses. The epistemology of academic psychology in those days was that there was no satisfactory method of studying unconscious mental processes. Therefore, they could never be proven or disproven and were beyond the realm of science.

This was to change later on, however. Ironically, at the present time there is great interest in the experimental study of the unconscious, though this interest is directed at the cognitive unconscious rather than the dynamic unconscious, which has to do with ego-defense. Times change, and with this come changes in the way scientists think about their subject matter. The changes are probably not the result of empirical findings, but reflect a new way of thinking, a changed *Zeitgeist,* which is a German word for an outlook that suddenly becomes widely accepted when a community is ready for it.

Constant confusion is evident even today in psychology between epistemology, which refers to how we achieve knowledge, and ontology, which refers to our theory about the nature of mind and existence. If a concept, such as unconscious mental activity, is methodologically impossible to observe directly, then it is said not to exist.

Bargh and Barndollar (1995) have discussed this confusion, citing some examples from Searle (1992) to illustrate its foolishness:

> Imagine yourself completely paralyzed but fully aware. You can produce no observable signs of consciousness, and an outside observer would have to conclude that you were not, even though you yourself know you are. Searle also quotes the old joke about two behaviorists who make love, with one saying to the other afterwards: 'It was good for you. How was it for me?

This was an important lesson for me, a recognition that one is apt not to be taken seriously if one's ideas and research fails to conform to the existing ideology. Philosophers of science often take stands that later are abandoned (Kuhn, 1970). Ideas that earlier had been rejected later become the coin of the realm. This is also applicable to the emergence of cognitive-mediational views of psychological stress and emotion theory, and the psychology of coping, when behaviorism and positivism fell by the wayside.

THE COSTS AND BENEFITS OF COLLABORATING WITH COLLEAGUES

Before closing this chapter on the Hopkins years, I want to comment on the complications of collaboration in research with university colleagues. Over the course of my research career, I have done research with many university people. Most have been students, some undergraduate, but mostly graduate. The students are often paid for their research assistance, learn about research and have opportunities to publish, thereby achieving professional visibility. I have also worked with academic colleagues, especially in the early years of my professorial life, collaborating in planning studies, collecting the data, and writing them up for publication. I was fortunate in that most were impressive scholars and researchers, and interesting as individuals.

Collaboration with university colleagues is a mixed blessing because of two pervasive problems. The biggest problem is that if too much of your research is done with others, then at promotion time the question will inevitably arise about which one of you is mainly responsible for the work. Did you get a free ride because your colleague initiated most of the ideas, or have you been the main progenitor of the research, its analysis, and write-up? In the latter case, the colleague may have the same difficulty at promotion time if the answer is ambiguous.

This problem encourages faculty members to work alone. It also gives students problems too, because they often work in the shadow of a distinguished professor who may get all or too much of the credit for the work. On the other hand, sometimes the student gets too much of the credit. The truth is sometimes difficult to discern. There is no ideal solution, but one helpful strategy is to make certain that you publish some work by yourself, even while collaborating with someone else. With equal colleagues, first authorship may be rotated, but this doesn't solve the problem, because first authorship is not a dependable criterion of the balance of responsibilities, because sometimes the authorship sequence is simply rotated mechanically.

Joint research is not always an asset in other respects also. Collaboration sometimes speeds the work and makes completing certain features of it more efficient. More often, however, it takes much longer to plan, conduct, analyze, and write up the work with two or more differently focused colleagues than when you work alone. With inexperienced students, it may take twice as long, because you must rewrite much of what they do; they are still learning, but need the opportunity to try their hand even if it is not yet professional.

Successful collaboration requires compatibility of work styles, which is something like the problem of marriage when the union is between two people of different temperaments and preferred ways of living. Sometimes collaborators cannot maintain the same work schedule, and you sit around waiting for them to turn in needed work, such as editing the manuscript you drafted. Some colleagues are better organized than others; some forget to contact you when they are supposed to or when there has been an unexpected change in the situation.

I've had many collaborators and the contrasts among them can be illustrated by looking more closely at how the work styles fitted with my own patterns in two very different cases. Although both had strong opinions on what we were doing and how we should do it, our work styles in each case were dramatically different. I won't identify them by name to avoid any embarrassment.

When one of the collaborators and I wrote an article together, one at the typewriter, the other sitting or standing nearby, each of us would verbalize what we wanted to say so we could get it down quickly on paper. Then it had to be edited carefully. We were both task oriented. Neither of us seemed determined to control the way it was said, and both quickly sensed when we got things more or less right regardless of who had verbalized it. In the main, we worked efficiently and without much conflict, and our egos did not get in the way. Only a few other times in my career did things go so smoothly.

In the case of another collaborator, however, there was considerable tension, I think because he always wanted to say it his way, which tended to get my dander up. His ego seemed to be involved in the writing of every word. Whatever I proposed, he would change, and I always felt that writing or planning together was an enervating contest of wills. He was an able researcher, and we got the job done, turning out provocative and valuable studies, but we also wasted much time on egocentric competition.

Problems like this continued throughout my research career—they are inevitable—but the issue of credit became less important as I achieved a major reputation as a scholar and researcher on my own. By having done much well-received research individually, as well as with quite a few different colleagues, there was less likelihood of review committees raising the possibility that the main progenitor was someone else.

The complexities of working with other persons tend to discourage professors from collaborating, which, ideally, could bring diverse talents to bear on the challenging theoretical and research issues with which we often struggle. We are pushed to tend our own gardens, so our names might become identified with important ideas and findings. Though often a pity, this follows an individualistic, competitive tradition, which results in what is viewed as a zero-sum game. It is the dominant reality of academic life.

My five years at Johns Hopkins were extraordinary in what they taught me about psychology—that is, the epistemology, ontology, and politics of the field in those years; the academic values; how to do research; and what happens when one publishes research that deviates from the ideological stance of the times. I had a lot to learn as a nearly green 26-year-old when I started academic life in 1948, but I was getting there.

In chapter 5, I accept another academic appointment, this time at Clark University in Worcester, Massachusetts.

REFERENCES

Allport, F. H. (1955). *Theories of perception and the concept of structure.* New York: Wiley.

Bargh, J. A., & Barndollar, K. (1995). Automaticity in action: The unconscious as repository of chronic goals and motives. In P. M. Gollwitzer & J. A. Bargh (Eds.), *The psychology of action* (pp. 457–481). New York: Guilford.

Bricker, P. D., & Chapanis, A. (1953). Do incorrectly perceived tachistoscopically presented stimuli convey some information? *Psychological Review, 60,* 181–183.

Bruner, J. S. (1990). *Acts of meaning.* Cambridge, MA: Harvard University Press.

Bruner, J. S., & Goodman, C. D. (1947). Value and need as organizing factors in perception. *Journal of Abnormal and Social Psychology, 42,* 33–44.

Chun, I, & Sarbin, T. R. (1968). Methodological artifacts in subception research and the tendency to reify: A rejoinder. *Psychological Record, 18,* 441–447.

Eriksen, C. W. (1956). Subception: fact or artifact? *Psychological Review, 63,* 74–80.

Exner, J. E. Jr. (1995). *Issues and methods in Rorschach research.* Mahway, New Jersey: Erlbaum.

Howes, D. (1954). A statistical theory of subception. *Psychological Review, 61,* 98–110.

Jessor, R. (1996). Ethnographic methods in contemporary perspective. In R. Jessor, A. Colby, and R. A. Shweder (Eds.), *Ethnography and human development: Context and meaning in social inquiry* (pp. 3–14). Chicago: University of Chicago Press.

Kuhn, T. S. (1970). *The structure of scientific revolutions* (2nd ed.). Chicago: University of Chicago Press.

Lazarus, R. S. (1949). The influence of color on the protocol of the Rorschach Test. *Journal of Abnormal and Social Psychology, 44,* 508–516.

Lazarus, R. S. (1956). Subception: Fact or artifact? A reply to Eriksen. *Psychological Review, 63,* 343–347.

Lazarus, R. S. (1974). *The riddle of man.* Englewood Cliffs, New Jersey: Prentice-Hall.

Lazarus, R. S., Eriksen, C. W., & Fonda, C. P. (1951). Personality dynamics and auditory perceptual recognition. *Journal of Personality, 19,* 471–482.

Lazarus, R. S., & Lazarus, B. N. (1994). *Passion and reason: Making sense of our emotions.* New York: Oxford University Press.

Lazarus, R. S., & McCleary, R. A. (1951). Autonomic discrimination without awareness: A study of subception. *Psychological Review, 58,* 113–122.

Lazarus, R. S., Yousem, H., & Arenberg, D. (1953). Hunger and perception. *Journal of Personality, 21,* 312–328.

Lewin, K. (1946). Behavior and development as a function of the total situation. In L. Carmichael (Ed.), *Manual of child psychology* (pp. 918–970). New York: Wiley.

McGinnies, E. (1949). Emotionality and perceptual defense. *Psychological Review, 56,* 244–251.

Rorschach, H. (1921). *Psychodiagnostics.* Bern: Huber.

Searle, J. R. (1992). *The rediscovery of the mind.* Cambridge, MA: MIT Press.

Shaffer, G. W., & Lazarus, R. S. (1952). *Fundamental concepts in clinical psychology.* New York: McGraw-Hill.

Stendler, C. B. (1950). Sixty years of child training practices. *Journal of Pediatrics, 36,* 122–134.

Willems, E. P., & Raush, H. L. (1969). *Naturalistic viewpoints in psychological research.* New York: Holt, Rinehart, and Winston.

CHAPTER FIVE

Clark University in Worcester, Massachusetts

I had been successful at Johns Hopkins, publishing research that gained national attention, and I was respected and liked by graduate and undergraduate students. Bernice and I had enjoyed our 5 years in Baltimore, building a family and career. It was also the most normal period we had in our marriage and it was the longest we had lived in one place thus far. We understood that we would have to leave Hopkins roughly by 1953, though this date was not inflexible. Under the circumstance, one hopes for an attractive job offer. It came from Clark University in Worcester, Massachusetts. I was offered an associate professorship and the position of Director of the Clinical Training Program. In most universities, tenure comes with an associate professorship, but this was not Clark's policy. My salary would be a modest $4,200 for the academic year (9 months). I left Hopkins in 1953 making $3,900 and, as you will see, departed Clark in 1957, still making less than $5,000.

But I was happy to accept the Clark offer. It had a solid reputation as a small, private university, with students from all over New England and New York City. Like Hopkins, it had a distinguished history, having hosted Sigmund Freud's only visit to America. Its first president was G. Stanley Hall, a pioneer of developmental psychology in the United States. Like Johns Hopkins, Clark had started out as a graduate school, but later added an undergraduate program to broaden its appeal and increase income from tuition.

In those years Clark had a small Psychology Department of roughly six regular faculty members. Several clinical affiliates, who worked at nearby clinics and hospitals, also contributed to the Department's educational program by teaching some of the clinical courses and supervising trainees. The Department was chaired by a distinguished European psychologist, Heinz Werner, who was in his mid-60's. Because of

Werner's interests, the emphasis in the department was firmly focused on developmental psychology. In addition to Werner and now me, the regular faculty included Robert Baker, Tamara Dembo, Gordon Gwinn, and Seymour Wapner.

In 1953, Worcester was a modest sized city of about 50,000 people. I first traveled to it alone to find a place to live, and rented a typical upstairs apartment in an old two-story detached house—something like the old Victorians in New York City—on a quiet, tree-lined suburban street, located about 5 miles from the university and the downtown area. The house had dark wood panels, bay windows, and old-fashioned rough soapstone set tubs in the kitchen; one never sees them today and porcelain is used to make the sink bright and smooth. I had the shortest commute to work I would ever again have in my long career, fewer than 10 minutes. Today it takes me 45 minutes to reach the university.

We set off in our car with our two babies, Nancy at age 6 weeks and David aged 2 years, our furniture coming separately on a moving van. Within days after our arrival, Bernice was invited to a faculty wive's tea, which was reminiscent of teas at Hopkins where the wife of a senior faculty member played the "colonel's wife." In other words, rather than acting like any other faculty wife, she constantly pulled rank on the wives of the junior faculty.

In any event, what happened at the Clark tea led to our first contact with the President of the University. As she was leaving, she backed her car into another, took down the license number and called the owner later, only to discover it was President Jefferson. He turned out to be a very pleasant and decent man whom we both liked. But what a way to be introduced!

Our formal introduction to the faculty and students came at a reception at the beginning of the semester. The 75 members of the faculty, all in cap and gown affixed with the colors of their alma mater, and their wives in long proper gowns, stood in a long receiving line. Each student—there were hundreds—would proceed down the receiving line, shaking hands with both the faculty member and his wife, and then being handed off to the next one in line. The previous faculty member would turn to the faculty member to his left and say, Professor whatshisname, this is Mr. or Miss so and so, and then after a hello, a few words, and a handshake, the student moved on. Given the anonymous patterns of life today, I suppose the face-to-face quality of this ceremony could be considered charming, but it was also a tedious social event, and very hard on the hand used for greeting, and the legs and back from standing in one place so long.

Compared with universities I had encountered earlier, Clark was a rather intimate place. The faculty was expected to attend graduation and a baccalaureate service in cap and gown and sit on the stage. I was not much for pomp and circumstance, and it is the only university at which I regularly attended these functions during my career. With so small a faculty, if you were missing there was an embarrassingly empty chair to indicate one's absence.

Worcester, Massachusetts (pronounced Wusta), situated in the middle of the state, did not look impressive when we first drove into the city limits in the summer of 1953. Satirized in the deprecatory comment from the 1937 Bostonian novel, *The late George Apley,* by John P. Marquand "But she's a Worcester girl," Worcester suffered from its proximity to Boston, which was the business and intellectual hub of the state.

As we drove into the city through an ugly factory and slum area after leaving the main road, Bernice dubbed it the "grey city." The houses were, in the main, drab and old-fashioned. The community was stagnant and conservative in the extreme. I can recall being asked by a female neighbor how long we would be living in Worcester, and after indicating that it would be at least 4 or 5 years, we were told, "Well then, it hardly pays to get to know you."

When we needed to go to the local bank to borrow $600 we were asked why people with our income would need to borrow money. We eventually got the loan, but were astonished that a bank would be so reluctant to loan its money to people with a secure job. This city showed little evidence of economic vitality. Few people moved in or out and there was little in the way of new building.

In Worcester, frugality was the watchword. One did not buy new shoes until it was no longer possible to repair the old ones. I was told that Jonas Clark, who founded the University, had not been sure the school would survive, so he designed Jonas Clark Hall, an old cavernous building of four stories where psychology was housed, to accommodate a shoe factory if the University fell on hard times. This was the culture we joined when I took the appointment as a faculty member of Clark University.

I remember walking the four flights of steps to the main office of the Department many times with Heinz Werner whose 65 years reached the top huffing and puffing less than my 31. He is shown with the other core faculty in Figure 5.1. He told me he had learned as a mountain climber not to talk while climbing, and to breathe deeply. But I think I was inadvertently patronizing the "old man" by being impressed that he could remain alert and active in meetings that lasted several hours.

FIGURE 5.1   The Core Psychology Faculty at Clark.
Clockwise around the table (from left): Dr. Tamara Dembo, Dr. Seymour Wapner, Dr. Robert Baker, Dr. Gordon Gwinn, Dr. Richard Lazarus, and Dr. Heinz Werner of the Psychology Department staff.

To a young man, such longevity seemed awesome, but as I approach 80, I no longer consider it remarkable at all.

In the early days of our residence in Worcester, we would sometimes go to Boston for dinner and theater. It was an hour and a half drive one way. We also drove to Boston once a month with our daughter Nancy to visit an orthopedist at Peter Bent Brigham Hospital, because she had a partially clubbed foot, which required therapy. The therapy worked and she was never again troubled with the problem.

The main road to Boston, about 40 miles east, was a three-lane highway, among the most dangerous roads ever built. In this respect it was similar to the old road between Baltimore and Washington, DC. The danger came from the fact that the middle lane could be used for passing in both directions, and at 40 or 50 miles an hour on a busy day, trying to pass in the center lane was not a safe maneuver. Worcester suffered from its closeness to Boston but, for us it was not close enough, so we went there less and less.

TAKING AN ADMINISTRATIVE JOB—
A MAJOR MISTAKE

I had been appointed the Director of the Clinical Training Program at Clark, so I was committed to an administrative role. Most of our clinical graduate students did their internships either at a number of Veterans Administration (VA) Hospitals and Clinics in the area, Worcester State Hospital, the Worcester Youth Guidance Center, and child-guidance clinics in Boston, the most famous being Judge Baker.

One of my responsibilities was to visit these internship centers to evaluate and contribute to internship training. The VA paid a consultants fee of $25 a day for these visits, and I spent about 4 days a month traveling to VA hospitals at which we had Clark students. The hundred dollars a month made a big difference in our income, but it used up too much time, and it had gotten difficult to do without the extras this provided. It was a financial trap I didn't like.

On some of these trips, such as to Northampton and Brockton, Massachusetts, I had to drive an hour and a half each way. Although the visits could be interesting, the VA hospitals were all a substantial drive from Worcester and in each case I had to commit a full day's time, during which I gave lectures and seminars and talked with the trainees. In some cases, such as Northhampton, it was possible to get in some recreation as well as business. In the late afternoon, I played tennis with the VA Chief Psychologist, Ike Scherer, and we would have dinner together before I took off for home.

Because of the widespread impression that the Northeast is highly urban, I was always amazed at how rural most of Massachusetts was. I would go many miles without seeing a town or a gas station. On the trip to Northhampton, I traveled the route taken by the infamous tornado of 1953, passing the rural section in which it was originally spawned. I could see the destructive swath it created before it got to urban Worcester, where it did substantial damage.

The Clinical Training Program was augmented by the presence of the chief psychologists in charge of training, Les Phillips at Worcester State Hospital, and Ted Leventhal at the Worcester Youth Guidance Center. These talented men added much to the Clark program, giving it great breadth and intellectual diversity. They maintained a close relationship with the Department, teaching some of its courses, supervising students in research, and advising the department on policy issues connected with training. Much of my time was spent working closely with them. Bernice and I spent many evenings with Les Phillips and his wife Eleanor. Les was ambitious, competitive, smart, and opinionated. We argued often, which we both enjoyed. I liked both of them, and so did Bernice.

The social atmosphere of the Department reflected the way many small, close-working professional groups behaved, recognizing that tensions among its personnel should be avoided. To prevent destructive competition, power struggles, ego-conflicts, and resentments from getting out of hand, we strove to live together in harmony, at least as much as possible.

Inevitably, however, there were power struggles and resentments, and I considered it part of my job to deal with them as constructively as possible. Occasionally deprecatory comments about this or that individual would crop up as one ambitious affiliate of the Department would try to upstage another, or a regular member would seek more power than others welcomed.

My most serious interpersonal problem surfaced fairly soon after I began to function as Director of Clinical Training. I was challenged by a man who believed I had usurped the position he should properly have held. In his eyes, Werner had appointed me as Director of Clinical Training behind his back. That was too bad, because I liked him as a person. I thought he was very decent, ethical, and able, but when he insisted that he was more qualified than I to be the Director, which, I suppose, could have been true on the basis of his much greater experience, a political struggle ensued. Simply put, whatever other construction might be put on his efforts, he wanted my job and I wasn't about to let him have it.

Among the faculty, I think I was more respected as a scholar than he, and it would have been a serious political mistake for Werner to have caved in to his demand. But I had no intention of ceding my role to him. I also knew Werner disliked my competitor for some reason, and didn't respect him either, so I had little real anxiety about my position. The struggle was ultimately resolved in my favor, but it led to ill will and much to my regret was the only seriously troubled relationship I had while at Clark. Even though I prevailed, I didn't enjoy the struggle. My antagonist later left the university, which is why he doesn't appear on the core faculty photo, and I never saw him again.

Although I was responsible for clinical training, I never had much formal training myself, except the supervision that Dean Shaffer gave me in my therapeutic work at Hopkins. Nor did I have the time to see patients at Clark. My knowledge and good sense in this area was never in question, but if I was to continue in my role as Director of the Clinical Training Program, I felt the need of proper credentials as a clinician. At the time, there was a growing movement toward formal accreditation for professional psychologists, and this was also beginning to be required at the state level throughout the country.

In 1954, I learned that the American Board of Examiners in Professional Psychology was planning a 2-day exam, the written part to be held in Boston on November 11–12 1954, the oral in New York City, in May 1955. The written part included multiple choice and essay questions about all sorts of issues pertaining to clinical theory and practice. On the later oral portion I was assigned a patient who needed to be seen on intake—that is, I had to do the initial interview from which diagnostic and therapeutic decisions would be made.

My patient was a woman who appeared to be suffering from depression. I had about 4 hours to make the clinical evaluation, including writing up my report with its recommendations about treatment. Later, I was interviewed by a board of clinical experts, none of whom I knew, and I was carefully questioned about my judgments. The central issue concerned whether the patient was a suicidal risk and, if so, what should be done. The woman's presenting problem reminded me uncomfortably about the Iranian student I had seen at the Hopkins clinic who committed suicide. But I was now better prepared for this test case by what had happened at Hopkins, which forced me to read and think a great deal about this kind of case.

I have little memory for most of the details, but I passed the exam and was given diploma number 1215 of the Board of Examiners of the American Psychological Association, becoming a Diplomate in Clinical Psychology on August 31, 1955, 2 years after coming to Clark. This diploma strengthened my academic position by proclaiming my clinical competence and skills. It also proclaimed to the world that not only was I properly qualified for my role as Clinical Director, but also for clinical practice. I had no intention of engaging in further practice after my years at Hopkins, but I could have done so if I wished.

SOCIAL LIFE

In 1956, a new housing development was constructed in the northern part of Worcester, and we decided to buy one of the houses on the G. I. Bill, with its federal guarantees of a low down payment and a modest mortgage interest rate. This acquainted us rapidly with the totally new pleasures and obligations of homeowning, and expressed our postwar desire for a suburban way of life.

Our life in suburbia was pretty standard. Bernice worked part time taking care of the books for my research grant. She made enough money at this to pay for baby sitters and small household items. We took the kids on trips, for example, to Benson's animal farm in Southern New Hampshire. Bernice obtained her first used car. Figure 5.2 shows Bernice and I in the snows of Worcester in December 1953, with Nancy in a baby carriage.

One of my major forms of recreation was tennis with Bob Baker, and volleyball, which was played mostly by faculty men who were far more advanced in age than I. I remember their knee bandages as a symbol of the discrepancy in our ages. One man even wore a corset on top of his shorts and shirt. But we played well as a team. When we were challenged by a student group, despite the age and physical health gap, we beat them easily; the students all wanted to be individual stars, whereas the faculty played as a team, setting the ball up for spiking at the net.

RESEARCH

The period at Clark provided me with my first substantial research grant money, which could support graduate students to do data collecting and made more elaborate research possible. At Hopkins, I did all my own data collecting, but at Clark it was largely done by graduate students, which was far more efficient for me. The main theme of this research, much of it performed with Robert W. Baker who also managed the campus clinic, had to do with the personality variables that could account for individual differences in stress reactions, and in coping with threat. This was a continuation of work I had initiated at Hopkins.

The personality variable to which we gave the most attention was motivation. The late 1950s were characterized by much interest in motivation and its measurement, stimulated by the impressive theoretical ideas and research of David McClelland. I had theorized that psychological stress only occurs when what is truly important to an individual is at stake.

As I look back, the most important research I published at Clark (Vogel, Raymond, & Lazarus, 1959) was performed on this question with two graduate students, Bill Vogel and Susan Raymond (who later became Vogel's wife). It demonstrated that what we most desire also makes us most vulnerable to stress when that desire is threatened. In contrast, what we desire least is much less likely to lead to stress. This

FIGURE 5.2   Nancy at 5 months in a baby carriage, December, 1953.

is a theme I carried over in later years to the emotions. There is no potential for stress or emotion if we don't have a stake in the outcome of an encounter. Other things being equal, the bigger the stake the stronger the emotion.

In the actual research, we asked high-school students to record in a diary how they spent their time over a 2-day period. From this information, we could gage the comparative strength of two common goals: achievement and affiliation. Those with high-achievement motivation greatly value competition against a standard of excellence. Those with high-affiliation motivation greatly value engaging in warm, friendly relations with other people. One can, of course, value both, but many people make a choice between one or the other based on their relative personal importance, which is reflected in how they spend their time.

On the basis of this diary-based information, we formed two groups of 20 students each. One group had a strong achievement goal and a weak affiliation goal. The other group had a strong affiliation goal and a weak achievement goal. Those high in achievement motivation spent most of their time studying and competing, whereas those high in affiliation motivation spent most of their time socially engaged with others.

The actual experiment was somewhat complicated and I don't need to describe it in detail here. Rather, I want to provide only a broad sense of what we did and found. The students were asked to perform certain tasks, which we characterized for them in two different ways, one as a test of academic and intellectual ability, the other as a test of the ability to have and sustain warm, friendly interpersonal relationships.

Half of the group with high-achievement motivation was given the academic instructions, and half the group with high-affiliation motivation was given instructions focused on friendships. The group with a strong affiliation goal was given the same two sets of instructions, half of them one set, the other half the other set. In this way, an equal number of each group was threatened in both their strongest and weakest goal direction. Degree of stress was evaluated by means of automatic nervous system reactions, such as pulse, blood pressure, and the resistance of their skin to an electric current (the galvanic skin response).

Our most important finding was that those students who were threatened in the area of their strongest motivation showed much higher levels of stress reaction during the test than those who were threatened in the area of their weakest motivation. In other words, if you are performing a task the result of which is not very important to you, your level of stress will be less than on a task whose result is very important. Therefore, to predict individual differences in stress reactions, one needs to know something about the strength of the goals that might be engaged in threat situations.

As I assess my research accomplishments at Clark, the bottom line is that, although I published some interesting and worthwhile studies, I do not regard it as up to the standard of quality and quantity I had attained at Johns Hopkins. In my 4 years at Clark, I published eight research articles, some of them quite mediocre. I still look on this period of my career as a transitional one in which I had not yet found the best academic situation for me.

For one thing, after a few years there I had become conscious of the enervating features of an administrative role. Though I believe I played that role competently, my main interests were in research and teaching, and the way my job was defined frustrated these main interests.

As was the case in graduate school, I was again troubled by colitis, which sapped some of my energy and deflected my attention from my may goals. This symptom suggested to me that I was under strain, and not in the academic role and setting most conducive to self-actualization. Bernice too was not enthralled by living in Worcester, and we both had been pretty sure we would ultimately leave. The main question was where and when.

TIME FOR A CHANGE

There were other factors in my dissatisfaction with my situation at Clark, which had to do with career aspirations and whether I was getting what I should be on the basis of my work. Within a few years after I got there, I began to feel that conditions were not favorable enough for me to remain a permanent member of the Department. I was overloaded with work and my position as Director of Clinical Training left me too little time for research and writing. This problem was compounded by the stinginess of Clark salaries, which had trapped me into too much consulting activity to supplement my modest University income.

Then too, the culture of the Department centered on developmental psychology, and the faculty was too small to permit other theoretical foci to flourish. I felt I would have to remain at the periphery rather than at the center of psychology at Clark, and that wasn't acceptable to me. The Department did expand after I left, and became more competitive in its salaries, but while I was there it was slow to move into the mainstream of psychology and grow with the field as a whole. I felt I would stagnate if I stayed. This led to the urge to seek more fertile ground.

Toward the end of my third year, I told Heinz Werner I wanted tenure and an increase in pay. Though tenure was not so important to me—I was confident I could get good offers elsewhere—I felt it had become an almost universal perquisite in academic life and should not be denied at Clark. He suggested I see President Jefferson. The conversation with him was warm and supportive. I received a small pay increase, but was told that the policy was to reserve tenure for a limited number of the faculty, and only at advanced levels. I didn't like the outcome.

I saw academic conservativism as holding Clark back, as well as me. There was growing competition all over the country for first-rate faculty members, but Clark was not yet ready to enter the auction. The sum and substance of my situation, with which Bernice concurred wholeheartedly, was that we should be ready to leave when the right job offer came along.

The first glimmer of an opportunity took place when the Psychology Department at Rochester University invited me to give a colloquium to talk about my research on stress. I thought they might be looking me over for a position. I gave my talk but nothing happened. Maybe I was wrong about their interest in me. Maybe I gave a poor presentation, though I didn't think so. Whatever the reasons, it was a disappointment. I never found out the truth, and my impatience was growing.

The second job-related event was a real feeler from Syracuse University. They were looking for a personality psychologist, and I was one of the candidates who came to give a colloquium. I understood that Calvin Hall was also being considered. He had written a major book on personality theory with Gardner Lindzey, and was interested in dreams. Syracuse chose Hall, who accepted but, ironically, stayed only a year then left. I felt a little discouraged, and wondered whether the right offer would ever come. With later hindsight, however, I came to consider the failure to get the job fortunate, because had I accepted this job, it would have been very difficult, and certainly improper after only a year or two, to consider going to Berkeley when invited, as I was to be shortly. In the meantime, I still looked forward to the opportunity to make a significant change to a top-notch university where I could truly flourish.

The opportunity came in the form of a feeler from Alex Sherrifs, presented in a very flattering way and speaking for the search committee of the Berkeley Department. When I wrote back expressing interest, I was invited to have an interview with Leo Postman, who was then the Chairman of Psychology. Like me, he was also an alumnus of CCNY, who had graduated in the same year, 1942. We met at an Eastern Psychological Association meeting in Philadelphia. Leo indicated that the Psychology Department was prepared to offer me a tenured position as a top-level Associate Professor, and encouraged me to consider it.

I had hoped for a full professorship. During the course of the negotiations, I was told that in 2 years I would be put up for the full professorship, and that no problem was foreseen for a promotion when the time came. I considered pressing for the full professorship, but there were risks in this. I trusted Leo's integrity and decided to take the offer. In 2 years, in 1959, as expected, I became a full professor at Berkeley at 37 years of age.

The salary was a little less than $9,000 for the academic year, which at that time seemed luxurious compared with what I received at Clark. But I had not banked on the high cost of living in the Bay Area, which, despite the mild climate, ate up much of the salary increase. Our move to California from Massachusetts was expensive, but Berkeley provided half the cost.

When I told Heinz Werner I had accepted a job offer, he was taken aback and a bit irritated that I had not discussed it with him. I suppose he thought if I had pressed harder, the matter would again be discussed with President Jefferson, but he had not been very forthcoming about upgrading my position when I had approached him earlier. On the other hand, the way promotions are often obtained is by using another, better offer. I really wasn't enamored of my future at Clark and the job at Berkeley was simply too attractive for me to negotiate further. Berkeley was a distinguished institution, and no one I knew would have understood if I had rejected its offer. I accepted.

Our main reservations about coming to Berkeley had to do with leaving family and friends in the Northeast. In addition, the new job on the West Coast was far from the population center of the country, and of psychology. Being in California meant complications, such as the great distance to Eastern meetings, and to Europe. Asia had not yet become a new industrial and intellectual center, though later, in 1963, my family and I would spend a year in Japan for research purposes.

The trip to California began in mid-August 1957, with five of us in a 1956 Plymouth, the one with the big tail fins and a body so loose that it seemed to bend and twist with every rise and fall in the pavement. In addition to our two children, the fifth traveler was our dog, a beagle named Black Joe. We loaded up the car trunk with games for our kids, now 6 and 4, and at every breakfast stop they would each get a present, always a new game that could be played in the car to keep them amused for awhile. We planned the trip to be about 8 days, making sure to arrive when the moving van arrived.

We drove about 6 hours each day. Our route was the Northern one across the Pennsylvania and Ohio Turnpikes to route 30, which took us through the Midwest, the state of Wyoming, and Winnemucka, Nevada, thence on route 40 to Berkeley. When there was a time change as we went West, we still got up at the same hour so our trip began progressively earlier in the morning to take advantage of the coolest hours. Each day we tried to end up in the early or middle part of the afternoon at a motel with a swimming pool so the kids could let off steam, tire themselves out, then sleep at night. As we approached California, son David and I had our first taste of abalone, which we both loved.

The Central Valley of California and the ride through Sacramento was very hot—we had no air conditioner—but when we hit Vallejo, which is near the coast, it suddenly turned cool. It was the second time Bunny and I had experienced the coastal phenomenon of temperature shifts of as much as 40° as you move from inland to the coast or vice versa.

The first time had been a trip to California we made in the month of August, 1950 from San Antonio, Texas at the close of the research project with Jim Deese and his wife at Lackland Air Force Base in San Antonio, Texas. We had travelled through Los Angeles, California (via steaming hot Phoenix and Blythe, Arizona), then up the coast to San Francisco, thence to Lake Tahoe, and back to the East Coast. Going up the coastal road, Route I, we would go a few miles inland and sweat, then suddenly veer toward the coast with its cool marine air. We also discovered the phenomenon of all dry climates—namely, that you are hot when in the sun and cold in the shade.

On the California portion of our trek, there were as yet no freeways, and we had to drive slowly through the business sections of each town along the way to Berkeley from Vallejo, ending up at last at a motel on University Avenue a few miles from the campus. It was a pretty sleazy motel, but well located for our purposes, and it accepted pets.

With our arrival in the Bay Area, we were about to begin a new period in our lives. Beginnings are always exciting but also a source of anxiety, because there is no script, except when you look back as I am doing now. Until we arrived in California, Bernice and I had never stayed in one community longer than 5 years, but now, without realizing it, we were digging in for the rest of our lives.

It takes a series of five chapters to examine the important experiences and concerns of our 40-plus years at Berkeley, including academic and research activities, and ultimately my retirement years, beginning in 1991. The Berkeley years begin in 1957 with chapter 6.

REFERENCES

Marquand, J. P. (1937). *The late George Apley.* Newbury Port, MA: Little Book.

Vogel, W., Raymond, S., & Lazarus, R. S. (1959). Intrinsic motivation and psychological stress. *Journal of Abnormal and Social Psychology, 58,* 225–233.

CHAPTER SIX

The Early Years at Berkeley

A fter our arrival at Berkeley in August 1957, our first needs were to obtain the keys to the Tolman house we had rented, sight unseen, and settle into the community. Although West Coast people might refer to it as a charming, Berkeleyish house with a view of the Bay and San Francisco, we were greatly disappointed when we saw it. As with most such houses, it was on stilts on a steep hill.

We were concerned about our kids on their bicycles, inexperienced as they were with hills and narrow, winding streets on which two cars could not pass. The house itself was old and dark, and its layout was poor from the standpoint of the furniture we were bringing and our family needs. We didn't stay in it a single night. Instead we remained in the motel and went house hunting, and soon we were renting a small house in lower Piedmont, in the Oakland area south of Berkeley and the campus.

During our first months in the Bay Area we visited many well-known places, such as Monterey and Carmel, Mount Tamalpias, Napa and the Alexander Valley, the North Coast, and San Francisco itself, with its theaters and restaurants. One of our main disappointments was the discovery that the beaches of Northern California were not as good as Eastern beaches, and the water was too cold for swimming. One had to go south to the beaches between Los Angeles and San Diego to find water that was not bitter cold, or travel to Mexico, the Caribbean, or Hawaii.

Another disappointment was that Berkeley, Oakland, and San Francisco did not have summer as we knew it in the East. It was wonderfully cool for working, but seemed more like early spring than summer. The Berkeley Hills were also basically urban rather than suburban, though there were marvelous public parks with miles of wooded areas. One day, we drove east through the Caldecott Tunnel under the Berkeley hills, and discovered that on the other side the climate and terrain were altogether different. With prevailing westerly winds off the ocean, the farther away from the water you get the hotter it is in the summer and the colder in the winter. Contra Costa County was warm, sometimes very hot, but dry, as in the desert.

After a few months of renting, we bought a house in the suburban community of Lafayette, which then had less than 8000 people. The move meant I would be a long-distance commuter for the rest of my professional life. We lived in Lafayette for 32 years. In 1975, we discovered the San Joaquin and Sacramento river delta, where we bought a small condo on the water and a power boat.

PSYCHOLOGY DEPARTMENT POLITICS

In taking the Berkeley offer, I thought little about the downside of our decision. The main one, which tended to come up when I discussed the move with others, concerned the political problems of the Berkeley Psychology Department. I was told it was rife with faculty contention and bitterness. Being young and ambitious, I took the optimistic view that I could handle it, that I did not need a surfeit of warm, friendly relationships with other faculty, that I was an autonomous individual with my own research and teaching agendas. Bernice and I would find our own suburban soulmates and, indeed, we did.

There was some denial in this sanguine view, and quite a few years later when I was in my 50s, I experienced some distress over my sense of isolation and powerlessness. True to my vow after Clark, I avoided administrative responsibilities when I could, which left academic power in the hands of others, and made it difficult to complain or try to change anything. When later I suffered at the hands of the often arbitrary and unsupportive Berkeley administration, I seriously considered leaving, but never did. I shall examine this struggle in chapter 11. What needs to be said now, however, is that we embarked on the move to the Bay Area, not so much with any apprehension, but with anticipation and enthusiasm.

The Psychology Department was impressive, consisting of a substantial core of "old Berkleyans" who had achieved important reputations as leaders in their respective fields. The term "old" does not refer to age, but to the fact that they had begun their productive careers there, which distinguished them from mainly younger faculty who were rapidly arriving in the great expansion of universities in the 1950s and 1960s. The history of the Department greatly anteceded even the arrival of the "old Berkeleyans," having begun about 1900, when psychology was still part of philosophy.

Included among the old Berkeleyans were, in alphabetical order, Egon and Else-Frenkel Brunswik, Richard Crutchfield, Edwin Ghiselli, Harold Jones, David Krech, Jean Macfarlane, Donald MacKinnon, Nevitt Sanford, Edward Tolman (probably the most distinguished figure in the department when I arrived, but who died shortly after), and Robert Tryon. The Brunswiks, both distinguished psychologists, had been tragic suicides before I arrived. Others, such as Leo Postman, Donald A. Riley, Mark Rosenzweig, Theodore Sarbin, Mason Haire, and Read Tuddenham arrived later, but significantly before I did. Frank Beach came much later. My generation included Jack Block, Kenneth Craik, Stephen Glickman, Harrison Gough, Jonas Langer, Arnold Leiman, Gerald Mendelsohn, and Paul Mussen.

Th list of Berkeley faculty is grossly incomplete, and I have not tried to be meticulous about the sequence of arrivals. It doesn't include those of the last few decades. Nor does it include scholars, some of them distinguished, who had special appointments, for example, women who could not be hired because of antinepotism rules, and those who served in institutes, such as the Institute of Human Development, and were not officially listed as members of the Psychology Department. A few examples are Mary Jones and Jean Block, both now deceased. Those already named, as well as many who came after them whom I haven't listed, helped over the years to make the Psychology Department at Berkeley one of the most distinguished in the world. I was proud to be a part of it.

It is easy to criticize ratings of universities and their departments on all sorts of grounds, but during my presence there has never been any question that Berkeley ranked very high among the top 10 universities in the country, and by extension, the world. The most respected surveys, for example, that of the National Research Council, identified Berkeley in 1995 as number one because it had the largest number of departments in the top 10, with Stanford second, Harvard third, Princeton fourth, and MIT fifth.

Of course, individual departments vary considerably in their rating, despite a high overall rating for the university. My own sense is that Psychology at Berkeley has weakened substantially in recent years. The National Research Council 1995 ratings confirms this judgment, placing it ninth among the top 10 schools, below most other major departments on the Berkeley campus.

Notwithstanding arguments about who is fairest of them all, the warnings about contentiousness in the Department proved valid almost at the instant of my arrival. The conflicts within the Department and the ways they were dealt with played an important part in my own adaptation, and so I venture to describe some of those that seem important. I can't say whether these conflicts were more virulent and socially destructive than those that are endemic to most major academic departments. They have to do with the distribution of space, educational doctrines, ideologies about what constitutes good research, hiring priorities, teaching decisions, who is to be promoted or accelerated, personal squabbles for power and influence, who is to be the chairperson, the location of one's office, and so on.

Immediately on my arrival, I was invited to parties at which dissatisfactions were aired, decisions to redress them examined, and efforts made to enlist me in their group's struggle. I did get hooked in the struggle to create a clinical training program.

Before speaking of the negatives, however, I must say that in these early years Bernice and I did not feel isolated. We were invited to small dinner parties by older members from diverse fields of psychology, and these parties were usually pleasant and often gracious. They were efforts to welcome newcomers despite the overt conflicts that surfaced again and again.

There were almost never parties for the Department as a whole. One summer we gave such a party, inviting everyone to a dinner in our Lafayette home, which had several good-sized patios on which we had planned to serve. The number of guests came to 65, and consisted of faculty members and their wives. Many of them were people whose names I had known since graduate school, some of whose research and books I had read as a student. Unfortunately, it turned out to be a chilly and windy evening, and we had to abandon outdoor serving, cramming everyone into our modest-sized home. Everyone responded like good sports, and the party turned out to be one of great good cheer.

THE FIGHT OVER CLINICAL TRAINING

The most prominent conflict in the Department, a struggle in which I was directly engaged, was over whether we should have a clinic and a clinical training program. A number of departmental groups were opposed to it, including the "old Berkeleyans" and the biological–experimental faculty. These two groups pretty much controlled the Department, but a substantial number of other faculty members also considered clinical training to be damaging to scholarly and teaching concerns.

Ultimately, the strife led to a successful move to unseat the chairperson, Leo Postman, in a "palace revolt." It was led by Nevitt Sanford, and included a rather diverse group, including myself, Jack Block, Joe Speisman, Alex Sherriffs, and several others. Though the cause was just, I have always felt a little guilty over this, partly because Leo was a very decent person and had never done me any harm. But the field prejudices were offensive and powerful sources of contention, and although there might also be other agendas for some of the group, we all believed there should be a clinical program in the Department.

When the university administration got wind of what was happening, it decided that the department could no longer govern itself. There was evidence of tremendous ill will. The result was that a chairperson was appointed for Psychology, C. W. Brown, who had the power of an autocratic department head.

As a result of the bitter complaints of the more clinically oriented faculty, one of the demands of the university administration was that the Department would have a clinic that served nonstudents—there already was a mental health clinic for students at Cowell Hospital. The clinic would function as the center of a clinical training program.[1]

This decision required a search for a Director of the clinic and the Clinical Training Program. The search ultimately ended with a short list of two psychologists, Edward Borden and Sheldon Korchin. The choice went to Korchin, who set about establishing a clinic and a Clinical Training Program with a modest-sized clinical faculty of five members. This program was, in effect, being forced down the throats of the substantial number of faculty who opposed it.

I should speak a bit about what I see as the reasons for the prejudice against clinical psychology, which were complex and often obscure. The main overt reason was the conviction that clinical psychology— especially when devoted to professional practice—was intellectually and scientifically alien to the scholarly ideals of doctoral education. A less overt reason was the fear that a clinical training program would dominate the department, siphon off money, space, students, and other resources from the rest of the faculty, and threaten the place of traditional psychology. Nationally, the hostility to clinical psychology constituted a nonefficacious holding action against a very powerful, but unstoppable, postwar social movement, which would end with psychologists engaging in private practice in competition with psychiatry.

Much to my surprise I discovered that the worst enemies of clinical training were not confined to the biological-experimental faculty, as most of us who were sympathetic to such training had initially supposed. It

---

[1] It is noteworthy that one of the faculty members, Olga Bridgman, who had been a student with an M. D. degree at Berkeley, then a faculty member in 1915 after her Ph. D., could be said to have mainly clinical interests in children with problems of delinquency and dependency. So there was actually a modest precedent at Berkeley for clinical concerns.

also included faculty members in cognate subfields, such as personality, social, and industrial psychology.

But why would personality psychology faculty members feel threatened by clinical training and want to distance themselves from it? One would have thought that there would be a natural affinity between personality and clinical psychology. I think the answer is that at Berkeley the field of personality was centered at the Institute of Personality Assessment and Research (IPAR), which tended to equate personality with assessment. IPAR's central concerns were personality structure and its measurement, rather than personality dynamics and efforts to change it, which has to do with psychological processes rather than structure.

To faculty members identified with IPAR (with the exception of Jack Block, I believe, and myself, but probably for somewhat different reasons), it seemed important to distinguish personality assessment from clinical diagnosis and practice. There was anxiety that the identity of personality psychology would be co-opted by clinical training, and this made some of the personality faculty wary of joining forces with the clinical group. I believe this anxiety was based on a sense of vulnerability that could not be acknowledged—namely, that although once distinguished and ground-breaking, personality assessment at Berkeley had become ossified and out of date.

I say this knowing full well that at present the field of personality is dominated by research on what is known as "the big five," which refers to five core traits used in personality assessment, said to cover most of the individual variations in life style. There is no reason to criticize such research per se, but as a total approach to personality, the outlook is to my mind much too narrow and limited to questionnaire approaches to represent a field as rich and varied as personality (see Lazarus, in press, 1997).

The personality-assessment emphasis on superficial structure rather than process left out, and still does, too much that was essential to the field, especially psychodynamics, which centers on the ongoing and changing struggle to adapt and includes psychological development, motivation, the coping process, and defense. Although I identify myself with the field of personality, you can see that my outlook places me at loggerheads with what personality psychology focused on when I was active in the Department, and this is still true for me as an emeritus.

But to return to the struggle over clinical training, I think a similar anxiety, with a comparable sense of vulnerability, also existed among the social and industrial faculty. Industrial psychology was a field with some stars at Berkeley, such as Edwin Ghiselli and Mason Haire. They were keen to affirm their commitment to theory and research on social organizations, and to avoid the impression that industrial psychologists, who were being increasingly certified by the American Psychological Association (APA) for applied practice, were nothing more than mental health experts who consulted for industry about dysfunctional workers.

Social psychologists, such as Richard Crutchfield and David Kretch, also shared this zealousness about what they considered to be scientific values, which to them seemed threatened by applied work. And so they too wanted to distance themselves from clinical psychology.

Although the stance of these faculty members was largely self-serving, there was some legitimacy to their feeling that professional clinical psychology posed a threat. There has long been a major prejudice in psychology departments against an emphasis on clinical practice rather than theory and research.

Many departments fought against taking on clinical training programs—and some major one's, like Stanford, still refuse to offer clinical training. The rationale for this attitude is that a Ph. D. degree was primarily for scholars not practitioners. I was sympathetic to this view when I was just starting out. I saw the main task of psychology to be a search for an understanding of our humanity. Practice should be secondary to this and flow from that search. But this doesn't mean it should be ruled out. You already know I believe that some practice is important in acquainting psychologists with real human problems, which makes it less likely that they will settle for simplistic analyses of mind and behavior.

I felt that clinical psychology was being victimized unfairly and unwisely, and that regardless of the issue of private practice, the questions it dealt with were important and deserved a proper place in academic life. Clinical practice is an important source of understanding and, at least in theory, should not be the enemy of either scholarship or the search for knowledge. The issue had become little more than a naked power struggle within university psychology departments.

It is ironic that the worst fears of conservative academics who wanted to emphasize scholarly research in graduate study later materialized. Once most psychologists were to be found in universities. Today, practicing clinicians make up the lion's share of psychologists working outside of universities. The standards of excellence among some professionals seem also to have been seriously eroded in this rapid and massive growth of clinical practice. The largest percentage of professionals are highly trained and qualified clinicians who must be upset about what has been happening to those standards.

Consider, for example, what we see on television and radio talk shows. Psychologists, with minimal opportunity to study the people they talk about, often exploit unhappy people by giving them half-baked advice as public entertainment. What many of them do on TV violates the professional standards and code of ethics promulgated by the American Psychological Association designed to prevent harmful psychological practices.

All this is in the interests of earning the entertainment dollar, and operates largely at the lowest intellectual common denominator. Though I find some of the media psychologists interesting, bright, and witty, even impressive, on the whole they do a serious disservice to the responsibility of psychology to gain knowledge and help people in trouble.

This problem is not unique to psychology, but also exists in medicine, a profession whose medical association has long been little more than a trade union to boost medical incomes rather than to advance health services for the public, and which doesn't police its own incompetent and fraudulent doctors adequately. The almighty dollar has come to rule absolutely in our society, even in the helping professions, making a tragedy for physicians themselves as the unhappy handmaidens of corporate America, a shame for the once honorable profession of medicine, and a potential disaster for us patients.

Libertarians and political conservatives, which include most physicians, will disagree with what I just said, because they believe society benefits most when people are left alone by government to be self-serving. On the contrary, my view is that without careful regulation, the public interest is likely to be thwarted. There needs to be a wary attitude on the part of the public and a reasonable compromise between freedom and regulation.

Unfortunately, what I have said about the deterioration of standards of clinical practice in psychology adds fuel to a dangerous and unproductive schism between clinical practitioners and researchers. The harm done is that what research workers discover is ignored by clinicians, and vice versa. Research workers fail to get the benefit of the practical experience and observations made by sound clinicians. Yet, ironically, many of the best young people starting out on a career in psychology today have the good sense to opt for clinical training, which gives them the largest range of job options. A fine analysis of this schism has recently been published in the *American Psychologist* (Beutler, Williams, Wakefield, & Entwistle, 1995), the house organ of the APA.

Echoing an earlier time when there had been separate national organizations for research and applied psychologists, a major breakup occurred in the 1990s in the American Psychological Association, which had once been the single umbrella organization for all of psychology.

The APA came more and more to look like a trade union, like the AMA, with its key interests vested in preserving and enhancing the fee-based practitioner.

This has led many who were dedicated to the search for knowledge to break away from the APA. They formed a separate organization, the American Psychological Society (APS), with its own science agendas and meetings. I consider this to be unfortunate because it further divides the field and separates practitioner from academician. Like many of my ilk, however, I belong to both organizations to try to neutralize this split. I am not convinced, however, that the balance of research and theoretical interests reflected in what is published in the APS journals is representative of the importance or diversity of subfields in the science of psychology. Field bias and prejudice about what constitutes science remain alive and well.

Despite the fact that the worst fears of the opponents of clinical training came true, I do not think that those who fought against applied professional concerns acted wisely. It is not useful or responsible to attack practice, as so many academics did when they fought clinical training programs. Had they not been so prejudiced and self-serving, the outcome might not have been as negative as it seems today, because there is so little interaction between scientific and applied psychology. This is a dichotomy that shouldn't exist.

The interdependency between good science and good practice is highlighted by the continuing efforts of the best clinicians to profit from their experience by asking searching questions about what they do and developing general principles that take what has been learned through scientific observation into account. The viewpoint I have been expressing is also emblematic of those researchers who define science broadly and ecumenically, rather than narrowly and hierarchically, and who also have respect for efforts to understand and deal with adaptational failures.

Serious effort had been made in the past to bridge the gap between science and clinical practice. This effort led to the formulation of the "scientist–practitioner" model of clinical training, which tried to do more than lip service to both sides of the issue. Another model has been the university degree of Doctor of Psychology, which, as I understand it—though I have no direct experience with it—makes no effort to teach science to practitioners. But when all is said and done, I don't think these models have worked very well in practice. Except for university clinicians who truly resonate to the idea, there continues to be a void between those who are interested in practice and those who are interested in research.

We must also be careful not to idealize psychological science with a capital "S." Unfortunately, the present scientific enterprise in psychology is in a sorry state. In chapter 4, I criticized the methodological narrowness of psychology and its failure to progress. I might add to what I said there by saying sadly that the real problems of mind, the ones we all wonder about in our lives, are not much addressed in psychology.

No self-respecting writer or dramatist would describe or attempt to understand people in the simplistic and superficial way that psychologists do in their research. We are so enamored of analytic reduction that we constantly fail to resynthesize what we find into higher levels of analysis. We ignore what I consider the most important problem of psychology—namely, how we derive meaning out of our relationships with the social and physical world. Humans are the most complicated of all God's creatures, and I believe, despite contrary affirmations from those in the field who serve as official gatekeepers of research, we are making very little progress in understanding the way our minds work. The great problems of humankind are every bit as important as they ever were, but the way present-day psychologists address them seems to be mostly by avoidance. I believe I am expressing thoughts many of us have, both young and old. We can do better, and we certainly need to.

DEPARTMENTAL REORGANIZATIONS

To return to the Berkeley situation, the embarrassing period of receivership during which the Department lacked the credibility to govern itself eventually came to an end. It did so by an expedient device in which it was reorganized into three broadly based camps, one that included clinical, personality, and social psychology, a second that was identified as biological–experimental psychology, and a third that was called general psychology.

You might wonder why there were three groups, rather than two, and what the designation "general" stood for, as that term should presumably cover the whole field. The arrangement of the Department into three groups had a political motivation, because most faculty members in the general group could have found a comfortable place in one of the other two groups. The general group actually consisted of a strange admixture of social and industrial psychologists, a few concerned with measurement and statistics, and an occasional faculty member in other areas, such as developmental psychology, who preferred the company of this group.

The political motivation, expressed quite openly by some, was that when the two groups would become deadlocked, a third was needed to swing the voting outcome. Thus, if the biological—experimental and the clinical, personality, and social groups were deadlocked, the general group would have power beyond its small size and importance to control the outcome. The Department operated for quite a few years with this strange structure.

The three groups, and the subgroups within them, were quite autonomous in many ways. They were responsible for their own curricula and graduate-student selection. They were able to compete with other groups for resources, such as space and new faculty. Faculty appointments and promotions were still departmental functions, though groups now had greater power over them.

However, the granting of the Ph. D. degree was still to a considerable extent in the hands of the graduate division. To be advanced to candidacy, each graduate student had to pass an examination given by a mixed group of faculty, which included at least one faculty member from outside the group, and one from outside the Department. The dissertation was also supervised by a mixed committee.

As anomalous as this organizational structure was, it seems to have worked. Its main result was much less contention, and the feeling that the educational and research functions of professors were being influenced, or even managed, by people in cognate fields, rather than by those who had little knowledge or respect for one's subject matter. The bitterness that had characterized Berkeley psychology for so many years began to disappear, or at least go underground.

At length, the same fragmenting forces that created the three separate groups, each containing several different psychological subfields, led to still another Departmental reorganization. Subfields separated, and gained almost complete autonomy over the curriculum and academic requirements at the graduate level—and to some extent even at the undergraduate level. In effect, each subfield was promoted to its own quasi department. There was a separate faculty for each—namely, personality, social, clinical, developmental, cognitive, biological, and measurement.

A doctoral student now had to specify what his subfield was and meet its requirements, which tended to escalate until it was virtually impossible to give much time to the study of other subjects. The faculties and students were so zealous about preserving their respective subfields that attempts to join forces educationally—even when doing so would be in the interests of overall graduate education (such as having overlapping studies for personality and social psychology)—

were met by great resistance, and nothing was ever done until very recently when, in 1995, personality and social psychology came together. Present-day overspecialization threatens possibilities of subject integration and interfield communication. Psychology seems to have become permanently fragmented.

I'M DESPERATELY ILL AT 41

In 1960 I was appointed to the Berkeley Center for Social Science Theory. The appointment gave me a marvelous opportunity for interdisciplinary intellectual interaction that has now all but disappeared on the campus. Each year, six significant social scientists were freed from teaching for 1 of 2 years of the appointment. Our main obligation consisted of meeting regularly once a week to talk about matters of general interest, usually theoretical ideas and research related to them. During my membership in the Center, two of the faculty were from Economics. Theodore Sarbin and myself were from Psychology, Neil Smelser from Sociology, and Leo Lowenthal from Rhetoric.

The weekly interactions were sparkling. Each, in turn, would talk about what was most dear to us in theory. I was writing my 1966 book on stress and coping, so I spoke of the ideas I was trying to write about. Neil Smelser was writing his seminal book on the *Theory of Collective Behavior,* which appeared in 1963. Because Smelser's work was focused, in part, on panics and riots, the main concern being *collective* fear and anger, and mine was focused on psychological stress, the main concern being *individual* fear and anger, our work overlapped considerably. Ted Sarbin, with interests in the social context of behavior, was struggling with issues of role and identity. Leo Lowenthal was concerned with the contrasts between popular and elite culture.

Despite the great satisfaction provided by my Center appointment during 1962 and 1963, these years, especially the latter one, were devastating for me, for reasons that at first I didn't understand. I noticed it as a failure on my part to make satisfactory progress on my book. I experienced a great sense of pressure and anxiety, and in panic I wanted to withdraw from everything. I began to feel that I was in the wrong line of work, that academic life was too stressful for me to handle, and I assumed that all this had psychological origins.

But matters were to grow much worse. When Bernice and I would play cribbage, which we did often, I would occasionally find it difficult to sort the cards to play them properly. Something was very wrong with my ability to function. To sort my hand I had to count everything slowly and concretely. I couldn't put the cards together at a glance, as any good player can do. I had suddenly lost the ability to think abstractly. As this was going on, Bernice would see that at first I would grow pale then flushed as the attack was ending. An attack would last 5, 10, or 15 minutes and then it was over. We knew something was wrong with me, but had no idea what it was.

I went to the Kaiser Health Maintenance Organization (HMO), which was then providing our University-sponsored health care. The physician I saw did a blood-sugar test and diagnosed my problem as probably a functional hypoglycemia in which the blood-sugar level rebounds defensively 2 or 3 hours after a high-carbohydrate meal. He tested my capacity to store sugar by having me fast for 24 hours and found my blood-sugar level normal.

In his eyes, this reinforced the functional diagnosis, which is a term suggesting that there is no organic disease, but it also demonstrated his ignorance about how to diagnose the problem. He recommended that I reduce my carbohydrate intake sharply. I ended up drinking coffee with an artificial sweetener, and kept small packages of gruyere cheese handy to eat so as not to worsen the defensive rebound that would have come from candy or other substances full of sugar. I kept getting worse.

One evening during this period I frightened Bernice and the kids severely when I was accidentally awakened by my young son David in late afternoon after a party the night before, and I became agitated and talked crazy. Bernice called an ambulance, but I was hysterical and refused to go. Paramedics in California are not permitted to take someone by force. So she called a friend next door whom we trusted, and he patiently and gently convinced me I should go voluntarily in his car. During the first part of the trip to the hospital I was quite disoriented, but while still being driven in our neighbor's car I came out of it. Just as suddenly as it started, I was perfectly rational and no longer agitated.

The Kaiser physician suggested I be committed to a mental hospital where I might have languished in total medical ignorance and died. I don't begrudge this doctor his ignorance. His practice had never provided him with experience with the type of disease I had. What I am offended by was his irresponsibility in not checking out the problem with those who were knowledgeable. A friend and colleague at Berkeley, Paul Mussen, told Bernice that I was not psychotic, but seemed to be suffering from an acute toxic condition, because my attacks were always short-lived, which suggested a hormonal or neurotransmitter disease.

This experience, incidentally, and other horror stories, soured me on HMOs, even those that are supposedly non-profit like Kaiser, which are now being touted as good solutions to the modern crisis of health care. I am very doubtful about this. Kaiser was one of the earliest and best. One must remember that the lower the cost of its health care, the more income an HMO provides for its physician partners in the form of bonuses, or to the stockholders if it is for profit. This means that the decisions about patient care create the potential of a conflict of interest. We left Kaiser later for a private insurance policy, which was much more expensive but permitted us the choice of physicians, for better or worse. In my old age, when health care becomes a matter of constant concern, I fear being trapped in a self-serving health care system.

Anyway, our kids must have suffered greatly from my erratic behavior. I'm sure Bunny was beside herself with worry, and it must have communicated itself to them. On one occasion, I couldn't drive home from a ball game in San Francisco because I was seeing double.

On another occasion I had to go to Los Angeles to give an invited talk at an APA meeting. In light of my symptoms, I took a roomette on the overnight train, which seemed to me less stressful than an airplane trip. I was loaded with gruyere cheese packages in case I might need them during the trip. I woke up with a terrible attack, which seemed to last well into the night before it abated. Alone in the roomette, I experienced awful terrors, and kept eating the cheese to no avail. Without realizing it, had I eaten a candy bar I would have been fine.

I managed to give my talk with no problems, then the next evening I took the train home. Being hungry, I spotted a French restaurant at which I ate while waiting for the train. Discouraged about my condition, and throwing caution to the winds, I had a high-carbohydrate meal, ending with crèpe suzettes, which I dearly love. According to the diagnosis of functional hypoglocemia, I should have had a terrible attack as a result of this sugar overload, but instead had a peaceful and comfortable trip. This was to be one of the important clues that my disorder had been misdiagnosed.

What had happened was consistent with a rare ailment, called an *insulinoma,* in which a tumor of the eyelet cells of the pancreas, which make and secrete insulin, runs amok. When one's blood sugar rises above a set point, insulin is normally poured into the bloodstream, which withdraws the sugar and stores it in the liver. But because an insulin-secreting tumor operates outside the normal homeostatic process, it continues to rob the blood, and hence brain cells, of the nutrition they need to work. Tumor-induced hypoglycemia is, in a sense, the opposite of a diabetic crisis in which the body doesn't make enough of the hormone to keep the blood sugar from rising too much.

Anyway, frantic about what was going on, and at our own expense, I went to another physician, Marvin Epstein, whom I had consulted in the past, and he proposed the diagnosis of an insulinoma. This alert physician referred me to the Endocrinology Department of the University of California Medical School in San Francisco with that provisional diagnosis. I was hospitalized and there began a splendid 9-day effort by a young endocrinologist named Raymond Di Raimondo to track down what was wrong with me. To this day I remain impressed with this doctor's skill, diligence, and sensitivity.

When Di Raimondo did the fasting test that the Kaiser doctor had also used but botched by limiting the fast to 24 hours, my blood sugar was normal for 48 hours, but he waited still longer to terminate the fast. The next morning it plummeted. What the Kaiser doctor apparently did not know was that the liver can store sugar for 48 hours.

I liked Di Raimondo very much and appreciated his diagnostic effort and the way he related to me. I suppose he saw me as someone who wanted to understand what was going on, and at every stage he informed me, even about his own uncertainties. He explained that, because there were no definitive bases for a diagnosis, and the same symptoms could be brought about by many other disorders, such as the failure of the adrenal glands, the strategy was to try to rule out each one in turn. After 9 days of diagnostic testing, the decision was made to operate. The surgery was long and complex—6 hours. A benign tumor was, indeed, found on the surface of the pancreas and attached to the spleen, which was also removed.

Almost immediately after surgery, when the morphine had been discontinued, I was a new man, feeling absolutely brilliant in contrast to my long period of mental weakness. It took a few months to realize I had simply been restored to my normal mental powers, hardly genius, but at least able to function well. It was a magical cure, which saved my life.

I can't resist observing that there are some lessons here for psychology, which still seems unable to feel confident about the strategy of making inferences about what is happening in the mind from indirect evidence. All we can observe about the mind are the circumstances under which people act, their actions, their physiological reactions (if we are prepared to measure them), and their introspections. The endocrinologist in my case suffered from the same limitations in diagnosing my ailment. But with experience, knowledge, and care, he was able to locate what was wrong without being able directly to see the defects.

In other words, there is much art in psychology—even in its research—as well as science (see Deese, 1972). I don't fully understand why psychologists are so timid in their search for understanding. The stock and trade of our field, however, seems to presume certainty about issues rife with weak probabilities, ambiguity, and uncertainty, masquerading as clear objective evidence. Of course, it is seldom that lives are at stake in this game, as mine was, in the diagnostic workup of my disease.

What I have said about art should not be taken as a plea for casualness or sloppiness in the observations we make or the measurements we use. We need to be as precise as we can, but not fool ourselves about what precision means; it must not come at the expense of relevance, clear-headed reasoning, and ecological validity.

But to return to my medical cure, much before my surgery I had applied to the National Institute of Mental Health for a Special Fellowship to study stress and coping cross-culturally in Japan, to begin in August of 1963. I was awarded the grant and was to be the first Special Fellow in the United States to go abroad. We were due to spend the year in Tokyo during the 1963–1964 academic year until the insulinoma crisis surfaced. But 6 weeks after the surgery, I felt quite well and in mid-August my family and I, and pug dog, were ready to travel to Japan.

Chapter 7 describes our extraordinary year in Tokyo, and how it changed our lives.

REFERENCES

Beutler, L. E., Williams, R. E., Wakefield, P. J., & Entwistle, S. R. (1995). Bridging scientists and practitioner perspectives in clinical psychology. *American Psychologist, 50,* 984–994.

Deese, J. (1972). *Psychology as science and art.* New York: Harcourt Brace Jovanovich.

Lazarus, R. S. (in press, 1997). Coping from the Perspective of Personality. *Zeitschrift für Differentialle und Diagnostische Psychologie.*

Smelser, N. J. (1963). *Theory of collective behavior.* New York: Free Press of Glencoe.

Our Year in Japan

To study stress and coping in a foreign culture as an National Institute of Mental Health (NIMH) Special Fellow, I chose Japan for four main reasons. First, its outlook is strikingly different from that of Western countries. To do a comparative study in a European country, while easier, seemed potentially less informative. Second, Japan was technologically advanced, which would permit me to obtain psychophysiological measures of stress, such as skin conductance, in addition to behavioral and self-report data. Third, psychology in Japan was a substantial academic discipline, so I would have the advantage of sophisticated scholars there who would understand the reasons for cross-cultural research and be able to help. Fourth, by 1963, the American occupation of Japan after World War II had come to an end, and Japan was now emerging again in industry and science.

In preparation, Bunny and I read everything we could about the Japanese. We tried to study the Japanese language, but had only limited time and opportunity to do so. We talked at length to a friend and colleague, George DeVos, a distinguished anthropology professor at Berkeley who was greatly respected for his research and books on Japan. Through George, we met Japanese psychologists with whom he had collaborated over the years. Nevertheless, we remained quite innocent about the immense differences in the way things were done in our two cultures. Nor were we really prepared, knowledge-wise, for the adventure of living in Japan with our children and dog. We had to discover most of this for ourselves.

The Fellowship required that I have a university sponsor for my research project. But which university, and to whom should I write? When dealing with an unfamiliar culture, the standard operating procedures are obscure unless you have competent advice. After some thought and consultation, I wrote to the Waseda University Psychology

Chairperson, Professor H. Motoaki, indicating my wish to be affiliated with Waseda.

I chose Waseda because it was a highly respected private institution oriented more toward clinical psychology than any of its competitors in Tokyo. Keio University, another respected private institution, by contrast, emphasized social psychology, and Todai, the National University of Tokyo, which was the most prestigious of Japanese universities, emphasized traditional experimental psychology, which included perception, learning, and physiological psychology, an outlook not compatible with my psychodynamic way of thinking.

The interchanges that followed were, as the King of Siam said to Anna, the British governess for his children, a "puzzlement," and I had difficulty inferring what was going on. I learned about some of what had happened after I had been in Japan awhile and, though I don't know the details, I could make some educated guesses.

A key problem faced by the Waseda University administration was to assess the position of the unknown American scholar who was being called a "Special Fellow." What is a special fellow? Was I a beginner, perhaps a student or a lowly postdoctoral fellow? Or was I an honest-to-goodness professor who should be given the academic privileges of Waseda University and membership in the faculty club? No one at Waseda knew, and without a mediator, which is the usual Asian way of negotiating and making decisions, the question of who I was couldn't be answered. They never sought the answer directly from me; that isn't the Japanese way. And I suspect that what I sent them left it ambiguous.

There were issues of protocol, for example, who should greet us when we arrived in Yokohama? I was a young man, so in their eyes it was improbable that I would be a significant American psychologist. On the other hand, if I were truly a professor at Berkeley, it would be insulting to undervalue my position. It took quite some time before I heard anything. Decisions take time in Japan because of the need for consensus among the interested parties.

Fortunately, they decided to treat me as a senior professor and everything was arranged in our favor. I didn't realize that to invite me as a foreign professor meant that a member of the Psychology Department would have to be assigned to take care of me and my family. It had to be someone who could manage English well enough to communicate and to translate for the others, few of whom could speak the language. This would be a demanding assignment for that person. The one selected was M. Tomita (first names are not much used in Japan), who was then a junior faculty member with whom Bernice and I developed a lifelong friendship.

THE TRIP AND OUR ARRIVAL

Because of my recent surgery, we decided to go via a cruise ship on which there would be a physician. We booked passage for August 1963, on the President Cleveland bound for Yokohama. It was a small ship that carried fewer than 400 passengers. Among our effects were some trunks and about 20 cartons of books and papers, including a portable typewriter (I was hoping to make progress on my book on stress and coping while in Japan) and clothes for the four of us for a year.

Going by ship was expensive, but turned out to be a fortunate decision. We had two small, inside staterooms—no porthole or window—with upper and lower berths—not great luxury compared with some of our later cruises, but certainly adequate. Besides, none of us would be in the room very much except at night when it was dark outside. Instead of being catapulted in one day from San Francisco to Tokyo, as we would have by airplane, we had a leisurely trip, and the time changes were mercifully gradual, amounting to 9 hours over the 13 days of the voyage. There was also a special program for the children, which kept them happy and involved. The only stop was in Honolulu for a few hours.

Our pleasure was enhanced by the fact that a large proportion of the passengers were navy and air force officers and their families who were moving to Japan to take up duty there. We made friends with some of the military passengers, especially with one family named Breen and another named Connors. Bud Breen was the assistant Naval Attaché in Tokyo. Joe Connors was an Air Force lieutenant colonel, hoping to make full colonel. Both had children, which kept our kids happy, and we would see much of them in Tokyo.

When we arrived in Yokohama, we were met by Professor Tomita and a number of Waseda graduate students who had come in several cars to greet us and help us with our things. Our first meeting proved very amusing. We had been prepared to greet our Japanese hosts with a bow, knowing this was their tradition. They, in turn, were prepared to shake our hands, knowing this was our tradition.

There followed a remarkable, almost comical episode in which I first initiated a bow, Japanese style, and Tomita simultaneously started to put forth his right hand to shake mine, American style. Seeing his hand come forth, I quickly aborted the bow and put my hand out, and seeing the beginning of a bow, he likewise abandoned the handshake and quickly shifted to the bow. Visualize what a camera might have caught of the motions involved, which could be speeded up or slowed down to change the tempo of the action and its feedback reactions. The zigzagging back and forth went on for a few moments in the form of a Chaplinesque dance between American and Japanese.

The first crisis we encountered at the port of Yokohama was that the immigration authorities insisted on quarantining our year-old pug dog, Madame Pompadour. We had been advised incorrectly by the Japanese consulate in San Francisco about the timing of the rabies shot, but they would not bend their rules despite the fact that she had her shot early enough to be more than adequately immunized against the disease. Negotiating about this took quite some time, and we were distressed to have our dog led away to a public health pound for about 2 weeks of observation. When we got her back in Tokyo, she had picked up an assortment of Japanese intestinal worms, but otherwise she was none the worse for wear.

It might amuse you to learn that in Tokyo in 1963 Japanese veterinarians made house calls. When we needed a doctor for Pompey, he would come to our house to check her out, prescribe some medication if necessary, then leave. One time we complained to the vet that she would urinate on the floor at night. "American dogs are used to warm houses," he explained, and he was right. The kerosene heaters were turned off at night. She stopped doing this when she was allowed to sleep with Nancy.

WE NEED A TOKYO HOME

We were driven in heavy traffic by Tomita to the International House, a hotel for foreign celebrities and intellectuals in one of the downtown areas of Tokyo, where we stayed for about 2 weeks. After the destruction of the War, there was construction everywhere in Tokyo, including the building of new subway lines for the growing city.

The International House was spare but clean, and Tomita visited every day. Our most pressing problem was finding a place to live, which was very difficult. Housing was usually arranged for foreign business people by their companies, and they were usually put up in commodious, but very expensive, American-style apartments downtown, for example, in the Roppongi district. We began a week or so of responding to ads for rentals all over the city. Tomita drove us to each place and talked for us with the Japanese owners. It was hot, sticky, and tiring, and took a long time to find a suitable place to live.

We finally found an unfurnished house in Ogikubo, a middle-class suburb at the last stop on the subway line and a considerable distance west of downtown Tokyo. Downstairs, except for a small room with a

Japanese style Ofuro (bath) and gas heater, the house was American style, with a kitchen and living room, but upstairs there were two Japanese-style tatami bedrooms in which we slept on the floor on a thin foam mattress. There was no central heating, so we had to use kerosene heaters to keep warm in the winter.

The rental was $250 a month, more than we received for our modern, spacious Lafayette furnished home. We needed to buy a considerable amount of furniture, which we did at Isetan's department store. We also needed cooking utensils and other accoutrements of a household, such as an electric rice cooker. The expense was considerable, but there was no way to avoid it.

The landlady, whom we knew as Iwamoto-San, did not speak a word of English, but she was friendly, and with the aid of a jibiki (a Japanese–English dictionary), and extensive charade-playing, we struck up a warm friendship. She was a divorced lady, not a good thing to be in Japan. Her family, however, who had owned a miso company, had left her a considerable income. Miso is a tasty soup, which comes as a powder, and is now served by many Japanese restaurants in the United States.

Mrs. Iwamoto also took us to the main Kabuki theater in Tokyo, all dressed up in her kimono, and tried the best she could to inform us about Kabuki lore and plots, buying us brochures written in English. We would see her on almost all of our later visits to Tokyo. She later married a gentle and pleasant psychiatrist by the name of Shigeta.

We enrolled our children in the American School in Mitaka, a private institution a long bus ride west from Ogikubo. One of its peculiar features was the policy, encouraged by American business families, to make life in Japan a little bit of America. They were concerned that their children might return to the United States as cultural strangers and have trouble fitting in.

This laudable aim, however, led to overkill in the form of isolation from the Japanese culture. Rather than becoming immersed in it, they defended against it, and remained largely ignorant of its characteristics. They also arranged the school schedule and its holidays so that they didn't overlap with the Japanese holidays. This added to the absence of interaction between American and Japanese children. "A little bit of America" came to be a self-protective cultural enclave, which failed to promote Japanese–American relationships. Isolation from the indigenous culture was also characteristic of military families.

In light of this school policy, such interaction for our kids was more difficult than it should have been. Interested in meeting Japanese kids, David and Nancy took to using board games, such as checkers, to overcome the language barrier. This was quite useful, given their natural reserve toward the Japanese, which had been fostered by American television's war movie references to the "dirty Japs," and the like, which were bound to foster fear and prejudice.

One of the most interesting, and for foreigners, exasperating features of life in Tokyo in 1963 was that, except for a few main routes, which had been labeled during the military occupation as A street, B street, and so on, there were no street signs. All signs are printed in Kanji, Japanese–language ideographs, which do not constitute a phonetic alphabet with Roman letters. Kanji are almost unreadable to foreigners without training. In addition, Japanese homes did not have precise street addresses. So, if you wanted to have someone visit you, or if you wanted to visit them, the first such trip was something of an adventure.

Under these circumstances, to find a place, you needed precise instructions and a map, which specified rough and ready landmarks, such as a store, an unusual building, train tracks or stations, and so forth, rather than street addresses with house numbers. So foreigners had personal cards printed with small maps, which could be given to friends. We also had calling cards, which is a Japanese custom, identifying who we were, one side printed in English, the other side in Japanese Kanji.

Our son David, who was 12 years old at the time, missed his bus one evening coming home from a school affair and had to take the train. A teacher made sure he got on the right one. But when he got to the Ogikubo train station, which was a long walk from where we lived, he had to take a taxi the rest of the way. This was quite a challenge, because it was necessary to tell the driver in Japanese when to go left, right, or straight ahead. Hidari means left, migi right, and masugu straight ahead. One also added something polite after the direction, such as please, so one said "Hidari itte kudasai," meaning go left please, and so on. It was dark and our 12-year-old must have been quite scared, and we were worried too by his lateness, but he managed to carry it off and get home safely. We were quite impressed.

Banking was a time-consuming problem in 1963 Tokyo. Everything had to paid in cash, and with an exchange rate of 365 Yen to the dollar, cash seemed like play money and took up too much space. Checks were not used and there were no credit cards. Our money arrived from NIMH as a monthly check in American dollars. Because the local branch would not accept American dollars, we first had to take the check to the central bank downtown, which itself was quite an excursion. It had to be deposited there to our account and changed into Yen. Then, each week Bernice had to make out another check for Yen, which could be cashed at the local bank branch near our house, and which drew on the Yen deposited downtown.

Most bank personnel had never seen a check before, so she had to see a manager each time to obtain cash in Yen. A passport was needed for these transactions. After a while, however, they got to know us. Our transactions were always done over our signature. Japanese citizens, on the other hand, used an authorized red Kanji stamp to identify themselves when making a transaction, which served as a signature does in the United States and legitimized their transactions.

OUR INTRODUCTION TO THE PSYCHOLOGY FACULTY

As might be expected, one evening shortly after we settled into our new home, Bernice and I were invited to a dinner party with the psychology faculty at Waseda University. Tomita told me they would appreciate a short speech in which I would say why I had come and what I hoped to accomplish. We sat at a long table, Bernice and I in the middle. She was the only woman.

I still remember a few things about the evening, which was in my eyes extraordinary, but something of a strain. When I gave my speech, I spoke slowly and briefly, indicating my wish to compare Japanese and American patterns of stress and coping, and the reasons for my choice of Japan. I also spoke of the book I was writing. Tomita translated. When I finished, Tomita asked if I were willing to answer some questions. I was delighted, because I thought it meant they had understood me and we would have a meeting of the minds. But what followed was altogether unexpected.

The first question was "How old are you?," which took me by surprise. I thought the question implied that I was very young. I had always looked young for my age. So, laughingly, I said I was 41, and indicated awareness of my youthfulness in a culture that venerated age and experience. I pointed out that in the United States, people are impressed by youthful virtuosity, not age. We were, in fact, a young country, with a frontier tradition, individualistic, and competitive. There was no reaction that I could see. Perhaps they didn't understand, but I never found out.

The second question was "Please tell us about your family." I was floored. What could I say? In my response, I stumbled inadvertently into a hornet's nest. I thought they were really asking about my descent, so I told them that my parents were the children of poor Jewish immigrants from Romania and Russia who were not educated or well-fixed financially. In effect, I came from very humble beginnings, but in the best American tradition, I was proud of having obtained an advanced university degree and having achieved a solid reputation as a research scholar. Then I made a major blunder. As a joke I said "Even my dog has a better pedigree than I."

As soon as the words got out of my mouth I realized this was a faux pas, because it flew in the face of Japanese family tradition. But my remark was simply ignored. Little did I know at that moment that no one had understood what I had said. It is doubtful that anyone at the table that evening understood the word "pedigree." So they responded with polite silence. It took me many years of lecturing abroad to learn to avoid making jokes; they usually fall flat, because the nuances and double entendres that make an intended joke funny are rarely understood by those for whom English is a second language.

The evening continued with some further pleasantries and good cheer, with members of the faculty making welcoming comments, most of them in Japanese, translated by Tomita, expressing the hope that we would enjoy our stay and I would be able to complete my research. There were no substantive questions or comments about the contents of my speech. Later, of course, as I became more familiar with the problems of communication, I suspected that only a modest proportion of what I had said had actually gotten through. It was the worst bane of our year in Japan, the uncertainty about whether or not we were being understood.

I had been told by American social scientists that they had never been invited to any of the homes of people in Japan, but were usually entertained in restaurants. One reason for this is that Japanese homes are quite small. A visiting room that is made presentable is used for friends, but there is a reluctance to have foreigners as home visitors. Another possible reason is a certain wariness of outsiders.

Luckily we never experienced this problem. Early on we were invited to the homes of Tomita and his intimate friends, and we were entertained generously. Perhaps the times were changing. Perhaps it was because we had them to our home. Perhaps our formal position made such invitations mandatory, or at least more desirable. Perhaps we had somehow gained their trust. We never knew why our experience turned out to be so different from that of other professionals who had come before us and felt isolated.

Tomita was a wonder. Because he told us about it 1 day, we knew he was somewhat annoyed at being at our beck and call, and at first I think he felt demeaned. He always did the work cheerfully, however, and I think in the long run he gained from all his trouble, which was considerable. It was the Japanese way, to be outstanding hosts, more attentive than we would be to anyone in the reverse position. His English was not very good in terms of grammar and pronunciation, but he was an extrovert who tried, and he used creative ways of communicating. We understood him better than anyone else we met in Japan except Americans. He was also smart and had strong opinions.

For example, his view of the War was that Roosevelt precipitated it treacherously by making demeaning economic and military demands that Japan simply could not meet. The attack on Pearl Harbor was a response to the last straw of disingenuous negotiations. In effect, Japan was reluctantly forced into the War.

We decided not to challenge him in this view. In general, our impression was that Japanese are far more jingoistic than Americans, and they avoid being placed in positions that might lead to criticisms of their country or people. To this day, I avoid criticizing Japanese whom I do not like, even to Tomita. American intellectuals, on the other hand, freely criticize their country, their colleagues, or even their politicians. To them, it is what democracy means, and being patriotic means caring and wanting to improve the way things are. Only several decades later did we begin to talk candidly—but only a little—about conditions in the world, life in the two cultures, and problems in Japan. On this visit, however, if we wanted to have a comfortable and friendly relationship, it was obvious that we would have to inhibit our natural tendency to make candid political and social judgments.

STRUGGLES WITH THE JAPANESE LANGUAGE

We spoke the Japanese language at about the level of a 2- or 3-year-old, enough to get along, "Hello, Goodbye, Thank you, Pleased to meet you, Where is the toilet?, How much does it cost?, Does this train go to . . .?," and so on. You know, the sort of phrases found in a Berlitz language guide. When we first visited some of the local Ogikubo stores near our house, the proprietor, especially if she were female, would hide lest she be embarrassed by not being able to deal with foreigners, who were seldom met in the outskirts of Tokyo, and because they couldn't speak our language. We actually saw them run away so they wouldn't have to confront us. Later on, they got more used to us and we got to know them a little bit.

But we had not been prepared for the tremendous difference in the accents with which the Japanese and we spoke their language and ours. Before leaving for Japan, I had briefly entertained a few Japanese visitors at Berkeley who wanted to see the University. I remember such a visit by Professor Sagara. I took him around the new building, Tolman Hall, constructed for the Departments of Psychology and Education. He tried valiantly to speak English, but I could hardly understand anything he said. It was a terribly embarrassing and exhausting struggle to interact with him.

Several months after we came to Japan, I met him again and had no trouble understanding him. So I said "Professor Sagara, I'm impressed with how much your English has improved." No response. He looked dour. Later, when we were alone, Tomita said that Sagara understood what I did not, that it was not his English that had improved but my ear for Japanese speaking English. I was properly chastened.

This incident helped us understand some of our own difficulties in communicating when we spoke Japanese. For example, early on we would practice things to say, and then speak directly to a taxi driver. No response. No sign of recognition that we were speaking to him in his own language. What was going on?, we wondered. The answer finally came to us. Just as Sagara's accent was unintelligible to us when he spoke English, so was our's unintelligible to the Japanese driver who saw two Caucasians seeming to speak an unknown tongue, say, English or German, and assumed they were speaking a foreign language.

The psychological set was wrong and we finally realized that first we had to get his attention to the fact that we were speaking Japanese. We would then begin by saying in Japanese "We are speaking Japanese" "Nihongo de," at which the driver would usually recognize what we had said and could then respond. It's not just knowing the words, but knowing how to say them that counts.

Our greatest frustration during that year was that we never improved our Japanese much for two main reasons. First, everyone there wanted to learn English, and second, the academics could not communicate with us in Japanese on anything more important than the basics of polite behavior and the mundane mechanics of living. Nothing intellectual or abstract. So we were encouraged to speak English not Japanese. We had needed much more language training than we had been able to get before coming to Japan. Too bad, but that was the reality. The Japanese expression for this statement, incidentally, is "shgategenai," which Tomita translated as "that's the way the ball bounces."

GETTING AROUND IN TOKYO

I found myself uncomfortable at being dependent on taxis and trains to go places in Tokyo. The drivers, and Tokyo traffic, scared me to death.

The pattern seemed chaotic, a form of anarchy, and I hated to rely on someone else I didn't trust rather than doing it myself. I decided to buy a car, and Tomita arranged for a used car we could afford, an English stick-shift Austin. In those days Japan had no automobile industry, and the Austin later became the model for the first Japanese Datsuns. Because Japanese drove on the left side instead of the right—as in Great Britain and Australia—the wheel and gear shift were on the right side, so one had to learn almost anew how to drive. Only on the American military bases did people drive on the right side of the road, another little bit of America abroad.

Driving at first was a struggle, especially when I had to turn left. Pretty soon, however, I became just as crazy as I thought the Japanese drivers were. But most important, I began to discern some order in the Japanese driving pattern, though it still seemed pretty wild. Japanese streets were typically so narrow that two cars could barely pass on the same street. Telephone poles sat a foot or two out into the street, and you had to drive around them. There were also five kinds of moving objects competing for the narrow road space, cars, small three-wheeled trucks (these were later banned in Japan because they were so danger-ous), motorcycles, bicycles, and pedestrians. In the beginning it seemed as though I was going to hit the pedestrians or the bikes and motorcy-cles, whose drivers never turned to look as we brushed by them. But if you worried too much about this you would be unable to drive at all.

Here are some of the rules of the road I discerned in Japan: First, the bigger the vehicle, say a truck, the more likely it was to be given the right of way. Second, the most important unwritten rule was not to look the other driver in the eye. Third, the second rule favored the for-eigner. If you looked, the other driver would know you saw him and would assume the right of way himself. Nobody would challenge him except a crazy foreigner. So, if you were obviously foreign and you did not look the other driver in the eye, he would remain wary, and you got the right of way. Fourth, if you were stopped by a policeman, as a foreigner you could draw on the expedient of not understanding what he was saying, leaving him preferring to send you on your way rather than going to the trouble of trying to deal with you.

At Shinjuku, a major section of Tokyo and in 1963 an intersection on the way to where we lived from downtown, about 10 lanes of cars would line up at the traffic signal, row on row. When the light changed from red to green, they all gunned their engines to gain an advantage in order to squeeze into two lanes. To move leisurely at this intersec-tion would put you at the end of the pack, often to have to wait until the light changed again.

I would gun my terribly underpowered car as hard as I could, and often made it through the intersection among the first or second cars. It became a regular game to me, and I wished I were driving a high-powered American car that could easily beat out everyone else. I suppose, however, that the most important reason I often prevailed was that the more prudent Japanese saw little sense in trying to compete with a foreigner who couldn't be trusted to use good sense. This is the way we drove around Tokyo all year. And somehow we never had a problem.

THE DAILY PATTERN OF OUR LIVES

My days in Japan took on a consistent rhythm, which was to work on my book all morning on the portable typewriter I had brought with me. Then, close to noon, we ordered lunch, which was brought hot on a bicycle from a local food shop. I especially liked tempura soba with two large shrimp (ebi futatsu), and assorted sushi, which was much more expensive. Most Japanese wives did not cook but obtained food in this way. Today, Americans have caught up with this tradition of takeout food, but Japanese get it delivered to their homes.

Two afternoons a week I would drive to the University. There I met with four graduate students who were assisting me in my research, which I will describe a little later. One was an advanced male graduate student by the name of M. Kodama. The three others were women, but I only remember the names of two, Hasegawa-san and Shioriri-san. Both are now married and professional psychologists. Yoko Hasegawa later became Yoko Kosugi. One of my most interesting experiences was to attend her wedding, done in traditional Japanese style with formal Japanese dress. Figure 7.1 is a photo of Mrs Kosugi in her wedding dress.

On other afternoons, we would wander about Tokyo, visiting places we had heard about, and taking snapshots. We did much walking around Ogikubo. The only big department stores were downtown, and they were worth visiting in themselves. But the local streets were fascinating, filled with all sorts of vendors—family shops dealing in tatami, fish, rice, baked goods, flowers, noodles, and other wares. In those days, there were no large supermarkets, as are common in the United States, though in later years such markets began to appear, wiping out many of the neighborhood stores. On the local streets, the smells were intriguing and nothing like those in American cities. The streets were always bustling with all sorts of people going about their business. Just walking around looking and smelling, and occasionally buying and

FIGURE 7.1 Yoko Hasegawa weds Kosugi-San.

tasting, was a major form of pleasure and relaxation. It was a pleasant and relatively easy life for us.

In 1963 there were no sewers, only septic tanks. Tokyo had an institution that we had never before encountered, referred to by Westerners euphemistically as "honey pot trucks." Like our garbage trucks, they would regularly come to every house. Their function was to suck out untreated sewage from septic tanks, presumably to take it to treatment plants. Their operation created an unmistakable odor, which could be sensed even from afar. To speak more directly, they stunk to high heaven, and with a distinctive odor I had never before experienced. I suspect they no longer exist in modern Tokyo, but because on later visits we stayed in hotels, I cannot be sure.

Big changes began to occur in Tokyo at about the time we were going to leave. The city was preparing for the Olympic games, which were to be held in Tokyo the very next year. The Japanese were ashamed of some of their customs, which they felt would be criticized by visitors. So the authorities engaged in a major propaganda battle to curtail them. There were large signs on the streets that read in Japanese "No urinating in the street." During our year in Japan, we had frequently seen men peeing in public. Our 10-year-old daughter, Nancy, was flabbergasted when she saw this. Our 12-year-old son David actually took a picture of this, which is in our photo album. This custom rapidly began to disappear at about the time we were ready to leave.

I might note in passing that when I visited public toilets in Japan, I would often find women cleaning out the urinals or brushing down the stone floors. I'm told that the same pattern is still found in France. The restrooms in train stations were for both men and women together. It took a little time to get used to, but the women never showed any curiosity about the exposure of the male genital. The Japanese are not as hide-bound as we, and natural body functions, such as elimination, as well as nudity, are accepted comfortably.

Japanese houses were generally open with rooms only subtly separated from each other by movable shoji screens. Because our's was half Western style, this internal openness was absent. Japanese houses are also closed off from the street by walls, however, and our house, as well as the others in the neighborhood, was surrounded by a stone ditch in which rain and waste water would run off. When we took a bath and let the water out it flowed right into the street.

And when we would drive home in our car, we had to open the outer door to allow the car into the car port, thence to the garden area or the house proper. In effect, privacy is preserved between the residents of a house and the outer world, but not within the house inside. A diagram describing this pattern can be found in a small book by Rapoport (1969) on how culture influences the houses in which we live.

Those who have spent time in Japan also know that the Japanese flush toilet is different from the Western version. In the West, one sits facing forward, looking away from the wall, rather than toward the wall as in Japan. The Japanese toilet is on the floor and one squats over it. The first Japanese maid we had didn't know how to use our toilet, and one day Bunny found her perched on it in the Japanese direction, literally standing on the toilet seat with bended knees. But we were no more sophisticated about the Japanese toilet. On one of my visits to Tokyo a few years later, I stayed with the Tomitas and had to use their Japanese toilet. I couldn't figure out how they did it, and since I was ashamed of my ignorance, I never mentioned it, but somehow managed.

Because I was a retired army officer, we had access to the military bases, which provided an island of American experience in a sea of predominantly Japanese relationships. Typically, on Sunday, the whole family would go to the officer's club at the Sanno hotel, where we would have an American meal, or an Americanized Japanese one. Often the children would see an American movie. At home on the TV we watched Japanese programs, or American programs, such as "Outer Limits," all in Japanese. Years later we finally found out what these wonderful programs were all about. But at Sanno, it was all American. There we bought the best of liquor at a very low price. I would often bring scotch, which was highly valued in Japan, to parties hosted by the Japanese.

The Breens played bridge, and they also lived in Ogikubo—being only the Assistant Naval Attaché, I suppose he didn't rate a fancy place downtown. We spent many an evening that winter in either of our houses. When we played in ours, we huddled next to the big kerosene heater, drinking Black Russians, an oversweet combination of vodka and Kahlua. To hold the sweetness down, we used a high proportion of vodka, so we were often playing cards in a pretty looped condition. Pompey, our dog, sat near the heater perched on three or four silk zabutons (cushions). Japanese winters were not severe, but without heat it was still cold and damp, and there were occasional light snow storms.

Speaking of kerosene heaters, most houses in Japan did not have central heating, and the main method of keeping warm was kerosene. The heaters had to be filled every day, which was done by the maid. They were well made, but still created the danger of asphyxiation. We had bought a large vented one, a monster that sat in the living room, which our landlady, Iwamoto-San regarded with some skepticism, though when we left she incorporated it in her own house next door.

One day disaster struck. The maid had done the wash and hung it up all over the living room to dry. Something clogged the heater and within a few minutes, everything on the first floor was covered with a coating of soot. We needed a repair man who, in the characteristic Japanese fashion, sat for about an hour drinking tea with us before getting to work. Given this experience, and many others like it, I have never given way to the popular notion of efficient Japanese workers, though I don't know the pattern there today, almost 40 years later. They work long hours, but take long, frequent breaks. I am convinced Americans work harder than those in any other industrial economy.

On the other hand, one gets the opposite impression when, every morning in downtown Tokyo, one sees workers in business suits scurrying frantically from crowded subways to their business offices lest they be late. This creates the sense that the Japanese work scene is frantic during work hours, though relaxed in off hours, often with the help of alcohol.

I should say something about our use of house servants in Japan. After the war, few Japanese families had servants. Most maids worked in American households and had been employees of the American occupation forces. We were told that they were not readily employable in the Japanese economy, presumably because to the Japanese they had an unsavory reputation, contaminated by American social and work standards.

We had several housemaids over the year of our stay, and they lived with us, working from morning until night at the going rate of $1 a day with 1 day off a week. You might think that with a full-time servant, we must have lived like millionaires in Japan, but please spare us any envy. Even with a live-in maid, Bernice worked harder there keeping house than in the United States. In Japan in 1963, there were no washing machines, dryers, dishwashers, garbage disposals, or vacuum cleaners, and it took constant effort to manage the household. We had never before fully appreciated these labor-saving devices, which are taken for granted in middle-class American households. Things have changed now, and labor-saving household appliances are staples in Japan too.

At Christmas time, Tokyo is all lit up celebrating the holiday, with Santa Clauses, Christmas music, and stores all decked out like ours in the States. But it is an imitation Christmas without its religious significance. The Japanese are mostly Buddhist Shinto, with only a small population of Christians.

When we were living in Japan, most Japanese were totally unaware of the multiple religions in the West, including the many Christian sects. Foreigners are all the same—that is, Christians. This limited view has changed substantially, however, in modern Tokyo. Because we are Jewish, we had no Christmas tree, and our maid, Yukiko-San, who seemed to us to be the most intelligent and literate of the maids we had, expressed wonder about this.

When we explained that we were Jewish, it was obvious that she did not understand—she spoke very little English. She assumed we belonged to some esoteric Christian sect. Finally, one day, she said knowingly to Bernice "Annu Franku," Ann Frank, that is, the "u" standing for the Japanese speech pattern of adding an extra sound after a consonant at the end of most words. We realized that she had looked into what we had told her and now had some grasp of who we were.

We were surprised at the Japanese emphasis on Christmas. The main Japanese holiday, and it is a big one, is New Year. Christmas is just tacked on to the time of the New Year, which extends much longer into January than ours. I suppose the Japanese like the color and decorativeness of the Christmas holiday, which relates to the brilliant lighting for advertisements along the Ginza and in other areas of Tokyo, such as Shinjuku, and is good for business.

OUR TRAVELS IN JAPAN

The Japanese are constant and intrepid tourists, and they visit tourist places religiously, even in their own country. I remember a number of overnight trips we took, most of them not far from Tokyo. One was to Lake Hakone in the early fall while it was still mild. We stayed overnight at the hotel and took a rowboat out on the lake. We went by train, but coming back we traveled on a cable car, which provided spectacular mountain views. In the winter, we visited Lake Yamanaka, which offers the splendid sight of Mount Fujiyama, if it is clear. We have some marvelous photos of the mountain in weather that was clear as a bell, which some of our Japanese friends envied, because most of the time the sacred mountain is obscured by clouds or haze.

In the late fall, we went to Nikko, which is an interesting and colorful Shinto shrine a few hours by train to the North. I remember the beautiful Japanese maple tree in deep rich red color outside the hotel, of which we also have a photo. We bought one later for our Lafayette home, and enjoyed it for years in front of the house. One of the sights at the shrine in Nikko is the famous three monkeys, "Hear no evil, see no evil, speak no evil." "Hear no evil" has the monkey's paws over the ears; in "see no evil," the paws are over the eyes; and in "speak no evil" they are over the monkey's mouth. We had been excited at the prospect of seeing it, but close up it was something of a disappointment. It is a very small, not very colorful wood carving panel, which is crowded among a surfeit of other objects. Had it been displayed by itself, it might have been more impressive.

We took quite a few other trips, but one is particularly worth describing because of its unique experiences. Waseda University maintains a small residence in Kamakura on the ocean southeast of Tokyo, about a 2-hour drive. A large part of the trip is just getting out of Tokyo, which even then had the most congested traffic I have ever encountered, though Seoul, Korea, which we visited in 1996, is just as bad, if not worse. It is clear that economic growth must be paid for by the ills of automobiles and urban and suburban over-crowding. We drove to Kamakura, as did a dozen or so other members of the Psychology Department and their families. We were guests of the Department.

One of the things I remember was that we took a Japanese bath. But with our hosts' sensibilities about our American shyness about naked-ness, the men and women were separated rather than, as usual, being together. The water was so hot I could barely get in. Knowing our aversion to extremely hot water, the bath had been kept at a lower temperature than Japanese normally prefer, but for us it was still too hot for comfort. On another occasion in Kyoto, we and the kids went to such a bath in a small Japanese hotel, a ryokan. A Japanese family arrived in the altogether, and we had our first experience of naked mixed bathing. We were a bit uncomfortable, but it was really not all that bad.

But the excitement of the trip to Kamakura had only begun. My son David and I got into bathrobes and put clogs on our feet, and with Tomita and a few other men, took a walk on the boardwalk and down-town, where we visited a pachinko parlor. It was warm, and the area was filled with people. Pachinko is a mindless slot-machine game in which you push a lever, which sends a steel ball coursing down an obstacle course, racking up a score depending on where it falls.In the pachinko parlor, one sees dozens of Japanese men and women work-ing the machines, sitting for hours and never looking up from what they are doing. Unlike our gambling slot machines, there is no money to be made in pachinko, at least as of 1963–1964, only credit for more games. It seems like a form of self-hypnosis. We also stopped off for some sake—or maybe it was a coffee shop for ice cream and Japanese cakes, which I have never learned to like because to me their sweet-ness has an odd taste.

One of the major trips of that year was a several-day-long visit to Kyoto, once the seat of Japanese rule, where everyone visiting Japan must go at least once. I was invited by Professor Haruyo Hama and Professor Matsumoto to give a talk to the Psychology Department at Doshisha University, and she and her staff hosted the four of us and took us to various places around the city. I can remember a tea cere-mony in a Zen chapel. Our hosts explained everything to us. One high-light was a visit to Katsura Villa, a spectacularly beautiful setting of classical Japanese one-story wood-frame buildings, situated in a watery setting and reflecting past Japanese ruling dynasties.

Dr. Hama was an interesting and unusual professional woman in a country in which women did not often play such roles. She actually had been born in Mongolia and, despite this cultural handicap, had become a significant person in academic life. She also spoke English quite well. This, and other impressive sights in Kyoto, including an impressive Buddha, gave us much pleasure on our visit to this culturally important city, which the United States spared from destructive air bombing during the war.

On a later visit to Doshisha University, we discussed a cross-cultural research project, which would compare Japanese and American ways of coping with bereavement. We had in mind to compare two conditions of loss, one in which the death was sudden and unpredictable, providing no opportunity for anticipatory grieving, and another in which the death was slow and drawn out as a result of an extended illness, such as cancer, with the bereaved person having ample time for anticipatory coping. We wondered whether the anticipation would make a difference in the success of the grieving process, and what similarities and differences there might be in the two cultures.

To this day, I believed that this would have been a difficult yet very worthwhile cross-cultural research project, but it never came off, and I still have some regrets. What happened was that when I came back to Berkeley, I was overburdened with work on the NIMH research project and my teaching duties. Another reason was the tremendous resources a project of this kind would have required.There was also the problem of communication. Language difficulties with cross-cultural research are daunting, and both the Japanese and American ways of coping would have to be examined in depth for this kind of study to be sound. Governmental research support would also be needed, and without travel money during the planning stage, a sound project would not be possible. Nevertheless, had we pursued it, it might have turned into a most distinctive and important cross-cultural research project on stress, emotion, and coping, one that still cries out to be done.

The social activities I most enjoyed in Tokyo were sushi parties with Tomita and his friends at a local Ogikubo sushi shop. The stalwarts of that group were Tomita, Professor Miwa (a physical chemist), Mr. Tominaga (a high-school teacher of English), and several other men whom we met socially on visits to Tokyo over a period of many years. This group had originally comprised members of Tomita's singing club, but it eventually narrowed to just these few families. Only men attended the sushi parties. In Japan, all-male recreation is more or less the rule.

We would all drink sake, and I would frequently bring a bottle of Johnny Walker Black Label scotch. In contrast to scotch, I learned that sake, if you drink too much of it, will produce a terrible hangover. According to Japanese custom, a younger person keeps filling an older person's sake cup and so, when my cup was empty, which was often, the person sitting on my left always made sure to fill it. Even though the cups are very small, one can drink an awful lot of the stuff under these conditions.

The Japanese take pride in the freshness of their raw fish. I enjoyed sashimi and sushi, and as it appeared that I had highly ecumenical tastes in food, my Japanese hosts enjoyed testing the limits of my tolerance with exotic variations. There was one occasion, however, at which my capacity was exceeded. The drinking and eating had begun, and a large sliced whole fish was brought to the table. Along with the others, one by one I picked up a few slices with my Ohashi (chopsticks) and started to eat when suddenly, the fish began to move up and down, as if breathing. Tomita pointed out that this showed how fresh the fish was; it had just been killed. Watching it reflex made me slightly nauseous, as did trying to pop into my mouth small crabs with large eyes seeming to burst out of their sockets. We all realized that I had not yet become fully Japanized, and some of my Western tastes still remained.

At these sushi parties, I would come home very late because they would go on and on, long after I was ready to quit. But I was at first unwilling to offend my hosts by making known my readiness to leave. I soon discovered that, as I was the honored guest, my Japanese companions were also reluctant to call things to a halt. I eventually came to understand that if a party was ever to end, I had the responsibility for calling it quits.

CULTURAL CONFUSIONS

The problem of ending parties illustrates a common complication in intercultural transactions. The more we interacted with our Japanese friends and hosts, the more we discovered cultural differences in the rules for social engagement. Some of these were trivial, but others were quite important, and we struggled to understand how we were expected to behave.

With respect to trivial ones, I remember a time when four graduate students were about to enter an elevator of the campus building that housed psychology. Every time we would approach the open door, we all stood there for a few moments. Who should go first? I would stand back in the American fashion of those days waiting for the female students to proceed, but all four of them would stand back awaiting my move into the elevator. We would do this again and again, laughing, until I finally realized that we had to negotiate a solution. Needless to say, being in Japan the solution was for me to go first, and once this became institutionalized we no longer had to do the "After you, Alphonse" routine.

Japanese men always walk in front of the women when going anywhere. One of our most amusing experiences took place when Motoaki later visited us in California. Contrary to what he had done in Tokyo, he now followed Bernice when they walked into a room, in a corridor, or on the street. So she said, "Professor Motoaki, how is that in Tokyo you always walked first, but here I walk first?" His smiling answer was "When in Rome. . . ."

Motoaki usually spoke in Japanese, with Tomita translating, but now and then he spoke some English, and we found he had more mastery than we had originally supposed. He was a very dignified man. I think, like me, he found it undignified to speak another language badly, so he was inhibited about trying. To be good at foreign languages, it helps to be extroverted, like Tomita, and not concerned about making mistakes.

Another cultural difference had to do with the role of women in Japanese society. Women, at least on the surface, subordinated themselves to men and were self-effacingly polite. In private, however, they typically manage the money, and do not kowtow to their man. However, we were surprised at the aggressiveness of older women whom we ran into—I should really say they literally ran into us—in department stores or in other public places. They shoved us aside mercilessly (though everyone was considerate of our young children) when seeking merchandise or attention from clerks, or in trains or subways and crowded streets. Sometimes I would be bruised as a result of such encounters. We were at first perplexed, but in time we learned what was going on. There are two principles, which help explain the anomaly.

First, when women get married, they are expected to live in the home of their mother-in-law, where they are the low person on the totem pole, and are severely restricted socially. They were, in effect, under the power of their husbands' mother who was apt to act in a tyrannical way toward them. Ultimately, however, as they become middle aged, they are freed from this tyranny when the couple and their children are able to live in their own home. At this stage of life, downtrodden for much of their adult lives, they abandon their inhibitions and turn their long suppressed hostility against others—for example, their own daughters-in-law.

The second principle is that Japanese social life is filled with obligations, or "on," which is the Japanese word for this, to people within the family and social group. Therefore, adding any more unnecessary obligations would be avoided like poison. So a differentiation is made between those toward whom one has clear obligations and others outside one's own group who can more or less be ignored. People on the street, in the subway, or in a department store, are strangers, and one need not feel an obligation toward them. To feel obligated is one of the most troubling experiences of Japanese social life.

This cultural outlook was well described by American anthropologist Ruth Benedict (1946) in her classic wartime work on Japan, *The Chrysanthemum and the Sword.* I'm confident that this is why Tomita would have preferred not to have the job of catering to our needs. Once such an obligation is accepted, however, it is rigorously pursued.

Other cultural differences, however, seemed far more important from the perspective of relationships with our Japanese friends. One of the most striking was the matter of gifts. It is customary to give a small gift when one visits. We were the recipients of many, some of them substantial, as when our whole family was treated by Tomita and his friends to elaborate dinners in Japanese restaurants. Nor do I ever remember paying anything at the sushi parties. This pattern continued in later visits Bunny and I made to Tokyo.

I also remember when Motoaki took us to his favorite bar and I drank and danced with one of the geishas. And on another occasion, we were invited by Motoaki and his wife to a very fine restaurant where we ate exquisitely prepared food and drank to our heart's content in a private room with magnificent service. Such dinners are very expensive, and we had similar experiences in later years as well. But one must be careful not to give an inappropriate gift, meaning one that is too expensive, because it might heavily obligate the recipient.

On one of our later visits, when I had been invited to give the foreign scholar's lecture to the Japanese Psychological Association held at Waseda University in the late 1980s, we wished to reciprocate for the great generosity of our hosts. When we expressed this wish to Tomita, he understood, and we arranged to pay for a restaurant dinner party with drinks for a considerable number of guests. Beforehand, we agreed on the approximate amount we would pay, and the dinner went off as planned. However, afterward Tomita told us apologetically that the amount was considerably more than we had agreed to. We said it did not matter, but it was clear the group wanted to make up for this by again inviting us to another dinner.

The dinner was enjoyable, but we would have preferred to have used the time differently (see Figure 7.2). We had very little time to ourselves in the 2 weeks we were in Tokyo. We had only one evening left that was free, which Bunny and I had hoped to spend by ourselves. But it was clear that our friends felt it was terribly important to have this second dinner. The excessive size of our gift to them made them feel uncomfortable and they wanted to make things right.

FIGURE 7.2   Our friends at the Ogikubo Soba restaurant.

MY JAPANESE RESEARCH

The primary reason for being in Japan was the potential for research comparing stress and coping in Japanese and Americans. Waseda University, represented by Tomita, made this research possible by making four first-rate graduate students available to assist me. We negotiated how much they would be paid from my NIMH research grant at Berkeley. I can't remember how we arrived at the figures, but it seemed fair to me and consistent with normal rates of pay in Japan.

The basic research plan, extremely ambitious in its design, was to show a stressful movie, and a benign control movie, to American students in Berkeley, and to Japanese students at Waseda, while recording their skin conductance and obtaining subjective reports of distress. These were obtained at frequent intervals during the film when a series of blank film leaders interrupted the film contents so distress could be rated. The American version of the study had already been completed at Berkeley (see Speisman, Lazarus, Mordkoff, & Davison, 1964).

The stress movie was a silent film made by Geza Roheim as part of an anthropological study of a male rite of passage in an aboriginal tribe, the Arunta, which lived in the Australian outback. What made the film stressful was a series of six operations performed with a stone knife on the underside of the penis, which was cut almost to the urethra. The operation is called subincision and was clearly painful and dirty, with maggots inserted into the wound as part of the ritual.

In addition to the film, four different orientation soundtracks, designed to influence how subjects appraised the movie's contents, were played as though they were part of the film. These were the main experimental conditions of the study. The four soundtracks were as follows: *intellectualization,* in which subjects were implicitly encouraged to gain emotional distance from the stressful contents of the film, just as an observing scientist would while watching it; *denial* in which subjects were told the procedure was not threatening or bothersome to the natives; *trauma* in which the threatening contents of the film were emphasized; and a *control* condition without soundtrack. There was also a separate control film about rice farming in Japan, a benign movie comparable to the one on corn farming in Iowa that we had used at Berkeley for the same purpose.

The research session began with the subject being told about the study. Then there was a benign period of just sitting quietly after the electrodes were placed on the arm in order to obtain a calm autonomic nervous system baseline against which to compare the stress film. Finally, the subject would watch the film itself. The research assistants' task was to run the Japanese subjects individually until the requisite number had been tested. Two Japanese research assistants ran each subject, one handling the equipment, the other interacting with the subject.

Two identical experiments were performed, one with 80 undergraduate subjects, the other with 48 subjects between 36 and 58 years of age. This had the purpose of contrasting younger Japanese, who might have begun to shift away from traditional cultural patterns, with older Japanese who were educated in traditional ways. They were ultimately combined because their reactions did not differ. In addition, we tested the Japanese subjects, as we had the Americans at Berkeley, with the Minnesota Multiphasic Personality Inventory (MMPI; Hathaway & McKinley, 1943), translated into Japanese, to identify personality characteristics that might have influenced how they reacted. All the procedures matched exactly what was done in Berkeley. The instructions and soundtracks were also carefully translated into Japanese by Tomita.

It took most of the year to complete data collection and analysis, and the study (Lazarus, Tomita, Opton, & Kodama, 1966) was published after I returned home. With respect to reported ratings of distress, and looking only at this kind of data, we found basically the same pattern in Japan that we had previously reported for American subjects. The denial and intellectualization passages significantly lowered ratings of distress while watching the film compared with the trauma soundtrack, which raised stress levels well above the distress reported for the control version of the film, and the separate control film. In effect, in both cultures the pattern of reported distress was the same.

What was strikingly different, however, was the skin conductance data, that is, the physiological indicator of stress level. Compared with their reactions to the benign control film, the American subjects reacted to the film with marked elevations of skin conductance above baseline levels, especially during the portrayal of the stressful operations compared with neutral events.

The Japanese subjects, on the other hand, did not show ups and downs in skin conductance commensurate with the events portrayed on the film. And the benign control film resulted in almost as much elevation of skin conductance in the Japanese subjects as did the stressful film. To put it a bit differently, compared with the Americans, whose skin conductance was highly selective in response to the stressful and benign film events, the Japanese showed little of the stimulus-controlled variation in stress levels in their psychophysiological reactions. Had we not looked at the skin conductance data, we would have concluded mistakenly that the stress process was no different in the two cultures (see Figure 7.3).

Our Japanese colleagues and we believe that the reason for this was that Japanese subjects were unusually sensitive to the experimental situation as a whole. They reacted with marked apprehension to just being observed, regardless of what was being shown on film. Their reactions, therefore, were not responsive to the two different kinds of film contents, the benign and stressful events. They reacted throughout the experiment as though they were under stress. Whatever differences there might have been in reactions to the events in the movie were, therefore, obscured by this more general source of apprehension in Japanese culture.

This fits the picture drawn by much psychological research of Japanese children as being more threatened by social censure than American children, who are accustomed to parental scolding. The Japanese college students felt uncomfortable under scrutiny, not only by Japanese in authority but foreigners, a feeling that was absent or minimal among the American students. Americans are used to detached medical examinations and survey research, which asks personal questions without making them uneasy. The two cultural groups are not different in anxiety level, but in what makes them anxious.

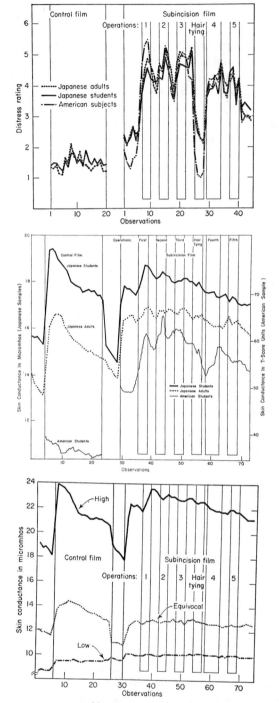

A. Mean ratings of distress during control and *Subincision* films by Japanese adult, Japanese student, and American student samples. (Subjects made one rating after each 25-second film segment.)

B. Mean skin conductance during control and *Subincision* films and during baseline periods for Japanese students and adults and for American students. (The conductance measure is the highest conductance reached during each 25-second film segment and during each 25-second period during base-line periods. No recordings were made during the base-line periods for the American subjects.)

C. Mean skin conductance during control and *Subincision* films and base-line periods for Japanese subjects divided according to their skin-conductance patterns into high-fluctuation (N = 69), equivocal (N = 31), and low-flat (N = 28) groups.

FIGURE 7.3   The main cross-cultural findings. (From Lazarus, Tomita, Opton, and Kodama, 1966).

TIME TO LEAVE

We left Japan the next summer, a little short of a year after we arrived, donating our Isetan furniture to Tomita and his friends, whose financial resources in those days were modest. On our many trips back to Japan, as recently as 1993, we have seen some of these pieces still in their homes. Before we left, Iwamoto-San gave us an outdoor party in the back yard. She bought lots of goodies, including expensive sushi, which she knew I loved. It was a generous and warm gesture.

The trip to Yokohama by ship, the President Cleveland, had been so delightful that we decided to spend our last cent on the return trip on the President Wilson, and on two Plymouth Valiants, which we bought at a substantial discount in Tokyo, to be delivered by a Berkeley dealership when we got back. The return voyage was quietly pleasant, but not as exciting as going, and although we were keen to get back home, we experienced some sadness about leaving.

We invited the Breens, Connors, and the Japanese with whom we had gotten intimate to a shipboard departure party. The emotional reactions and tears from our Japanese friends came as a surprise and contradicted our Western assumptions about the detachment and inscrutability of Asians. We were also surprised at the depth of our own emotions on that departure. As is traditional at such parties, we served champagne, whiskey, and snacks, prepared in the ship's kitchen. There was also the traditional confetti and band at the sailing, and then we settled down to 13 days of shipboard relaxation and fun.

When, at last, early in the morning the ship passed below the Golden Gate Bridge in sunshine under an almost cloudless sky, we were very excited, having been away so long. It was a thrill to be back. I took dozens of photos and still have them, and hundreds of photos of our experiences in Japan.

When we got to our Lafayette home, we discovered that an enormous amount of damage had been done by our American tenants. We had rented our house to an Education professor from the Midwest, and assumed incorrectly that they were responsible people who would care for our home as we would have theirs. So much for stereotypes about who will make a good tenant.

Our tenants had lied to us about how many people would be living there, and about their promise to return our home as we had left it. We found gum under the dining-room table, initials carved on some of our wood pieces, sand in the garbage disposal and the dishwasher, both of which were ruined, damaged and missing silverware, and other totally unjustified destruction. When we telephoned them about this, they were offensive and nasty. This experience angered and saddened us, but our insurance covered some of our losses, and what happened did not dim our pleasure at returning home and once again sleeping in our own beds.

The next day, Bunny and I picked up our two new cars in Berkeley, and in the evening we went to Ondine's in Sausalito where we had dinner and watched the summer fog creep over the hills and across the Bay. We resumed our lives in the Bay Area hardly suspecting that the year in Japan had changed our lives forever.

THE IMPACT OF THE YEAR IN JAPAN
ON OUR LATER LIVES

Our stay in Japan had been a remarkable experience. We had established lasting links with many we had met there, and others we were to meet subsequently. Within the next few years, I sponsored numerous young Japanese scholars at Berkeley who spent 6 months or a year there as academic visitors. From time to time I had the impression that with respect to Japanese psychologists I was substituting for the American embassy. In most cases, Bunny and I would invite the visitor to our home for dinner, usually with Berkeley graduate students or faculty.

I cannot list all the visitors, only some of the most important. There were four visits by Tomita, one in 1966 for the purpose of solidifying our joint research in Japan, which we were about to publish, another when he was on his way to Europe, and still another on his way to Europe for a meeting. The fourth visit was to the 1990 Centennial celebration of the American Psychological Association in Washington, DC. Tomita had been designated the representative of the Japanese Psychological Association. There was an opportunity for him to stop in San Francisco en route, and to consult about what he should say about this at the meeting.

One of Tomita's visits occurred over the Jewish Passover holiday. We had the most hilarious Passover anyone could imagine, with the Japanese Tomita singing "O Solo Mio," Mary's (David's wife) Italian Catholic father playing the accordion, and a Jewish physician friend giving a medical account of the 10 plagues visited on the Egyptians at the time of the exodus. A completely polyglot enterprise racially, culturally, and religiously.

Except for a brief mention of him as one of the research assistants, I have not yet said much about Kodama, a warm, gentle man who came to dinner with us in 1980 on his way to Europe, and then again with his wife and daughter in 1996 on their way back from Montreal and the International Congress of Psychology. He played a very important role in our research in Japan, having been the senior graduate research assistant on that project, the one who was most informed about psychophysiological equipment and procedures. Later he became a professor and married, and he and his wife, a professional psychologist, entertained us a number of times in Japan on return visits.

We entertained Professor Motoaki and his colleague, Professor Shigehisa at our home for dinner in February 1990. (Figure 7.4 presents a photo of Motaki and me.) They came to the United States on behalf of the newly created Japanese Association of Health Psychology, of which he was the first president. He also visited Berkeley on the occasion of an APA meeting in San Francisco in late summer of 1991. With him came a delegation of officers of the Japanese Association of Health Psychology. They visited the Berkeley Campus and graciously purchased copies of my new monograph *Emotion and Adaptation,* which was being featured at the APA meeting by Oxford University Press. Ceremoniously and with pleasure, I signed their copies in my Berkeley office, and gave them a tour of the campus. Like most traveling fathers and grandfathers, they bought sweatshirts for their children and grandchildren, monogrammed with the Berkeley logo, at the University student store.

In October 1991, Nancy's family went to Tokyo as her husband Rick had business to conduct with a Japanese real-estate-investment firm. On that trip they visited Tomita and his friends, including our landlady, Iwamoto-San, who had become Mrs. Shigeta, all of whom had met Nancy as a child in 1963. Then, in March 1993, some of the friends of Tomita, now our's too, Professor and Mrs. Miwa and Mr. Tominaga visited the Bay Area for a holiday. They stayed at the home of our daughter Nancy and her husband Rick, and our granddaughters, Maiya and Ava Rose. They had dinner with our son David and his wife Mary, at their home with our other grandchildren, Jessica and Adam, and also with Bunny and me in our home.

Most extraordinary of all has been the number of times Bunny and I were invited back to Japan and were entertained there. What is especially noteworthy is that on all these visits, often as long as two weeks, our travel expenses and local hotel and meals were paid by one or another Japanese organization. Our plane travel was always business class on these special visits. In appreciation, I gave a number of extra lectures. On two of these occasions in the early years, I also stayed in Tomita's home.

I made one visit alone in May 1968 in connection with the World Congress of Psychology meeting in Tokyo. I was royally entertained by

FIGURE 7.4   Professor Motoaki and I on the Berkeley campus.

Tomita's friends, the Kodama's, and Motoaki. Bunny and I have been back four other times, first in March of 1970 on our way back from India, where I served as academic representative for Berkeley in trouble-shooting some problems in the University's Education Abroad program.

But our most fabulous visit was in September 1983, when I gave one of the rare foreign scholar's addresses to the Japanese Psychological Association meeting, which was hosted that year by Waseda University. We were put up for two weeks in a fine hotel in Shinjuku, which offered a view of Mount Fuji. I also lectured several other times in Tokyo.

I gave my talk in a large auditorium without air conditioning on a steamy day that was nearly 100°, and thereby hangs an amusing tale dealing with sex roles. It took a few hours of speaking and standing at the podium because there was a translator who would regularly report what I said after I had spoken a paragraph or two. This doubled the time of my address.

As a result of the heat, Tomita and I were provided with a pitcher of water (see Figure 7.5B). After the session, Bernice, who was also sitting on the platform, endeared herself afterward to the more liberated

FIGURE 7.5   Photos of special address to Japanese Psychological Association (JPA), September, 1983.

Japanese women by half-jokingly muttering aloud that this arrangement was sexist. "Goshujin (honorable husband)," she said, "was given something to drink, but not me, and I'm just as hot."

All along, Bernice had managed to be seen by the Japanese men—who, wanting to preserve their masculine prerogatives, have long felt distaste for assertive American women—as the "good Japanese wife," one who deferred to her husband and attended to his needs. But now, in this outspoken comment, though she said it with laughter and good humor, she had also endeared herself to Japanese women by being outspoken about her rights. She seems to have had the knack of endearing herself to both sexes, becoming an attractive role model for completely opposite reasons. Quite a feat, it seemed to me. I was impressed!

On that trip, incidentally, we again visited Doshisha University in Kyoto, where I gave another lecture and we spent time with Professor Hama and her colleagues. I remember eating a picnic lunch of sushi on top of a mountain nearby on a warm, lovely day, and on another occasion visiting Lake Biwa to the Southeast with Hama.

In October 1988, I was invited to a conference on issues of psychology and health in Kitakyushu, Kyushu. I found that meeting frustrating, because there was absolutely no interaction about my paper on work stress (Lazarus,1991), or any other for that matter. I gave my paper under time pressure to a very large audience who asked no questions amid too many other speakers. The program was too tightly organized to leave time for discussion and the meeting was so unproductive I attended only a few sessions.

Then, on the way home, we stopped in Tokyo where I spoke to another group and responded to a panel of psychologists and psychiatrists who asked me questions or gave critical comments on what I said. A small book entitled *Measuring Stress to Predict Health Outcome: A lecture by R. S. Lazarus, Ph. D.* appeared in 1990, Edited By S. Hayashi, MD, published by Seiwa Shoten. Hayashi has also visited the Bay Area several times. In 1991, incidentally, my 1984 book with Susan Folkman, *Stress, Appraisal, and Coping,* was reprinted in Japanese through the Japan UNI Agency, Inc., of Tokyo.

I enjoyed this Tokyo meeting because of the active interchange it made possible. It was arranged by Motoaki and by charging a fee to the audience, provided the funds for us to stay several days in Tokyo. We were able to visit Tomita and friends, who organized dinner at a soba shop, which included Iwamoto-San (now Mrs. Shigeta).

Finally, in July of 1993, Bunny and I attended the International Congress of Health Psychology, where I gave two lectures with simultaneous translations, and two additional lectures to other groups in Tokyo with the usual type of translation. We spent about 10 days in Tokyo on that interesting visit.

You can see that our lives have been much affected by the year we spent in Japan in 1963–1964. As it gets late in our lives, both ours and theirs, we have the most warm feelings for the people we met there, and for the graciousness with which they dealt with us. Our photograph albums are filled with pictures of all these visits, and the people I have mentioned in this account. Periodically, as in the writing of this autobiography, Bernice and I review these albums and we think back on the times they reflect. Our children sometimes do too.

In chapter 8, I return to Berkeley during the Vietnam War demonstrations of 1964. Mostly, the chapter covers my research on the use of motion-picture films to induce stress in the laboratory. This research lies at the heart of my theoretical approach to psychological stress and the emotions, and particularly the central constructs of appraisal and coping.

REFERENCES

Benedict, R. (1946). *The chrysanthemum and the sword.* Boston: Houghton-Mifflin.

Hathaway, S. R., & McKinley, J. C. (1943). *The Minnesota Multiphasic Personality Inventory.* New York: Psychological Corporation.

Lazarus, R. S. (1991). Psychological stress in the workplace. In P. L. Perrewé (Ed.), Handbook on job stress. [Special Issue] *Journal of Social Behavior and Personality, 6,* 1–13.

Lazarus, R. S., Tomita, M., Opton, E., Jr., & Kodama, M. (1966). A cross-cultural study of stress-reaction patterns in Japan. *Journal of Abnormal and Social Psychology, 4,* 622–633.

Rapaport, A. (1969). *House form and culture.* Englewood Cliffs, NJ: Prentice-Hall.

Speisman, J. C., Lazarus, R. S., Mordkoff, A., & Davison, L. (1964). Experimental reduction of stress based on ego-defense theory. *Journal of Abnormal and Social Psychology, 68,* 367–380.

Berkeley, the 1960s

When I returned to Berkeley late in the summer of 1964, momentous things were taking place on the campus, in the country as a whole, and in the world. To a considerable degree, these events flowed from our ill-fated slide into the Vietnam War. The 1960's were to change the country forever. Before I return to research and theoretical efforts that followed my stay in Japan, I should devote modest space to these events. They had an important impact on all our lives whether or not we realized it at the time.

STUDENT PROTESTS OVER THE VIETNAM WAR

It is not my purpose to give a detailed historical account of the Vietnam War, yet it would be useful to recapitulate some of it as prelude to the protest movement that students at Berkeley and as a member of the faculty, I had to confront beginning in 1964.

We got into the war slowly, almost without deliberate intent, after a period of French and Japanese rule. Since 1940, there had been scattered communist guerrilla resistance to foreign occupation and rule. The guerrillas, led by Ho Chi Minh, were called the Viet Minh (Hallstead, 1978). President Truman supported the French in its struggle against the Viet Minh. They were decisively defeated in 1954 at Dienbienphu. The French remained in the South, but ultimately left, leaving South Vietnam to the American puppet dictator, Ngo Dinh Diem.

The United States later escalated its aid, and sent a modest force of combat personnel, the first ones being killed in 1959. What was called the second Indochina war began against the National Liberation Front, which ultimately came to be referred to by its enemies as the Viet Cong. In retrospect, one thinks of the falseness and folly of the domino theory, which was constantly given as justification for the Vietnam War. Barbara Tuchman's (1984) colorful phrase, "The March of Folly," comes to mind as we survey this tragedy.

159

In any case, the major escalation of the Vietnam War took place after the Gulf of Tonkin incident in 1965 in which some of our ships patrolling the area were attacked under ambiguous conditions. President Johnson used the incident as an excuse for this escalation. This resulted in the Gulf of Tonkin resolution by Congress to respond aggressively to any future attacks, and we were then really in the war in earnest. I am constantly amazed at and offended by how easy it is for our government to commit the lives of its countrymen for self-serving international games that are not in the interests of the country or wise policies from a humanitarian standpoint. Vietnam was a striking example, and there continue to be others.

But to turn now to the antiwar demonstrations on the Berkeley campus, as early as 1960, a somewhat disorganized peace movement existed in the United States, made up largely of pacifists, socialists, and communists who wanted radical social change and only later set its protest sights on the American role in Vietnam. Even before the Gulf of Tonkin incident and the escalation of the war, a student-protest movement had already begun on the Berkeley campus.

Students for a Democratic Society (SDS) had demonstrated in 1964 under the rubric of the Berkeley Free Speech Movement (FSM). A socialist leader of this movement, Jack Weinberg, who became famous for the statement "Don't trust anyone over thirty," was arrested for setting up an unauthorized table on the Berkeley campus to proselytize for the Congress of Racial Equality (CORE). After the arrest, the police car holding Weinberg was surrounded by large numbers of students and for 2 days he and others used its roof to give speeches against the "establishment."

The growth of the protest movement really began in earnest in the succeeding years with teach-ins and other types of demonstrations, which took place with increasing frequency on many American campuses and in many large cities. In 1962 we had only 12,000 military personnel in South Vietnam. At the peak of American troop involvement in 1968, 549,000 soldiers were there in a losing effort to subdue the Viet Cong and support a corrupt and inept dictatorship in Saigon. A chronology of protests (Heath, 1976) during those years reveals an expansion that matched the progressive escalation of the war. The list of protests across the country grew from less than half a page long in 1964 to over four pages in 1970. The Vietnam War finally ended in 1973 with President Nixon's order for withdrawal of all our combat troops.

The university administration, in fact most of the faculty at the time, believed the Berkeley Free Speech Movement was a response to local problems on our campus, which called for local solutions. The administration, faculty, and students were slow to realize that the student problems set in motion by Vietnam were national rather than local and applied to a great many universities throughout our country. Indeed, they were soon to become worldwide (DeBenedetti, 1990), suggesting that youth everywhere were deeply troubled by the condition of their societies and concerned about their own futures.

Beginning in 1964 after our return from Japan, and continuing until the end of the war, academic life was more and more disrupted by sit-ins, teach-ins, meetings, demonstrations, and the boycott of classes. It was as if the students blamed the educational enterprise for what they saw as the evils of our society—in effect, extending the meaning of that denigrating phrase, "the power structure," to include the university itself as the enemy.

I have always regarded the attack on the university as foolish. It was, however, reasonable to protest the war, and other negative features of our society, and I had my own beefs with the Berkeley administration. Like a large proportion of the faculty, I agreed that the war was foolish and immoral, and that the draft was inequitable, as it was easy for students to gain deferment. It was a perfect example of a war we should never have fought. But it didn't make sense to assault the university, which not only offered the best chance of free and open discussion of ideals and knowledge, but provided tuition-free education to qualified young people, which is no longer the case today.

Faculty opinion about the issues varied considerably, ranging as always from highly conservative in the sciences, math, engineering, law, and medicine, to the liberal left in the humanities and social sciences. As both a social and biological science, psychology was rather conservative, much to my surprise, though we had a few rabble rousers.

But the protest movement had been taken over by angry, extreme left-wing youths who were less interested in the war than social revolution. It was no longer really a peace movement, but a fractionated army of protesters against almost everything capitalism stood for. Many of its participants were professional radicals, who were attracted to Berkeley and other campuses because they saw the protest movement as fodder for their many dissatisfactions with society. In any case, the antiwar movement rapidly lost its central focus and spilled over into vandalism against local merchants, whose store windows were broken and their merchandise trashed. It all began to look pretty irrational.

The university administration did not know how to deal with the problem, and often fumbled badly, thereby further encouraging the protesters and enlarging the disruption. Much of the public was offended by what it saw as privileged young persons—and faculty too—biting the hand that fed them, and were increasingly disgusted by what was happening. Especially in the early years of protest, instead of helping to fire up the public against the war, it only turned the public and the politicians against the university.

The university tried to fight back by creating layers of administrators to preserve its reputation and cultivate its badly needed state money. The bloated administration we ended up with over the next decades had its origins in an effort to control the political and economic damage. Nevertheless, it was not long after Vietnam that California began for the first time to charge high fees and, later on, tuition for students.

I am not suggesting that this was a direct result only of the Vietnam protests—economic factors, changes in the political climate, and changes in the population of California had much to do with it. I am saying, however, that the protests against the university and the society helped to turn many people against higher education, especially when it was being publicly supported.

I have never bought the notion, promulgated by many of the Baby Boomer generation who look back on those days nostalgically, that the protests were a successful, morally upright, and realistic social movement. Most of the histories I have read of the Vietnam protest movement were written by people who were imbued with its causes and who romanticized youth protest for its own sake.

Later on, as it became clear we were not winning the war and the death toll mounted, though bitterly divided, the country finally turned against the war. I believe this might have happened sooner had the protest movement been more sensitive to public attitudes, eschewed the trashing of businesses and other radical extremes, emphasized the war's folly, and explained the disingenuous nature of its rationale, and its great social costs.

In any case, doing one's academic work got more and more difficult in those years. Our attention was diverted from intellectual issues to political ones. Less attention was given to course work and seminars were often lackadaisical. The whole educational enterprise suffered.

I did the best I could to further my research project about which I felt sanguine, and to teach my subject matter as best I could, while anxiously watching the rapid drift of the university, country, and world to political and social anarchy, a drift that continues today. But in spite of the disruptions, the period was enormously productive for my research and the expansion of my ideas about stress and coping.

EARLY RESEARCH AT BERKELEY

A primary requirement of stress research is to measure the stress reactions it causes. One could, of course, ask subjects how they felt during stressful experiences, which would provide useful information. But there are good reasons for not putting all one's measurement eggs in the one basket of self-report, which is subjective and, therefore, always somewhat suspect.

To evaluate this limitation and compensate for it, we can turn to behavioral measures, and physiological measures that are highly responsive to stress—for example, autonomic nervous system reactions, such as skin conductance and heart rate, or adrenal gland hormones. When these measures disagree with the evidence from self-reports, we are alerted to the possibility that something might be amiss in the inferences we might make about the stress reactions experienced.

To obtain physiological data, one needs a modest psychophysiological laboratory. This was made possible by the grant from the National Institute of Mental Health (NIMH) which, happily, was approved just before I left Clark University. It permitted me to hire graduate students who could help set up the lab equipment, learn psychophysiological methods, and obtain and analyze data. I also obtained a research grant from the National Science Foundation for the cross-cultural research I did in Japan.

Two bright and talented graduate students, Arnold Mordkoff and Leslie Davison, worked with me in those early days. I also began to collaborate with a young clinical faculty colleague at Berkeley, Joseph C. Speisman. Our early work was done in old, dingy, and inadequate quarters in the Life Sciences Building where psychology was housed. Joe left Berkeley after a few years to take a position with the NIMH, which dealt with clinical training programs, and after some years there, he joined the faculty of Boston University where he ultimately became a full professor and chairperson of the Psychology Department.

After working and publishing with me for a number of years while he was completing his doctorate, Arnie Mordkoff obtained an attractive academic job at New York University. His main interest lay in the psychophysiology of cardiovascular disease, and he published some fine articles on this and related subjects. He achieved a reputation as a promising young scholar-researcher and was quickly promoted. Then suddenly one summer, he was killed in a tragic accident before he would be able to realize his promising academic career. When Les Davison finished his degree at Berkeley, he took a position at the University of California at San Francisco, where he pursued research on brain damage. He lived in San Francisco with his wife. He too died prematurely.

Now that I had a psychophysiological laboratory and funds for research from the NIMH, it was possible to develop an innovative research program that could draw on the theory of psychological stress and coping I had been developing.

A training grant from the Rehabilitation Services Administration (RSA) provided substantial additional resources, making it possible to expand the program greatly. The RSA training grant came about because that agency realized it lacked a forceful program of research to deal with the psychological problems of people who suffered from disabilities as a result of accidents, for example, spinal-cord injuries with varying degrees of paralysis.

As a result, I met with a small group of psychologists for several days in Miami Beach, Florida, to discuss what might be done to enhance research on the psychological problems of rehabilitation. It was chaired by Emory Cowen who later became a major figure in community psychology. The committee also included Abe Luchins, whose research on psychological rigidity was well known, Bruce Thomason, and Mort Weiner. Our committee made the recommendation that training grants be established to groom budding psychologists to be able to do research in a rehabilitation setting (see Cowen, 1960).

I applied for one such grant, which was approved and awarded for a period of 5 years. Stress and the need to cope with it is severe when a man or woman suffers such an injury. After the medical dangers have more or less passed, spinal-cord-injured patients need to restructure their lives and learn how to function adequately, maintain satisfactory morale, and be productive citizens.

Although we trained a number of doctoral students, and completed considerable research, the RSA program was a failure with respect to the agency's objective of hiring researchers who were skilled and knowledgeable about stress and coping. For reasons that are still not clear to me, the agency made no effort to set up jobs in rehabilitation centers for the graduates of these programs. It was as if no one working at RSA knew that these training programs existed. None of my graduates was ever approached about a job, nor was I asked to recommend any. It did facilitate the research of my students and postdocs, however, and provided jobs for my predoctoral graduate students. It also helped me to advance the cause of stress and coping theory and research, for which I am grateful.

The combined NIMH and RSA funds made it possible for me to hire Edward M. Opton, Jr. after he finished his doctoral training at Duke, and James R. Averill when he finished his postdoctoral work with M. E. Wenger, a distinguished professor of psychophysiology at the University of California at Los Angeles. Opton and Averill overlapped for several years on the project, and both spent about 5 years with me at Berkeley.

These outstanding men and a number of graduate students can take considerable credit for the success of our research project.[1] Ned Opton eventually left to go to law school to pursue his long commitment to ensuring social justice, and has worked for many years as an attorney for the university. Jim Averill went on to become a professor at the University of Massachusetts at Amherst, where he has become a distinguished figure in the psychology of emotion.

In the remainder of this chapter, I examine what I think was distinctive about my theoretical approach to stress and my research discoveries with a minimum of jargon, so that nonpsychologists too might understand its rationale and main features.

MY APPROACH TO PSYCHOLOGICAL STRESS

From the beginning of my education in psychology, I was greatly influenced by several generations of distinguished psychologists who adopted or leaned toward a subjective approach to theory. This assumes that our emotions and the ways we act and react depend on how we evaluate our experiences in the world. This doctrine overlaps with the movement I referred to in chapter 4 as the *New Look in Perception.*

The most important grandfathers of this approach to the mind were Kurt Lewin, Henry Murray, and Gordon Allport. Later advocates include Solomon Asch, Harry Harlow, Fritz Heider, George Kelly, David McClelland, Gardner Murphy, Julian Rotter, Edward Tolman, and Robert White. I had the privilege of interacting with Asch, Harlow, McClelland, Murphy (who served as an early mentor), Rotter, Tolman, and White.

Although the important thinkers just named were revered as distinguished personality and social psychologists in academic life, radical behaviorism still dominated psychological thought and it did not really

---

[1] Graduate students included Elizabeth Alfert, Carlyle Folkins, Reuven Gal, Carlyle Folkins, Asher Koriat, Karen Lawson, Edward Malmstrom, Alan Monat, Rachel Melkman, Mark Nomikos, and Neil Rankin. Gal, Koriat, and Melkman were Israeli graduate students who obtained their doctorates at Berkeley. Gal later became the chief psychologists for the Israeli armed forces. All of these students appear as authors on published papers emanating from the Berkeley Stress and Coping Project.

lose its cachet until roughly the 1970s. Behaviorism defined psychology as the science of behavior rather than the science of mind. In an effort to be ultrascientific, it inveighed against subjectivism—for example, the notion that beauty is in the eye of the beholder or, as expressed in the oft-quoted line from Shakespeare, "There is nothing either good or bad, but thinking makes it so. (Hamlet, act 2, sc. 2, l.).

Because we cannot know what is in the mind directly—it is private and known only to oneself—this doctrine affirmed that psychological processes can only be inferred from the observable conditions that affect it and from observations of the reactions they produce. This important half truth is one reason why behaviorism gained prominence.

However, its distrust of speculation about the mind, and its extremely negative opinion of the utility and validity of what people tell us about what is in their minds, made it difficult to advance psychological knowledge. Behaviorism was enamored of a very narrow philosophy of science called logical positivism. This viewpoint considered two kinds of statements, first naming, second description of what can be observed in the world. All other kinds of statements—for example, metaphysical, poetic, value judgments, and hortative efforts to influence—were divided into what was called emotional, statements, or nonsense.

All this was justified as an effort to clean up the language of science and eliminated terms that had no objective referents. What was excluded, of course, were any speculations about what mind is like and what is important in our lives. It simply went much too far, and ruled out what today we would regard as proper subjects of scientific study.

Ultimately, behaviorism could not provide a suitably rich and accurate understanding of how our minds work and, for that matter, even how the animal mind works. Today, in most social sciences, including psychology, we have been moving toward a multivariate systems model of mind and behavior, which is a far more sophisticated approach to adaptation in the human animal, the most complicated of God's creatures. There is also increasing use of a narrative approach.

Allow me to apply what I have been saying about psychology in general to the subject matter of stress and coping. Traditionally stress has been viewed as either harsh environmental stimuli, called stressors, or the disturbed response to them, called stress reactions.

Examples of such *stressors* include natural or man-made disasters, such as earthquakes, floods, hurricanes, wars, physical assaults, life-threatening diseases, social insults, chronic social tensions (for example, within the family or at work), difficult-to-manage work or school situations, or failures at school or job. These events threaten a person's well-being and even survival, result in physical or psychological harms (or losses), and signal the threat of harm in the future. *Stress reactions* can be illustrated by emotional distress, disruptions of work and social functioning, and by bodily changes, which, if sustained, might result in psychosomatic or life-threatening diseases.

Notice that this traditional way of thinking focuses on observable stimuli (physical and social stressors) and disturbed reactions to them, both psychological and physiological. It follows the behavioristic tradition of stimulus–response (S–R) psychology. Left out of the equation, however, are important products of mind—namely, thoughts, interpretations, judgments, and diverse goals and beliefs, which lead to individual differences in reaction to the same environmental conditions.

The new doctrine, which is actually as old as the ancient Greeks, is often referred to as *cognitive mediation*. It simply means that all environmental stimuli, stressors included, are filtered through a mind that thinks and evaluates before they lead to a reaction. It could also be described as S–O–R psychology, rather than the simpler S–R psychology, with the O standing for organism, but which really refers to properties of the mind, such as thoughts (cognitions) and desires (motives or goals).

An essential ingredient of this way of thinking is that, to understand how people adapt to the circumstances of their lives, we have to view what happens in terms of the *relationship* between a particular person, with distinctive goals, beliefs, and ways of coping, and a particular environment, with its own special demands, constraints, personal resources, and opportunities. Stress should be defined as a kind *relational meaning*, constructed by the person out of the person–environment relationship. It is also no longer sufficient to think in terms of a passive organism reacting to environmental demands, but we must consider what happens psychologically as a result of active decisions and choices by people who confront situations relevant to their well-being.

Here, for example, is a man who is thoroughly convinced of his self-worth, who reacts to an offensive remark directed at him with disinterested amusement. Here is another man with a vulnerable self-worth, who hears an innocuous remark as an insult that demeans him and arouses his ire. Here's a woman who believes that men wish only to subjugate her to their sexual whims. As a result, she takes her date's somewhat outmoded courtesies, such as moving her chair for her to sit down at the dinner table, as an offputting sign of male chauvinism, and will have nothing further to do with him. Here is another woman who views men as she remembers her father, gentle and caring, and who interprets the same courtesies as evidence that he is a thoughtful and respectful companion. This is a kind of commonsense psychology, because it is the way most people intuit what is going on in their lives.

The scientific tasks of formal theory and research are to examine in detail how this works.

Stress, and the emotions that arise from it, consists of diverse kinds of relational mismatch between two interacting forces, an environmental situation and a personality, which determines whether an event is reacted to as harmful, threatening, challenging, or benign. The general form of the mismatch is that environmental demands exceed the person's resources to manage them. To be hard pressed is to be stressed; to be overwhelmed is to be defeated, at least for the moment. Stress is not just an environmental stimulus or a response, but a *troubled relationship* between a person and the environment.

Appraisal is the central construct of all cognitive mediational approaches to stress and coping, and the emotions. As persons, we are constantly appraising what happens to us from the standpoint of its significance for our well-being. This significance, a form of relational meaning, differs to some extent from one person to another. Differences in appraisal help us understand the inevitable individual variations in reaction under the same or similar environmental conditions. Modern psychology has been slow to think relationally, and to realize that personal meanings, constructed by the mind on the basis of the nature of the person–environment relationship, are the coin of the realm.

Early on, I also realized that it was not just stress that was important in human health and well-being, but *coping* too makes a major difference. If we cope effectively, stress is reduced or at least under control. If we cope ineffectively, then stress is increased. This doesn't mean, necessarily, that good copers have low stress. Some good copers take more risks and strive to accomplish more, which could increase stress, though perhaps it is a different kind. Nevertheless, there is, in the main, a reciprocal relationship between the quality of coping and the degree of stress. And if we want to know about how stress affects our health and well-being, we need to study coping too.

Mainly what I contributed to appraisal theory and the psychology of coping was to take somewhat vague and inchoate concepts, which had been around in one form or another for a long while, and make them sharper, more precise, and central to psychological stress, and the emotions. The concept of appraisal had already been drawn on in other works related to stress and the emotions.

For example, two research-oriented psychiatrists, Grinker and Spiegel (1945), had written a book dealing with the stresses faced by military air crews during World War II. The men they studied had developed emotional disorders as a result of the continuing and prolonged stress of air combat. It was an early version of what today is called *posttraumatic stress disorder.* Though their use of the term "appraisal" (p. 122 of their book) was casual rather than systematic, they used it to refer to the subjective basis of threat created by combat conditions.

In an extremely important monograph centered on cognitive mediation, Magda Arnold (1960) used the term "appraisal" as the central construct in a two-volume work on emotion. Her work represents, I believe, the first truly systematic use of the concept in a serious theoretical treatment of the field of emotion. Her book influenced me to abandon the term, "perception" (apperception, which means to see through, would have been a better word), which I had originally used in its broadest sense to imply personal meaning, and employ appraisal systematically because it clearly denoted evaluation (see Lazarus, 1964; and Speisman, Lazarus, Mordkoff, and Davison, 1964).

For Arnold, appraisal was an instantaneous sensing of harm or benefit. I drew on her usage, but gave much more emphasis to the deliberate search for knowledge about the environment and one's own personal goals and beliefs, all of which are needed to properly construe what is happening. I originally thought of appraisal as based on thoughtful evaluation, which depended on many factors, but in recent years I realized, as Arnold suggested, that appraisal is often rapid rather than deliberate, also often unconscious, and despite its complexity, almost instantaneous.

My research also provided substantial empirical support for this emerging approach to stress and coping. Later (Lazarus, 1991a), when I applied these concepts to the arousal of emotion, they had to be refurbished considerably to identify the relational meanings that lie behind each of the emotions, and to spell out the links between emotion and coping. But more about this in chapter 10.

MY FIRST MAJOR STRESS AND COPING MONOGRAPH

The reader already knows that I worked on my book on stress and coping while in Japan, and that during the last year or so of my pancreatic illness I was unable to make satisfactory progress. By the time I returned to Berkeley in the summer of 1964, I had completed a draft of that book. I sought and obtained a sabbatical leave during the next academic year during which the book was finished. It was entitled *Psychological Stress and the Coping Process,* and published by McGraw-Hill in 1966.

This book presented a theoretical analysis of psychological stress, reviewed extensive research in the field from a cognitive–mediational standpoint in which appraisal and coping were the central constructs, and discussed a few emotions, such as anxiety and anger, both of which are apt to be aroused under conditions of stress.

During the first few years after my monograph on stress and coping appeared, there was little reaction, which was disappointing. It was reviewed favorably in *Contemporary Psychology* after a year or so, by someone I had never heard of. However, the review lacked the verve and the deep commitment of a dedicated expert in the field, and I was again disappointed.

I have long been convinced that this journal, which is the main book-reviewing journal of psychology, often does a disservice to authors by publishing reviews by only one reviewer and by not seeking their input in the choice of reviewer. In my judgment, the wrong person has invariably been chosen to review my work, usually psychologists who do not share my epistemological and meta-theoretical outlook, and sometimes reviewers who are in direct competition with my ideas and research—which makes intellectually for a questionable review.

I don't view this as malicious, but I see it as a result of a careless system in which, given the volume of books written, ignorance or hastiness about the best people to do a fair and meaningful review, and the absence of more than one reviewer, impairs the review process. Stress was a relatively new field when my book appeared, and the editorial committee probably did not at that time include an expert on the subject. But the author is never permitted any input, which is an arrangement supposedly designed to defend an independent choice of reviewers.

However, I think of this as rationalization rather than a diligent search for a proper review. The committee might have sought competent advice, and even consulted with the author, without having slavishly followed any specific recommendations. In typical administrative fashion in which one protects one's credibility, *Contemporary Psychology* erroneously presumes that an author's lack of input keeps the process fair and objective.

In any case, I consider myself lucky, because it could have been worse. Reviews of my books have usually been favorable, even when not well or accurately reviewed. My disappointment stems from the fact that reviewers have typically failed to understand or sympathized with my objectives as author, which provokes a distorted account for the reader.

I remember talking to Irving Janis, a distinguished social psychologist who had preceded me in theory and research on psychological stress, about the problem of getting a fair hearing and the attention of the professional world. Janis's (1958) book was a fascinating study of a

patient he worked with psychoanalytically and who, during his therapy, faced major surgery. It also reported a field study of a number of
people who needed surgery. Janis made me feel better by saying that
he had the same experience I did with his book, which was later considered of major importance. He told me that he too was concerned at
first that no one seemed to be interested, though this changed after a
time. I think things have gotten worse for young researchers today,
because of the tremendous overload of things to be read.

After a slow start during the rest of the decade of the 1960s, in 1989
my book was labeled a "citation classic,"[2] because by then it had been
cited over 1,150 times. I believe it greatly influenced the direction of
the field of psychological stress and coping, and later the study of the
emotions. Its influence spanned a number of different fields, including
psychology, sociology, anthropology, physiology, and psychiatry.

Two factors are probably involved in the frequently slow acceptance
of a monographic work. First, the author is usually impatient to see
reactions to his opus and fails to realize that it takes time for people to
obtain and read the work. Second, in my case and that of Janis, a major
change was taking place as psychology moved into the decade of the
1970s, often referred to as the "cognitive revolution," in which there
would be much more acceptance of cognitive–mediational approaches
to feelings and actions. My book appeared a bit too early, though this
later made me look prescient. Timing in what one writes is terribly
important. One can be too early or too late.

How Stress Is Usually Studied

In addition to being able to measure it, in doing research on stress it is
especially desirable to be present when it occurs. Ideally, we could then
notice visible stress reactions, ask those under stress to tell us what
they are thinking and feeling, and make sophisticated measurements of
their physiological reactions. Nowadays, the brain could be added as a
target of such measurement in light of new methods of brain scanning.

Because we can't anticipate very well when and where stress will
occur, however, we are usually forced to make observations after the
fact by having people reconstruct what happened. We must then rely
on what they tell us about it, which may suffer from inadequacies of

---

[2] Letter from James A. Mears, Senior Editorial Manager, July 14, 1989 about the *Science
Citation Index and Social Science Citation Index*. Philadelphia: Institute for Scientific
Information. At that time they had recorded 1150 specific citations to my book.

memory or defensive distortions. Yet, despite the methodological risks of reconstructing past stressful experiences, it is one of the most common methods of studying stress, emotion, and coping, and has its own special advantages, because people can usually provide unique insights into their private experiences.

Janis's pioneering clinical study of a patient facing the stress of surgery, and his field research on other surgical patients, is one important example of a retrospective analysis, though the observations took place very close in time to the event of interest.

Another important example is a study by David Mechanic (1962), who examined the stress and coping processes of graduate students who were anticipating a crucial examination to determine whether they could continue their studies toward the doctorate. Because many were likely to be flunked out by the exam, this was a period of several months of high stress, especially as the students had already invested 2 or 3 years of prior work on the degree.

As anxiety mounted with the approach of the examination, Mechanic explored in considerable detail the social support they were receiving from their spouses, how they coped with the continuing pressure, and the impact of the experience on social relationships with competing students during the several months before the exam.

The favorite method of doing stress research, however, has been the laboratory experiment, in which stress is aroused while the researcher is present to observe and measure it. In the 1940s and 1950s, experimenters created diverse stress conditions, such as failure on an important task, receiving painful electric shocks, plunging an arm into icy water and holding it there as long as possible, and criticizing subjects in ways that threaten their ego-identities, all in an effort to simulate real-life stressful experiences and study it in the laboratory.

Convincing subjects of the reality of the threat usually requires deception, about which there are some inherent downsides. One is that deception endangers the researcher's credibility and threatens the cooperation of the subjects. A second is that it is not easy to set up believable threats in the laboratory, so most of the stress conditions employed are just pale shadows of powerful natural stressors. A third is that the stress experiences possible in the laboratory do not match the wide range of harms, threats, and challenges found in nature.

How, for example, can one come close to the reality of the death of a loved one and how could a humane and moral scientist try to do such a thing without a clear understanding on the part of the subject that it was just a simulation? And if it is a simulation, it cannot begin to approach the psychological reality of such an experience.

The most important defect of laboratory research in general, with or without deception, is that although the main rationale for an experiment is to control extraneous variables, stress experiments are usually complex social events in which such control is not likely to be achieved. For example, though subjects are given the same instructions, each experimenter has a distinctive appearance, style, and manner, and each subject has an individual personality with a distinctive style of thinking and set of goals. This encourages diverse interpretations by subjects of what is happening, which greatly complicates the psychodynamics of the experimental situation.

STUDYING STRESS NATURALLY, YET IN THE LABORATORY

For a long time I wondered how to set up laboratory experiments without using deception, yet still make careful stress measurements. It dawned on me that the most natural way to arouse stress would be to show films dealing with emotional subjects. Drama has long moved people, and movies do too, whether they are performed in a theater or on our home television set. They draw on the natural human tendency to put ourselves in the shoes of others struggling with life's problems and to react emotionally, because we have experienced, or might experience, comparable events.

Movies and plays that fail to arouse emotions do not achieve major audiences. When we see a successful drama, it is as if we are the people being portrayed. Though a movie is ostensibly about others, in a sense it is we in the audience rather than those presented in the drama who are the psychological center of attention, and we react accordingly with the emotions conveyed by the actors, and by the situations in which the dramatist has placed them. In effect, the drama is really all about us, which is why we are moved. A recent book (Tan, 1996) provides a theoretical analysis of the structure of narrative films and a review of research on the emotions they provoke. Films are viewed by the author as emotion generating machines.

I was one of the earliest researchers, if not the first, to use films programmatically in research on the stress emotions. This approach made it possible to study the stress process without deception while it is occurring in the laboratory. The heading for this section of the chapter, which speaks about studying stress naturally in the laboratory, sounds like an oxymoron, but in using films to study stress, we can have our cake—that is, a degree of naturalism—and eat it too by being positioned to measure psychophysiological response variables of interest.

This early research with stressful movies went hand in hand with the cognitive–mediational, appraisal-centered view I espoused in my 1966 book. My movie methods were first described in great detail in a monograph (Lazarus, Speisman, Mordkoff, & Davison, 1962), which laid the groundwork for future research by demonstrating that a film could produce stress reactions and how these reactions could be documented. Between 1960 and the early 1970s, we used films as the main, but not the only, method of arousing stress in the laboratory.

The first film used by the *Berkeley Stress and Coping Project,* which is what we later called our research group, was about subincision, which is a male rite of passage employed by a Stone-Age tribe, the Arunta, living in the outback of Australia. It is a silent film presenting a series of six crude operations on the underside of the penis.

As I noted in chapter 7, I had obtained the film from a psychoanalytically oriented psychologist at Oslo University in Norway, Arvid Åas, who interpreted its emotional impact in terms of the Freudian concept of castration anxiety. The loss of or damage to the penis could, perhaps, be taken literally, but I think it makes better sense to view it symbolically as the threat of loss of potency. I recognized the castration implication, but was also aware through interviews with subjects of many other sources of threat in the film, depending on the person watching it—for example, pain, the crudeness and unsanitary conditions of the surgery, child abuse, hidden homosexual urges, people being entrapped by destructive social requirements that cannot be evaded, and so on, some of which were recorded in our research (see also Speisman, Lazarus, Mordkoff, & Davison, 1964).

In our research, we found no evidence of any difference in the degree of stress generated by the subincision film on college men and women. One could interpret this in different ways—for example, that women are also concerned with loss of potency, male or female, or that castration anxiety has no relevance to the threat communicated by the film— but I am not sure what is the best explanation of this surprising finding. In any case, the subincision film offered a rich and effective way to arouse psychological stress, and it was used in several early studies.

In our initial pilot studies, student subjects varied greatly in what they said about their experience in watching the subincision film. The most common reaction reported was distress, coupled with physiological confirmation of this in heart rate and skin conductance, which were measured continuously while subjects watched.

We also observed two other frequent but less common reactions. In one, which seemed to be an effort to cope by *denial,* subjects would insist that "It didn't bother me a bit." Despite the denial, however, subjects often showed marked physiological stress reactions, suggesting that the denial was not working (Weinstein, Averill, Opton, & Lazarus, 1968). Another reaction seemed to be an effort to cope by intellectualization or *distancing* oneself emotionally, as I now prefer to label the process. These subjects would make statements such as "The film was an interesting anthropological study; my reaction was no different than it would be to any other strange foreign customs."

The interviews gave us clues about how we might try to influence the way subjects construed what was happening, and to see how effective different defenses were in reducing stress. We produced our own sound tracks for the movie, which expressed the thought processes characteristic of different ego-defenses, such as denial and distancing. Then we determined to what extent these ways of coping affected the stress reactions aroused by watching the movie.

In chapter 7, I described one such experiment as part of the cross-cultural comparison of stress reactions in Japanese and Americans. More than any other research we did in those days, this method of manipulating appraisal by using sound tracks, and later, by using orienting statements that were played before the film was shown, caught the fancy of many psychologists and offered viable empirical support for an appraisal-centered theory of stress.

The idea for the study of distancing was reinforced by one of our earliest film studies. While I was running subjects, sitting there monitoring the instruments measuring heart rate and skin conductance and watching the subincision film, I noticed something peculiar. When I began doing this, the film seemed very stressful and unpleasant to watch. I was caught between two impulses, either to look away in anxiety or disgust or to give way to the fascination inherent in esoteric human events.

But after awhile, I got bored with the whole thing, and even wondered why the film was said to be so stressful. I recognized that by repeatedly watching the film, I had become "habituated," which means that it no longer aroused any emotion in me. As I implied by the quotation marks around the word habituated, however, putting this label on the phenomenon does not really explain what had happened psychologically.

What does it mean to say I had become habituated? The term merely describes a lowered level of stress, not how the change came about. That the film was no longer stressful to watch means some active psychological process had been going on. Becoming distanced, I suspected, is not something that happens passively, but one that requires effort, even if we are unaware of it.

At the time this research was taking place, the Vietnam War was being fought on American television, and a number of writers (e.g., Bernard, Ottenberg, & Redl, 1965) have discussed the process of distancing from the emotional experience of daily watching people being victimized by war on their television sets. Some of these writers expressed concern that the victims, viewed as enemies, were being dehumanized—that is, regarded as less then human, making it easier for viewers not to feel distress and to be unable to empathize with the plight of the victims. Dehumanization protected the viewer, but also contributed to the legitimation of evil. In other words, perhaps it is easy to distance ourselves and we do it too much, at the cost of our humanity.

In any case, it was as though I was now watching the film without paying attention to its emotional implications. I was seeing what was happening, but not assimilating its emotional significance, as if a filter had been placed over my eyes, which protected me from noticing the meanings that were threatening. Whether or not this is an adequate explanation of why we can watch wounded and dying people on TV without emotion, my habituation process while watching the subincision film seemed to be drawing on a classical defense against threat.

A later event was to change my psychological state dramatically by once again restoring the stress level with which I had originally reacted. When, in later research, I was creating sound tracks to test the idea that ego-defensive strategies, such as denial and distancing, could lower stress, the task of making the sound tracks forced me to watch carefully what was going on in the film and seemed to make it impossible to distance from the film's stressful contents. Watching the film once again became a highly stressful experience. I could no longer ignore the threatening nature of what was being shown. The proverbial protective filter over my eyes was gone.

When we distance ourselves psychologically from something disturbing, we treat what is happening in a detached, analytic way, downplaying or ignoring its negative emotional significance. Distancing is what paramedics have learned to do when they deal with bloody and mangled bodies after a car crash, apply emergency procedures to those still alive, or remove dead bodies after an earthquake.[3] It is a powerful way to do their job without becoming overwhelmed with distress.

Distancing is also what parents do who fear they would feel so distressed after a bloody injury suffered by their child that they couldn't

---

[3] For a detailed account of how this worked in the Loma Prieta earthquake in the San Francisco Bay area of California, see Stuhlmiller, C. M. (1996). *Rescuers of Cypress: Learning from disaster.* New York: Peter Lang.

act helpfully. Yet they manage to tie up the wound to staunch the blood, place the child in the car, drive to the emergency room of a hospital, and perhaps only after they have done what was needed, allow themselves to be emotionally distressed or to feel faint.

The same principle applies when medical students are introduced to the autopsy of a dead person's body. The procedures employed in the dissection are intuitively well designed to encourage emotional distancing. The face and hands, which provide a disturbing personal identity to the body being dissected are almost always covered. The body is covered, except for the portion being examined. No reference is made to the living identity and personality of the corpse, as that would add an emotional dimension to the procedure. The autopsy is treated seriously and professionally, and gallows humor, which often occurs in surgery, is discouraged.

In other words, every effort is made to keep the experience unemotional, because otherwise novice students might suffer too much distress, which would get in the way of learning and might even lead them to faint or be forced to leave. Learning how to be a good physician, nurse, or other health care worker involves learning routinely to achieve the necessary emotional distance to protect them against unwanted emotional distress without seeming indifferent.

Only later, incidentally, did I catch on that ego-defenses actually lower stress levels by helping a person construe what is happening as less threatening. In effect, defenses are forms of *reappraisal* in which the relational meaning of the experience is changed from threatening to benign. The concept of appraisal and reappraisal is, therefore, a more fundamental process than ego-defenses in our understanding of how we evaluate and reevaluate threatening events in our lives. What started out as research on ego-defense processes pulled us more and more into the realm of appraisal and reappraisal as the basic feature of the stress process.

The power of reappraisal to alter stress reactions is easily illustrated by a common experience many of us have had when we are made angry by a verbal insult from someone we love, such as a spouse, lover, child, or friend. Imagine the following scenario experienced by a spouse who has been insulted and made angry by his or her partner.

As the offended partner is about to retaliate, he or she suddenly recognizes that the offending person has been ill, or is struggling with major stress at work, and so is worn down or "stressed out" as might be said these days. It becomes clear that the offending person cannot reasonably be held responsible for what was said or done. There was no genuine malice, and no offense had really been intended.

This benign reinterpretation of what happened obviates what would have been the meaning: that the person who first felt assaulted had been demeaned. The partner must be excused as not responsible for what was said and done, and this appraisal or reappraisal eliminates any need to feel angry and retaliate to restore a wounded ego. Moreover, the process need not be considered a form of repression or denial as long as the reappraisal is fully believed and could reasonably correspond to reality.

The Effects of Denial and Distancing

Returning to our film research on ego-defense, as I mused about distancing, and the role of appraisal in psychological stress and the emotions, it seemed to me that we could do some experiments that would help us to understand better this process of protecting oneself against threatening events. We could encourage the film viewer to employ either of two types of defense, denial and distancing by means of sound tracks, and compare their capacity to reduce stress levels aroused by watching stressful film events.

I have already said much about distancing but less about denial, which is a different form of ego-defense. When a person engages in denial, the claim is being made that no threat exists. In Freudian terms, it is disavowed. The person may say, " I am not angry" or "seriously ill," and so forth, though that is not true. On the other hand, when a person distances psychologically from a threat, it is not being denied. That something emotionally disturbing has happened is acknowledged, but it is dealt with in a way that neutralizes or cools down any disturbance, a process that has also been called intellectualization.

In psychoanalytic thought, to disavow reality was said to be normal only in a young child whose ability to make distinctions between fantasy and reality is still shaky. As the child matures and becomes adult, however, and learns the realities of life, denial is regarded as pathogenic and pathological—in effect, it is said to be a regressive, psychotic process.

Eventually, I came to see that the pathological and pathogenic aspects of denial were often being overstated. In a 1983 chapter on denial (Lazarus, 1983), I argued that we all use denial to some extent, which, in its milder, more socially acceptable form, is akin to illusion— that is, a widely held, comforting idea about life and the world, which distorts reality and often depends on euphemisms. Because most people are convinced these illusions are true, and make decisions on the basis of them, they do not look crazy and are not necessarily harmful, though they could be under the right circumstances.

I have already described in some detail in Chapter 7, the experiments we did in Berkeley and Tokyo on sound-track interventions while subjects watched the subincision film, and there is no need to repeat them here. Several different versions of this research were done, some of which employed other films—for example, one in which wood-shop accidents were shown on film. We demonstrated that playing the denial sound track in advance of the film as an orienting statement had the same ameliorating effect on stress levels as sound tracks had (Lazarus & Alfert, 1964).

You will recall that what we found in this research at Berkeley, and with other films in which we manipulated how American subjects construe the events being portrayed, is that the *trauma* sound track markedly increased both the subjective and physiological evidence of stress, compared with the *control* film in which the subjects were told nothing. In contrast, the *denial* and *distancing* sound tracks markedly decreased the stress-response levels.[4] We spoke of this effect as the short-circuiting of threat, which uses the metaphor of an electric circuit to suggest that the appraisal reduced stress reactions in advance of their actual occurrence.

We also did a closely related subsequent study to learn what subjects might do psychologically to regulate their emotions while watching a stressful film (Korian, Melkman, Averill, & Lazarus, 1972). The wood-shop accident film, "It didn't have to happen," was employed. This film is narrated by a foreman whose apparent intent is to teach woodworkers about the way accidents happen and how to avoid them. It begins with a brief shot of a worker, Slim, being impaled by a board that flies from a circular saw and kills him.

A second accident shows how another worker, Armand, who is operating a milling machine, gets his finger cut off. First we see Armand working the machine with a missing middle finger. Then, in a flashback, we see him with all his fingers intact, and we instantly intuit that we are about to see him lose the finger. When the accident is shown, blood appears to spurt from the wound, and Armand holds his hand, minus the finger, in consternation and distress.

Subjects first watched the movie without any instructions. Then some subjects were instructed to *involve themselves* as much as possible in

---

[4] For summaries of this research and others like it see Lazarus, R. S., Averill, J. R., & Opton, E. M., Jr. (1970). Towards a cognitive theory of emotion. In M. Arnold (Ed.), *Feelings and emotions* (pp. 207–232). New York: Academic Press; Lazarus, R. S. (1966). *Psychological stress and the coping process.* New York: McGraw-Hill; and Lazarus, R. S., & Folkman, S. (1984). *Stress, appraisal, and coping.* New York: Springer.

the emotionally distressing events, whereas other subjects were told to *distance* themselves (we actually used the word detach) as much as possible from the experience. How they did this was left up to them.

Those who were instructed to involve themselves reported higher distress and showed greater physiological stress reactions than before. Those instructed to distance themselves showed lower stress reactions than before. All subjects were asked afterward what they did to regulate their emotional reactions. The most common strategy reported by those seeking to involve themselves was to imagine that the events were actually happening to them. Another common strategy was to think about and exaggerate the consequences of the accidents, or to imagine that it was happening to somebody they knew.

In contrast, the most common strategy for those seeking to distance was to remind themselves that they were watching a film rather than the real thing. They also concentrated on the technical aspects of the film. The strategies our subjects reported support the claim that denial and distancing are commonly used and readily understood ways of coping with the emotional distress aroused by stressful films.

By influencing how our subjects appraised what they saw, we had successfully manipulated their stress levels. All watched the same film, but their emotional response to that film differed greatly depending on how they were led to appraise its personal significance. We had verified a very powerful principle—namely, that the way people *appraise* the personal significance of what is happening affects their stress reactions and the emotions associated with them.

The Effects of Surprise and Suspense

The capacity of films to throw light on how stress works can also be illustrated by later efforts of my colleagues and me to study the part played by *anticipation* in the arousal and management of stress (Nomikos, Opton, Averill, & Lazarus, 1968). Again we used the film showing a series of wood-shop accidents, and as in previous research, we measured heart rate, skin conductance, and subjective distress.

Because the second accident in this film involves a flashback in which the viewer realizes that Armand's accident is about to be shown, there is a period of anticipation before the dreaded event happens. We wanted to know whether the time a viewer had to anticipate the accident made any difference in the amount of stress that was aroused. By appropriate cutting and splicing of the film, we created two versions of the same accident scene. One was called *surprise,* in which some subjects waited only a little over 6 seconds for the accident to happen—very little warning time. The other was called *suspense,* in which other subjects waited for almost 19 seconds.

We found that the stress levels were far lower, both physiologically and subjectively, in the surprise condition than in the suspense condition. In effect, the longer subjects could anticipate the cutting off of Armand's finger, the more stress they displayed. This principle is one that dentists intuitively use when giving an injection, which most people find stressful. They don't wait around long before injecting the hypodermic needle into the patient's gums, but proceed without delay, which keeps the level of anticipatory anxiety from mounting. Waiting would simply increase the stress levels.

We also wanted to learn which portion of this experience leads to the most stress, waiting for the accident to happen or actually seeing the loss of Armand's finger—in effect, which is worse, the anticipation or the reality? The evidence was overwhelming. Stress levels rose sharply up to the moment of the actual accident, but at the point when the finger was cut off, the stress level was already beginning to come down. In other words, anticipating the event was worse than seeing it.

The most experienced and celebrated film directors, such as Alfred Hitchcock, intuitively understand very well how various dramatic devices work in producing reactions in an audience, and they use them accordingly. The flashback is particularly interesting, because it can be so readily used to create anxiety, which results from anticipation of a harmful event that remains ambiguous because we don't know exactly what will happen. I'm not sure whether directors who use flashbacks can always express in words the principles underlying how they manipulate emotions in their audiences, but they evidently know how to do it and succeed wonderfully. And Hitchcock was certainly a master at creating suspense.

Whenever I have lectured about this research with the wood-shop accident film, I always say that it is strictly a dramatization by actors, none of whom are actually injured. The accidents had to be faked; no one would have waited around long enough to capture such relatively rare events on film. Nevertheless, even though we know this, when we watch the film the accidents seem real rather than being enacted, and we are, perforce, emotionally caught up in them.

To come back to the important research issues of the experiment on surprise and suspense, there remained an unresolved theoretical problem. The anticipation times employed in the study were very short, less than a quarter of a minute even in the suspense condition. I suspected that things would be different if subjects had a much longer time for cognitive coping to occur—that is, for having reassuring second thoughts about what is about to happen. So one of my students designed a very different kind of experiment that allowed us to assess this question (Folkins, 1970).

The stress employed was the expectation of a painful electric shock. Each subject sat in a chair in front of a clock and a viewing screen on which instructional messages were flashed. They knew they would be warned about how long they would have to wait for the shock. The messages read "Shock in 5 seconds," and so on for several different waiting periods. Some subjects had to wait for 30 seconds, others 1 minute, 3 minutes, 5 minutes, or 20 minutes. No shock was actually used; just anticipating it was enough to arouse substantial stress, which was measured, as in the other studies, by continuous physiological recordings and periodic subjective reports. The experiment was over for each subject after the clock indicated that it was time for the shock to be given.

The results of comparing the amount of stress aroused in each of the periods of waiting were fascinating. Subjects who waited only 30 seconds and 1 minute showed higher levels of stress than those who waited 3 and 5 minutes. Those waiting 20 minutes showed the highest stress levels, which started to climb slowly after about 7 or 8 minutes from the time the shock was due, but rose dramatically in the last minute.

What could account for these differences? We had data that could help make this clear. As part of the experiment, a subsample of each group of subjects had been asked several times during the waiting period to tell us what they had been thinking while waiting. Their thoughts differed greatly depending on the length of the waiting period. For example, subjects waiting 30 seconds and 1 minute had few thoughts of any kind, expressed in one subject's statement that "There was not enough time to think of much of anything." What they did understand, however, was that they were about to experience something painful, so their stress level was high.

Those who waited for 3 and 5 minutes, however, had plenty of time to think reassuring thoughts about the upcoming shock. For example, they would say to themselves, not unrealistically, "I've been shocked before and it wasn't so bad, it's the waiting that's the hard part" or, "I'm sure that a university professor would not be allowed to really hurt me, it can't be so bad." In other words, if they had enough time to analyze the situation, they could reassure themselves that there was not much to be upset about. And cognitive coping lowered their stress levels.

But what about the rise in stress levels for those who waited 20 minutes for the shock? This group had the most time of all to cope cognitively with the threat of shock. Why didn't it help? What I believe happened is that a new, threatening meaning was added to the situation by the very long waiting period, and this undermined the effort at self-reassurance. The subjects told us that the long wait made the situation seem ominous. Anything one must await helplessly for so long couldn't be trivial.

The longer period of suspense had resulted in a build-up of stress, just as it had in the suspense condition of the flashback incident with Armand in the wood-shop accident film. We were observing a curvilinear rather than linear relationship between waiting time and stress levels. I imagine, however, that if the waiting period had been days or weeks, as it often is in real life, the early stages of waiting would have been more benign, because the stressful event was still very remote in time. We all know that eventually we must die, but the confrontation with death seems so far away in time, we are able to put it out of our minds.

What is really important in anticipatory stress situations is the opportunity provided in the waiting period to cope with the threat psychologically, and the meaning that is given to the experience of waiting itself. Very short periods of time, such as those in the surprise condition of the movie study, do not provide enough waiting time for subjects to think about the threatening implications of what is about to happen. The stress is high. Slightly longer waiting periods permit a build-up of threat, as in the 19-second period in which subjects awaited Armand's accident, and the 30-second and 1-minute periods of waiting for an electric shock. But there still isn't enough time for reassuring coping thoughts to occur, as is the case if you have a few minutes. And, as always, the individual differences are large.

We can conclude that, given a potentially threatening situation, the magnitude of a stress reaction depends on how a person construes what is happening—that is, what they tell themselves about it. Although many other conditions probably influence it, the amount of time for anticipation of the harm seems to be important in affecting this construal,[5] or as I label it, appraisal.

What our research in the 1960s accomplished was to focus attention on psychological stress as a normal but important feature of human life, not only in extreme situations but in routine events of daily living.

---

[5] See also the research of Monat, A., Averill, J. R., & Lazarus, R. S. (1973). Anticipatory stress and coping under various conditions of uncertainty. *Journal of Personality and Social Psychology, 24,* 237–253. Monat was also a graduate student working with me on these projects; after completing his doctorate he became a professor at the University of California at Hayward.

We showed that the way people appraise and cope with stress situations determines their levels of stress reaction, and that if we change these appraisals, stress levels also change.

This idea and the findings obtained implicated the coping process as a powerful antidote to stress. It was not until the late 1970s, however, that *The Berkeley Stress and Coping Project* began systematically to study the coping process, when we sought a method of measuring coping in the field and turned to studies of people who had to deal with stress in the natural course of their lives.

In the 1970s, the topic of psychological stress and coping had finally attained great professional and popular interest. Clinical treatment programs began to draw on psychological stress theory to design therapeutic interventions (Meichenbaum, 1977). What we did experimentally is formally similar to what *cognitive therapists* do when they help patients discover and change pathogenic ways of thinking and beliefs that encourage dysfunction and forms of distress, such as depression and anxiety. I was very pleased when one of the most creative and scholarly of the cognitive therapists, Donald Meichenbaum, and his coauthor Matt E. Jaremko, acknowledged this connection by dedicated their edited book to me and my work (Meichenbaum & Jaremko, 1983).

There was now also a thriving business, both professional and lay, in the management of stress, which extended also to industrial organizations (Lazarus, 1991b). Interest also spread overseas to other countries. The theory and research my colleagues and I published in the 1960s seems to have played an important role in this expanding interest and growing sophistication about how appraisal and coping processes worked.

Our research also demonstrate the validity of the point of the Hamlet quotation I presented earlier in this chapter about the role of thinking in making something seem good or bad. The ancient Greek writer, Epictetus, made a similar statement in *The Enchiridion* when he wrote: "Men are disturbed not by things, but by the view which they take of things."

During this period, radical behaviorism, the approach to mind that had dominated and, I believe, strangulated our field for three quarters of a century, had begun to lose its hold on psychology, which then turned once again toward the principle of cognitive mediation. Mimicking the ancient Greek interests of Plato, Aristotle, a Roman named Seneca, and the medieval Catholic Church, psychology was asking questions once again about the relationships among the three functions of mind: cognition, motivation, and emotion. But in saying this, however, I am anticipating my work in the 1980s, still almost 20 years away.

With the appraisal-centered laboratory research just described, my laboratory days were drawing to a close, and they ended in the 1970s. I was becoming convinced that the exciting, but complicated, issues and concepts of stress and emotion could be better addressed and expanded empirically by field research. My transition to the field is the central topic of chapter 9.

REFERENCES

Arnold, M. B. (1960). *Emotion and personality* (Vols 1 & 2). New York: Columbia University Press.

Bernard, V. W., Ottenberg, P., & Redl F. (1965). Dehumanization: A composite psychological defense in relation to modern war. In M. Schwebel (Ed.), *Behavioral science and human survival.* Palo Alto, CA: Science and Behavior Books.

Cowen, E. L. (1960). Personality, motivation, and clinical phenomena. *Psychological Research and Rehabilitation.* Miami Conference Report.

DeBenedetti, C. (with Chatfield). (1990). *An American ordeal: The antiwar movement of the Vietnam era.* Syracuse NY: Syracuse University Press.

Folkins, C.H. (1970). Temporal factors and the cognitive mediators of stress reaction. *Journal of Personality and Social Psychology, 46,* 839–852.

Grinker, R. R., & Spiegel, J. P. (1945). *Men under stress.* New York: McGraw-Hill.

Hallstead, F. (1978). *Out now!: A participant's account of the American movement against the Vietnam War.* New York: Monat Press.

Heath, G. L. (1976). *Mutiny does not happen lightly: The literature of the American resistance to the Vietnam War.* NJ: Scarecrow Press.

Janis, I. L. (1958). *Psychological stress.* New York: Wiley.

Koriat, A., Melkman, R., Averill, J. R., & Lazarus, R. S. (1972). The self-control of emotional reactions to a stressful film. *Journal of Personality, 40,* 601–619.

Lazarus, R. S. (1964). A laboratory approach to the dynamics of psychological stress. *American Psychologist, 19,* 400–411.

Lazarus, R. S. (1966). *Psychological stress and the coping process.* New York: McGraw-Hill.

Lazarus, R. S. (1983). The costs and benefits of denial. In S. Breznitz (Ed.), *The denial of stress* (pp. 1–30). New York: Free Press.

Lazarus, R. S. (1991a). *Emotion and adaptation.* New York: Oxford University Press.

Lazarus, R. S. (1991b). Psychological stress in the workplace, and commentaries. In P. L. Perewé (Ed.), *Job stress. A special issue of the Journal of Social Behavior and Personality* (Vol. 6, pp. 1–38). Corte Madera, CA: Select Press.

Lazarus, R. S., & Alfert, E. (1964). The short-circuiting of threat by experimentally altering cognitive appraisal. *Journal of Abnormal and Social Psychology, 69,* 195–205.

Lazarus, R. S., Averill, J. R., & Opton, E. M., Jr. (1970). Toward a cognitive theory of emotion. In M. Arnold (Ed.), *Feelings and emotions* (pp. 207–232). New York: Academic Press.

Lazarus, R. S., & Folkman, S. (1984). *Stress, appraisal, and coping.* New York: Springer.

Lazarus, R. S., Speisman, J. C., Mordkoff, A. M., & Davison, L. A. (1964). A laboratory study of psychological stress produced by a motion picture film. *Psychological Monographs: General and Applied, 76* (Whole No. 553).

Mechanic, D. (1962). *Students under stress.* New York: Free Press of Glencoe.

Meichenbaum, D. (1977). *Cognitive behavior modification: An integrative approach.* New York: Plenum.

Meichenbaum, D., & Jaremko, M. E. (1983). *Stress reduction and prevention.* New York: Plenum.

Monat, A., Averill, J. R., & Lazarus, R. S. (1973). Anticipatory stress and coping under various conditions of uncertainty. *Journal of Personality and Social Psychology, 24,* 237–253.

Nomikos, M., Opton, E. M., Jr., Averill, J. R., & Lazarus, R. S. (1968). Surprise and suspense in the production of a stress reaction. *Journal of Personality and Social Psychology, 8,* 204–208.

Speisman, J. C., Lazarus, R. S., Mordkoff, A. M., & Davison, L. A. (1962). Experimental analysis of a film used as a threatening stimulus. *Journal of Consulting Psychology, 28,* 23–33.

Tan, E. S. (1996). *Emotion and the structure of narrative film: Film as an emotion machine.* Mahwah, NJ: Erlbaum.

Tuchman, B. (1984). *The March of Folly.* New York: Knopf.

Weinstein, J., Averill, J. R., Opton, E. M., Jr., & Lazarus, R. S. (1968). Defensive style and discrepancy between self-report and physiological indexes of stress. *Journal of Personality and Social Psychology, 10,* 406–413.

The Berkeley Stress and Coping Project

Considering that this chapter is mostly about my research and thought, for those who have followed my family's fate closely from the beginning, including our youthful appearance early on, I should begin this chapter with a brief note that on September 2, 1972 Bernice and I celebrated our 25th wedding anniversary. One of the photos in Figure 9.1 shows us at home cutting the cake, and the other shows the six of us, without the grandchildren, all together in front of the fireplace, celebrating Bernice's 50th birthday on June 10th in our Lafayette home. I couldn't resist including this sign of progress and advancing age.

In this chapter I examine highlights of my theoretical and research efforts at Berkeley during the late 1970s and through most of the 1980s prior to my retirement from teaching in 1991. This period was preceded by a slow transition from laboratory to field research, and the decision to study stress, emotion, and coping in the daily lives of older people living in the community.

The Berkeley Stress and Coping Project had already passed through two very distinctive periods, or incarnations. The first, beginning with my arrival in Berkeley, and with funds from a research grant from the National Institute of Mental Health (NIMH), was devoted to the establishment of a psychophysiological laboratory, and the pursuit of film studies. We published a monograph reviewing some of this early research (Lazarus, Speisman, Mordkoff, & Davison, 1962, an article describing the sound tracks and orientation passages used to influence appraisal (Lazarus, Speisman, & Mordkoff, 1963), and other studies exploring methodological issues in psychophysiological research (Speisman, Lazarus, Mordkoff, & Davison, 1964).

The second incarnation, supported by the NIMH, a National Science Foundation (NSF) cross-cultural research grant, and a 5-year research

A. Cutting the cake on our 25th wedding anniversary on September 2, 1970.

B. Celebrating Bernice's 50th birthday on June 10, 1972.

FIGURE 9.1   We and our family in the early 1970s.

training grant from the Vocational Rehabilitation Administration (VRA), continued to expand this research and its theoretical underpinnings. During this period, we performed and published a great deal of research (e.g., Folkins, Lawson, Opton, & Lazarus, 1968; Nomikos, Opton, Averill, & Lazarus, 1968), and our Project gained widespread recognition. Our articles began to reflect an increasing interest in the emotions and in the coping process (e.g., Lazarus, 1968, Lazarus, Averill, and Opton, 1970, 1974). I have already covered the first and second project incarnations in chapter 8.

In the early 1970s, I was intellectually poised to begin a major transition from laboratory to field research. This actually took until 1978 when the third major incarnation of the Berkeley Stress and Coping Project got under way with a different set of personnel. This period lasted just about 10 years until 1988 when we closed down the Project shortly before my retirement from teaching in 1991. But I should spend some time describing the transition to field research, which preceded this third period.

THE TRANSITION FROM THE LABORATORY TO THE FIELD

I had become increasingly edgy about the heavy dependence of stress theory and research on laboratory experiments, a concern that kept growing as stress and coping theory expanded. There were many reasons for my change of heart, some having to do with the technical problems of arousing stress and emotion, others having to do with limitations of laboratory research in general.

For one thing, the films we were able to obtain were very limited in content, being mostly about assaults on the body. They did not permit us to sample the rich variety of stress emotions that should be studied programmatically. In addition, I was no longer convinced that stress and coping were best studied in the laboratory, even with films, which are capable of arousing emotional reactions without deception. I believed then, as I do now, that deception undermines experimenter–subject trust, making many findings suspect.

Also in those days, before psychophysiology had been computerized, the cost of obtaining and reducing to numbers recordings of heart rate, skin conductance, and other autonomic nervous system indicators of emotional reactions was very high in time, labor, and money. Although psychophysiological measurement had proven very useful, its high cost greatly limited the resources available for studying the most important psychodynamic issues.

Finally, emotions in the laboratory are not so easy to arouse and control. They are usually weaker than those that occur in everyday life because laboratory subjects do not have as much of a personal stake in experimental situations as they do in everyday life situations. In addition, the variety of coping strategies available to experimental subjects is sharply curtailed in comparison with the normal stress conditions of life. The laboratory is most suited to creating analogues of psychological processes to test well-formulated theories, but not for novel observation and description of the processes of interest.

Nor are our current theories comprehensive enough or sufficiently detailed to deduce precise hypotheses for laboratory testing, and the use of the term "hypothesis" has become mainly an affectation in our field when hunches, speculations, or ad hoc impressions would be more accurate. So I felt then, and still do, that the potential of laboratory experiments as a source of knowledge, especially in the context of seeking new discoveries, pales against the naturalistic observation of stress and coping processes in everyday life.

In 1972, along with Bernice, I also reached 50 years of age, and several other events contributed to my restlessness about the status quo. An NIMH research committee turned down a major application for funds, suggesting I needed to find a new research direction. Although it might have been a sign of hubris, I privately thought the unthinkable—namely, that envy and unreasonable nitpicking was involved in this decision, as few laboratories had been either as productive or influential in the field of stress and coping. But it is never fruitful to pursue a line of thought like this too far. One must roll with the punches and push on.

There were other important considerations that urged change. I was beginning to feel stale at Berkeley, and poorly integrated into the Psychology Department, especially the personality program. I found myself an alien in what I considered my own field. I resolutely resisted the conformity pressure, both in research and teaching, and steadfastly went my own way, but I felt isolated and not pleased about what was happening.

I was also receiving very tempting offers from other universities to accept special appointments at a high salary with attractive perquisites, appointments that would reduce my teaching and committee load and free more time for research. For now, however, it is enough to note that it became evident that family considerations made it all but impossible to leave without doing serious damage.

So, to help resolve these problems, I decided instead to try another way of doing research without abandoning my long-standing commitment to an already influential, but still incomplete, theoretical approach to stress, emotion, and coping. I wanted to study how these processes operate in daily living.

THE STRUGGLE TO CLOSE DOWN MY LABORATORY

It turns out that making the transition was far more difficult than I had anticipated. I had no prior experience with field research, and epidemiological studies with large samples and superficial observation turned me off. Large-scale populations were not compatible with my psychodynamic concerns with the individual and within-individual variations over time and across the circumstances of living.

These concerns called for in-depth study of individuals, using longitudinal research strategies in which the same individuals are studied repeatedly. But I did not wish to fall back on a completely ideographic style of research either, say, with an N of 1. Within-person comparisons have to be combined somehow with between-person comparisons to give them a normative base, which meant doing research in which the sample size had to be modest.

I began to think about the methodology that would be needed, finally settling on a research strategy, sometimes referred to as *ipsative-normative*, in which one paints a portrait of a number of individuals by observing how they act and react over time and across different life conditions. Because the number of research subjects would have to be limited in order to study the same persons over time and in a number of different settings, I could not hope to work with demographically representative samples. It would be necessary to choose a relatively homogeneous sample with a view to replicate each study and eventually to compare it with other samples so as to generalize more broadly.

Psychological measurement has long tended to emphasize stability—that is, it usually adopts a structural outlook—but I wanted my research to be change- or process-centered too, which is what stress is mostly about, because those under stress want to change the conditions making them distressed and dysfunctional. Appraisal and coping, and the emotions associated with them, would be the central foci of any such field research. I was confident it was possible, as well as desirable, to study the sources of stress in people's daily lives, how they coped with them, and how stress and coping might affect adaptational outcomes, such as morale, social functioning, and somatic health.

Thinking this way, however, does not provide an adequate blueprint for a funded research program. I remember giving lectures here and there about my conceptualization and what I wanted to do, and I look back on these lectures as being very incomplete. They would begin clearly enough, but when it came to the details about how I would go about measuring daily stress and coping processes, I was still vague, whether or not my listeners sensed it. I wasn't yet quite ready.

As I hinted earlier, abandoning an existing and well-functioning laboratory proved difficult. Even after funding ended, I couldn't easily turn off what had become a viable, ongoing research program. Students wanted to do their dissertations there, with its psychophysiological equipment, films, tried-and-true procedures, and research rooms arranged for observation on the fourth floor of Tolman Hall. The Berkeley Stress and Coping Project continued to publish experimental research and to turn out students with doctorates until the mid-1970s.

During those years, for example, two graduate students from Israel, Asher Koriat and Rachel Melkman, along with Jim Averill and I, studied what people do to regulate their emotional reactions (Koriat, Melkman, Averill, & Lazarus, 1972). Both have academic appointments now in Israel. Averill, Malmstrom (a graduate student), Koriat (another graduate student from Israel), and Lazarus (1972) did a study on habituation to stress. Another Israeli student, Reuven Gal, who had been the Chief Psychologist of the Israeli Navy and later became Chief Psychologist of the Israeli Armed Forces, did his dissertation on the role of activity in the regulation of stress in the laboratory. We published an article together showing that just doing something, anything, even if it had no chance of changing a bad situation, could often be stress reducing (Gal & Lazarus, 1975).

A little later, Alan Monat also needed the lab for his dissertation to follow up earlier experiments on anticipatory stress and coping under conditions of uncertainty (Monat, Averill, & Lazarus, 1973). He later became a Professor of Psychology at the California State University at Hayward, and teaches courses there on stress and coping. Together we published books on personality and an anthology of stress and coping, which is now in its third edition (Monat & Lazarus, 1991).

AN EARLY INSTANCE OF FIELD RESEARCH

Despite delays and uncertainties, my ultimate transition to field research is well illustrated by research I published in 1973 with a graduate student, Frances Cohen, as first author (Cohen & Lazarus, 1973). In time, after she completed her doctorate, Fran became a full Professor of Psychology at the University of California in San Francisco, where she continues to do research on stress and coping in a variety of illnesses.

What made our field study distinctive was that it compared a dispositional measure of coping with a process measure, testing the assumption that dispositional measures predict how subjects actually coped with actual threats in their lives. The threat in this study was a relatively minor surgical operation, either hernia, gall bladder, or thyroidectomy. The *dispositional measures* consisted of two scales of repression–sensitization.

The *process measure,* which was an analogue of the dispositional measure, was based on a careful interview with patients in the hospital the evening before the surgery when they were likely to be most threatened. To infer the coping process, the interviews assessed what patients knew about their disorder and the upcoming surgery.

They were said to be coping with a *vigilant strategy* if they had substantial knowledge, or were avidly seeking it. An *avoidant* or *denial* coping strategy was inferred if patients knew little, and obviously didn't wish to know, even if proffered. Such patients placed their trust in their physicians, often believing, quite erroneously, that they had the best surgeon for the job. Some readers may have noticed that this research is an extension of some of my earlier research efforts with respect to New Look issues of the 1950s. Important problems never die.

Contrary to what should have happened, we found that the dispositional measures were very poor predictors of the coping process displayed by subjects. Nor did they correlate with postsurgical measures of recovery, though the process measure did. Patients who employed an avoidant or denial process had a shorter stay in the hospital and fewer minor complications than those who coped with the threat vigilantly.

I have always interpreted this as the result of the tendency of hospitals to encourage the patient to accept complete control over their fate by doctors and nurses. Vigilance about what is happening, therefore, does little or no good, as others are in control. On the other hand, placing oneself in the hands of professionals, and attaining a passive attitude of "just relax and enjoy the vacation," are well suited to the hospital environment.

I should note, however, that this pattern doesn't apply to all medical conditions. In asthma, for example, which is typically an outpatient disorder, vigilance is very important as a coping strategy. Taking asthma medication at the first sign of an attack helps prevent an asthmatic crisis, whereas denial of the danger leads the patient to fail to take such medicines. This failure often results in the patient having to be hospitalized because of an attack that turns into a medical emergency (Staudenmayer, Kinsman, Dirks, Spector, & Wangaard, 1977).

Cohen and I concluded that the study of coping should be directed more at the active coping process used in managing threat, because trait or dispositional measures, at least in our data, were not effective predictors either of the process of coping or its outcomes. This conclusion has been supported by a related German study published recently (Krohne, Slangen, & Kleemann, 1996). As a result of this study, I became all the more convinced I was on the right track in focusing on process, and that it was time to leave the laboratory and study stress and coping as they occurred in the natural course of living.

My first effort to obtain research funds succeeded in 1978 with a grant from the National Institute of Child Health and Development (NICHD). It was part of a larger human development program-project at the University of California at San Francisco (UCSF), under the aegis of Marjorie Fiske Lowenthal. The mission of my subproject was to study stress and coping in aging. This began a research project that was to be enormously productive and influential over a period of 10 years. It was the third and last incarnation of the Berkeley Project.

THE BERKELEY STRESS AND COPING PROJECT, THIRD INCARNATION

As I hope is clear to the reader at this point, my substantive theory of stress and emotion focuses on two main concepts, appraisal and coping. It proposes that individual goals and beliefs interact with environmental demands, constraints, personal resources, and opportunities to shape the appraisal of what is happening, the stress reaction, and how the individual copes. An article in the *European Journal of Personality,* written toward the end of the project, pulled together both the metatheory, which consists of principles for thinking about phenomena such as relational meaning, theoretical propositions, and research findings over the nearly 10-year period of this research (Lazarus & Folkman, 1987).

The main task of our field research, which was supported for a time by the National Institute of Aging (NIA) and a special research grant from the MacArthur Foundation, was to identify and describe the emotions that flowed from stress, and the coping process employed to deal with both the provoking conditions and the emotional reactions. Sources of stress in the lives of people had to be described, as well as positive events too, and the role played by appraisal and coping as mediators of the emotional outcomes. These were all part of a multivariate system. I felt that too much previous stress research had involved testing of relationships by manipulating variables, and there had been too little of naturalistic, in-depth description.

My colleague in this research was Susan Folkman, who had first been a graduate student under my direction and whose doctoral dissertation in 1980 became the initial publication of the Project's third incarnation. Her dissertation used a special coping questionnaire, which I will say more about shortly. Folkman, who clearly demonstrated her talent for research and diligence even then, later became the project director and coprincipal investigator, and helped guide the Project, which was later supported by the *National Institute of Drug Abuse* (NIDA), until the Project closed down in 1988.

In 1984, we collaborated on a major monograph, *Stress, Appraisal, and Coping* (Lazarus & Folkman, 1984), which has also been used as a college textbook. Figure 9.2 shows me showing off this book in my office when it appeared. I believe it is the most heavily cited monograph in the field since then, both in the United States and abroad, and has been translated into many languages. After the Project closed down, Folkman took a position as a Professor of Medicine at the University of California in San Francisco, where she directs a major NIMH-funded research project on stress and coping in caregivers of partners who are dying of AIDS. This research continues to produce important findings and insights about coping (e.g., Folkman, 1997; Folkman, Chesney, & Christopher-Richards, 1994; Stein, Folkman, Trabasso, & Richards, 1997).

A number of others also participated in portions of the third incarnation of the Berkeley Stress and Coping Project. They include two faculty members, Judith Cohen, from the Epidemiology Section of the Berkeley

FIGURE 9.2 Showing *Stress, Appraisal, and Coping* in my Berkeley office.

School of Public Health, and James Coyne, from Psychology. Graduate students came from the UCSF Developmental Training Program, the Education Department at Berkeley, as well as Epidemiology and Psychology. They included Carolyn Aldwin, Patricia Benner, Francis Cohen, Gayle Dakof, Anita DeLongis, Gloria Golden, Rand Gruen, Alan Kanner, Ray Launier, Catherine Schaefer, and Judith Wrubel. Their names grace many of the publications of the Project during its 10 years of existence. Most have been quite successful after leaving graduate school, holding diverse positions as professors in other departments, research personnel, and practicing clinicians.

We studied several groups of older people ranging in age from 45 to 80, and carefully delimited demographically. Interviewers visited their homes once a month for a year to inquire about stress and coping in their lives, using a variety of measurement tools, including question-naires about daily hassles and coping. For this we innovated two main measurement devices, the *Hassles and Uplifts Scales* and the *Ways of Coping Interview-Questionnaire.* We also obtained life history and personality data. Each sample consisted of about 100 subjects, both men and women, similar in age.

Below I examine briefly some of the highlights of our research and thought during this period. I begin with the concept of daily hassles as an approach to stress measurement and follow with an account of our interview-questionnaire approach to coping.

STRESS AS DAILY HASSLES

Based on a measure of stressful life events introduced in 1967 by Holmes and Rahe (1967), attempts to measure how much stress a person had experienced in the recent past had been dominated for quite a while by life-events lists. Life events refer to major changes in one's living conditions, such as having to pay a mortgage, marriage, divorce, and death of a spouse. A reasonable assumption was that the more stressful life changes there had been recently, the more likely it was a person would become ill, presumably as a result of the extensive coping effort required.

Although a number of additions and changes were made over the years, the standard procedure was to give a weight to each event based on the degree of adaptational demands it made. Normative studies provided data on such weightings as subjectively evaluated by large and diverse population samples. This resulted in a method of obtaining stress scores based on how much change had occurred in any given person's life over, say, the last year or 6 months, regardless of whether the change was positive or negative.

The reasoning here, incidentally, was that even a vacation, or getting married, which are considered positive experiences, could be quite stressful in the coping demands it makes on the person. The higher the change score, the greater the stressful demands were said to be on the adaptational resources of the person, and the greater the potential for subsequent illness.

From its inception, the life-change method struck me as inadequate theoretically and practically. Most stressful demands in our daily lives are chronic or recurrent. Major changes, such as divorce or death of a loved one, are usually infrequent in our lives, but stress is, nevertheless, a daily part of our existence. I was convinced that the daily grind of even seemingly minor irritants, frustrations, and threats, such as problems of getting along with people, both at home with family members and lovers, at school with teachers and peers, and on the job with coworkers, were just as important in arousing stress as major life events, perhaps even more important.

So our research group set about developing a list of what we called *daily hassles* (Delongis, Coyne, Dakof, Folkman, & Lazarus, 1982; DeLongis, Folkman, & Lazarus, 1988; and Kanner, Coyne, Schaefer, & Lazarus, 1981). The resulting list contained 117 items, which could be grouped into eight major categories—namely, household responsibilities, finances, work, the environment and social issues, home maintenance, health, personal life, family, and friends.

It also occurred to us that people who experience a great many hassles, but who also experience many positive experiences, might be better off in health and well-being than those who had lots of hassles but fewer positive experiences. So we also developed a list of what we called *daily uplifts,* which contained 135 items, such as getting enough sleep, spending time with family, making a friend, getting good advice, and so forth. The hassles-and-uplifts questionnaires could be scored for both the frequency of these experiences and their intensity, as rated by subjects.

We even found a poem by Charles Bukowski (1980) that expressed the idea that little things may be as stressful as big things:

> *It is not the large things that*
> *send a man to the madhouse. . . .*
> *No, it's the continuing series*
> *of small tragedies that send*
> *a man to the madhouse*
> *Not the death of his love*
> *but a shoelace that*
> *snaps with no time left.*

In our earliest studies of this (e.g., Kanner, et al., 1981; Delongis et al, 1981, 1988), we pitted life events against daily hassles as a predictor of emotional distress and psychological symptoms in 100 middle-aged men and women who had been studied by means of interviews once a month over the course of a year. One of our striking findings was that daily hassles scores were more strongly related to emotional distress and symptoms of dysfunction than life events.

How could this be? From a commonsense standpoint, death of a spouse, divorce, a large mortgage, being sued or going to jail, are clearly massive stressors. Does it make sense that a concatenation of seemingly minor stresses could compete with major life events as a source of stress? There are several reasons why the answer is yes.

One reason is that people with numerous and severe daily hassles, which may constitute chronic features of their lives, may not have recently experienced any really major life events. High-scoring major life events, such as death of a loved one, are infrequent in most people's lives, but daily hassles are not. Therefore, most of the stresses experienced by the average person are not in the form of major life changes, but consist of seemingly minor daily hassles that plague them day in and day out.

Second, major life events, such as divorce or death of a spouse, also affect the pattern of daily hassles in a person's life. The two types of stress measures, daily hassles and life events, are, indeed, positively correlated. Life events produce some, though by no means all, of one's daily hassles, and it is the hassles that contain the immediate seeds of emotional distress and dysfunction. Let us look at this more closely by looking at two similar, yet importantly different major life events, divorce and death of a loved one.

Both these life changes result in chronic loneliness and make new daily demands on how the person must live, such as having to care for children, manage finances, repair the car, make one's own meals, and so forth. Many of these demands, which the person who is now gone might previously have taken responsibility for, must now be performed by the divorced or bereaved person, sometimes for the first time, and the inexperienced spouse may find them quite threatening.

Although the hassles produced by these two overlapping life events share much in common—the person is lonely, sexually needy, must take on tasks that were hitherto handled by the spouse, and so on—there are also important differences. For example, with the death of a loved one, the deceased spouse is no longer present physically, but there is no obvious personal rejection inherent in a death that is accidental or a result of illness. On the other hand, divorce invokes the image of a relationship failure, and often implies rejection.

Another factor creating major psychological differences between death and divorce is that the divorced person may still have to deal with the lost partner, who might remain in the same community. Often they must struggle together with contentious issues relevant to visitation rights with the children and other obligations from the past. There are, in effect, many divergent stressful details in the small daily annoyances produced by these two overlapping, yet different major life events.

Third, and most important conceptually, daily hassles are proximal events in one's life whereas major life events are distal. *Proximal* means that the person has already identified them as onerous, based on their intimate personal significance. So when one endorses an occurrence or relationship as a hassle, one has already acknowledged its stressful character.

Life events, however, are *distal* because they do not affect everyone in the same way. When one endorses a life event as having happened in the recent past, there is no clear implication about how it was experienced, or even that it was especially stressful. For one individual, a death may be a release from terrible obligations, but for another it is a deep, tragic loss. This also applies to divorce, which in one person might be an escape from a bad relationship, whereas in another it represents a personal failure and a severe trial. As such, the relational meaning of distal events needs to be known to predict how the person will react emotionally.

There is no inherent conflict between life events and daily hassles as measures of stress. Both deal with different, though related, occurrences in a person's life. As measures of stress, they supplement each other. Nevertheless, because of their proximal nature, I have always thought that daily hassles give us a more useful metric for considering the effects of typical stresses on mental health, and perhaps physical health too, than the rarer and more distal life events (Lazarus, 1984), and our research data and those of others support this position.

Daily hassles are not all equal in their capacity to damage health and morale. Some hassles are more central than others to a person's psychological economy, but what is central differs from one individual to another (Gruen, Folkman, & Lazarus, 1989). When we had subjects rate how central to their existential concerns a variety of their daily hassles were, we found that the ones they rated as central were better predictors of emotional and health problems than peripheral hassles, which had been just as intense when they occurred but faded away more quickly. People ruminate over central hassles day in and day out, and these hassles recur more frequently in their daily lives than peripheral hassles, probably because they represent, for given individuals, special areas of emotional vulnerability. This research was cross-sectional, not proscriptive, and the issue is far from settled.

Do daily uplifts buffer the negative effects of daily hassles—that is, do they protect the person against the damage stress does? The evidence is ambiguous. In some studies, people seem to gain such protection, but in others the evidence of this effect is absent. This is an important health-related issue that still needs to be resolved. As you will see, one reason for the confusion may have to do with the coping process.

COPING WITH STRESS

Coping has to do with the way people manage the conditions that arouse stress in their lives, as well as the stress state itself. As I said in chapter 8, effective coping reduces the stresses of our lives to more modest and acceptable proportions. It does so by leading us to make decisions that could represent a better fit with the realities of our lives and by making it easier to live with the emotional distress that life often generates. Effective coping should have salutary effects on our mental and physical health. Ineffective coping should magnify stress and lead to bad decisions about our lives and an increase in emotional distress which, in turn, could have damaging effects on our physical health.

To some extent, therefore, stress and coping could be said to have a reciprocal relationship with each other. When coping is ineffective, level of stress should be high; but when coping is effective, level of stress should be low. Coping is, therefore, an essential feature of the dynamics of stress and the emotions. If we do not give major attention to how coping works, we will fail to understand these dynamics. In my opinion, coping is one of two most important concepts in the field of stress and emotion, the other being appraisal.

Most of the early psychoanalytic interest in coping and defense centered on styles of dealing with threats to one's integrity—in effect, as a dispositional property of person rather than situation. A dispositional or trait view implies that individuals differ in the stable ways they cope with threat. The approach is typically a hierarchical one, which follows psychoanalytic views of development in that some types of coping, such as ego-defenses, are regarded as developmentally immature—in effect, either neurotic or psychotic—whereas others are normal and healthy.

The word "cope" historically has had many meanings, but its modern one seems to have originated about 1400 AD and referred to engaging an enemy in battle; and even more to the point, to contend or come to blows with a hostile force or agency, and to prove oneself a match for it (Oxford English Dictionary, 1970). The psychoanalytic concept of ego-defense deals with one type of coping—namely, the devices by which the ego protects a person from the conscious recognition of a threat posed by socially or intrapsychically proscribed impulses. Coping ultimately came to be a more generic concept, with defense being subsumed under it.

I have been a pioneer with respect to the topic of coping, about which there was, at first, relatively little enthusiasm in the biological and social sciences. My research and ideas first appeared in my 1966 book. Psychological interest in coping seems to have increased in the 1970s, as illustrated in the first edited psychological volume of articles devoted to coping and adaptation in 1974, in which my colleagues and I have a chapter (Coehlo, Hamburg, & Adams, 1974). Interest has mounted ever since (Lazarus, 1966, 1993; Lazarus, & Folkman, 1984).

Three very recent books attest to the growing maturity of the field of coping, one by Aldwin (1994) dealing with developmental issues, an ambitious handbook edited by Zeidner and Endler (1996), and an edited volume by Gottlieb (1997) on coping with chronic stress. In a foreword to that handbook, Carver (1996, p. xi) wrote that "The vast majority of the work done in this area has occurred within the past two decades." A recent literature search, reported in a chapter in this handbook by Costa, Somerfield, and McCrae (1996) identified 113 articles written about coping in 1974, 183 in 1980, and 639 in 1984, a high level of interest that has been sustained ever since, and may still be growing.

A major objective of our field research was to develop an adequate conceptualization of the coping process and to measure it in the lives of the people we were studying. There are three principles of coping when viewed as a process:

First, process means that coping constantly changes over the course of a stressful encounter and from one type of encounter to another. Coping, therefore, is always contextual, that is, what a person does to cope depends on one's personality, the kind of threat, harm, or challenge being coped with, the temporal stage of a stressful encounter, and which of several possible adaptational outcomes are of interest— namely, somatic health, subjective well-being, or social functioning.

Second, coping must be assessed as independent of its outcomes. It should be regarded as an effort to manage stress, which may succeed or fail. We need to understand the principles that determine when it will succeed or fail, and in what ways.

Third, coping consists of what an individual thinks and does in an effort to deal with demands that tax or exceed resources. These thoughts and actions must be measured to study the coping process.

With these principles in mind, our research group formally defined coping as constantly changing cognitive and behavioral efforts to manage specific external and/or internal demands that are appraised as taxing or exceeding the resources of the person (Lazarus & Folkman, 1984).

Looking more closely at the definition, the *process* principle is reflected in the words "constantly changing." *Effort* implies that anything a person thinks and does to alter a stressful encounter or condition is coping, regardless of how well or poorly it works. By using the word *manage,* we avoid equating coping with mastery. This means that avoiding, minimizing, tolerating, accepting, and defending against a bad situation that cannot be overcome all fall under the rubric of coping. *Taxing* refers to the need for substantial effort, which involves costs. Finally, *exceeding* refers to conditions of trauma in which the individual is overwhelmed and feels helpless.

To consider how coping is measured within a process framework, we need to recognize that asking patients with, say, breast cancer a very broad question, such as how they cope with their affliction, is likely to yield misleading information, because there are many different specific threats connected with the disease. We are not likely to discover which threat they are referring to from so broad a question.

The specific threats could vary greatly—for example, the danger of a return of the malignancy, uncertainty about what to say about the illness and one's emotional reactions to others, such as lovers, spouses, or children, whether treatment is worthwhile and if so, which one, dealing with possible disfigurement from treatment, and rearranging one's life to accommodate treatment, to name some of the most important ones.

Not only will the coping process vary with different threats, but some threats, such as the potential for recurrence of the cancer and the anxiety this generates could be coped with differently at different times during the illness. Thus, after the patient has gotten used to the postsurgical situation of mastectomy or lumpectomy, the main coping strategy may be avoidance or denial. As the time for a medical visit to reassess the situation grows near, however, vigilance and anxiety may mount, along with the occurrence of intrusive thoughts and images about what may happen.

For this reason, it is not enough to ask about coping with illness in general, but a more specific and detailed examination should be made of the diverse sources of threat and the timing of coping thoughts and actions, which will vary as the life situation of the patient changes. This requires that the same individual be studied over time and across diverse stressful transactions, which result from the overall illness. These ways of thinking about coping set our approach off from what had hitherto been the traditional structural view.

To measure coping as process and to study its changes over time and across diverse contexts, we created a procedure referred to as the *Ways of Coping Questionnaire* (Folkman & Lazarus, 1988), which became the most widely used quantitative measurement approach in research on coping. We asked our participants to reconstruct the most stressful experience of the past month, to indicate how they appraised what happened, and to identify the thoughts and actions that had been employed in coping with these stresses.

The questionnaire itself, which we used as the basis of the interview, contains 67 items, grouped into eight major strategies of coping derived from a factor analysis of data from our studies. Factor 1 is *confrontive coping,* illustrated by the statement "I expressed anger to the person(s) who caused the problem." Factor 2 is *distancing,* as in the statement "I didn't let it get to me; refused to think about it too much." Factor 3 is *self-controlling* coping, as in "I tried to keep my feelings to myself." Factor 4 is *seeking social support*—for example, "I asked a relative or friend I respected for advice." Factor 5 is *accepting responsibility,* illustrated by "I realized I brought the problem on myself." Factor 6 is *escape–avoidance,* as in the item "Avoided being with people in general." Factor 7 is *planful problem solving,* as in "I made a plan of action and followed it." And Factor 8 is *positive reappraisal,* illustrated by "I changed or grew as a person in a good way."

Our research with the *Ways of Coping Questionnaire* has produced many replicated findings about the coping process and how it works. The five most important of these, in my estimation, are as follows (see Lazarus, 1993):

1. In any stressful encounter, people use most or all of the eight coping strategies (Folkman & Lazarus, 1980). A probable reason for this is that most stressful encounters are complex and take place over a period of time. Thus, each facet, or the personal business being transacted in the encounter, may encourage different coping strategies, so that over the entire complex encounter with its many facets, people draw on all or most of the coping options. It is also possible that they try out different strategies in a trial-and-error search for a solution.

2. Some coping strategies are more consistently used across certain types of stressful encounters compared with others (Folkman, Lazarus, Dunkle-Schetter, DeLongis, and Gruen, 1986; Folkman, Lazarus, Gruen, & DeLongis, 1986). For example, an individual who uses positive reappraisal (e.g., "I came out of the experience better than when I went in") in one stressful encounter is apt to use it again in other encounters. The tendency to do this must be a personality trait. However, seeking social support (e.g., "I asked a relative or friend I respected for advice") is much more influenced by the situation than the personality of the individual. For example, if the threat being coped with is a source of shame, the individual is apt to conceal the problem from others, whereas that same individual may seek help from friends or family about a threat connected with the loss of a job because the company is downsizing (Mikulincer & Florian, 1996–97).

3. What people do to cope changes from one time to another, because the requirements of the situation change and call for different coping thoughts and actions. Thus, a student anticipating an important college examination is apt to cope by mobilizing to prepare prior to the exam, but after the exam is over and the results are being awaited, distancing becomes the preferred strategy (Folkman & Lazarus, 1985). Stressful encounters, such as exams, change in their emotional impact and coping requirements from one stage to another. So coping, and the emotional state associated with it change too.

Consider again the woman with breast cancer who has been treated surgically in hopes of defeating the cancer. Her state of mind and the way she copes will be quite different after being told there is a good chance the cancer has not spread than it will be if she learns it has recurred in another part of her body. The emotional problems that must be dealt with as the illness progresses are different, and so is the coping process.

This, incidentally, is why the same coping strategy, which has positive consequences at one time, or in one situation, may be counterproductive at another time or in another situation. In the example of the college exam, distancing prior to taking the exam is apt to leave the person unprepared and vulnerable, whereas after the exam and before the results have been announced, distancing is the most useful thing to do, as nothing of value can be done until the results are known, and the anxiety aroused would have no useful function. Similarly, denial that one is having a heart attack is dangerous, but after one is hospitalized and recovering, denial helps the person approach the situation more calmly and accept an exercise regimen that could be important in facilitating recovery.

An old psychoanalytic position about denial is that it is an immature coping strategy in childhood, but is pathological and pathogenic in adult life. Early on, I took the position that we all use denial, and that there are times when it is useful and other times when it is harmful. This means we need to identify the rules about when it is okay to deny and when it is not.

I wrote one of my favorite articles about this in Lazarus (1983), *The Costs and Benefits of Denial,* in which I argued that if denial of reality, such as the danger in an episode of chest pain or a suspicious lump, leads to the failure to seek medical help, it could be a counterproductive coping strategy. However, if nothing can be done to improve one's situation, the denial can make one feel better but poses no danger. Since then, there has been a growing consensus that the tendency to think positive and to be optimistic can often be psychological assets.

This article was reprinted a number of times in books dealing with terminal or life-threatening illnesses.

However, I began to believe that some of this sanguinity had gone too far, in particular, with respect to people who are suffering, or with terminal illnesses. They are really distressed but pressured by doctors, friends, and relatives, who can't face suffering or dying, to keep a stiff-upper-lip or have only positive thoughts. This pressure trivializes their distress and they are apt to feel isolated and inauthentic in their intimate relationships.

Therefore, I wrote a kind of antidote to my denial piece, entitled *The Trivialization of Distress* (Lazarus, 1985), which was presented in 1963 at The Vermont Conference on the Primary Prevention of Psychopathology, the second time, I am proud to say, that I had given a paper in this series. The paper (Lazarus, 1984) actually first appeared out of publishing order in a book of Master Series lectures published by the American Psychological Association, as a result of the kindness of The New England Press, which published the Vermont series. A photograph of the participants of that conference, many of whom are well-known, is presented in Figure 9.3.

4. When an individual under stress sees that nothing can be done to alter the situation, this appraisal encourages emotion-focused coping strategies designed to help an individual feel better. On the other hand, when an individual believes that the situation is controllable by actions aimed at producing change, problem-focused coping strategies are encouraged (Folkman & Lazarus, 1980). What helps most, of course, is to diagnose the situation properly to see what kind of coping is called for. Consider, for example, the epigrammatic motto of Alcoholics Anonymous, which, paraphrased, states: God grant me the courage to change what can be changed, the serenity to accept what cannot be changed, and the wisdom to know the difference.

5. What people do to cope influences their emotional state. If, for example, one assesses the emotion at the beginning of a stressful encounter, some coping strategies will lead to an improved emotional state and others will yield a worsened one. We have found that a combination of planful problem solving and positive reappraisal often results in changes in the emotion from negative to less negative or positive. Other coping patterns, however, such as confrontive coping and distancing, have led to opposite emotional changes—that is, to more negative emotions (Bolger, 1990; Folkman & Lazarus, 1988). Everything depends on the kind of threat being dealt with and the situation. I don't believe there are any coping strategies that are always bad or good.

Top rows: Kenneth Warner, Peter Nathan, Wilbert Fordyce, Albert Stone, Rudolf Moos, Stephen Goldston

Middle rows: Gerald Koocher, Robin DiMatteo, Dick Evans, William Haskel, myself, Charles Kiesler, George Albe

Bottom row: David Mechanic, Howard Leventhal, Sandra Levy, Margaret Chesney, James Rosen, Laura Solomon

FIGURE 9.3   Vermont conference participants, July 1983.

We have made only a bare beginning in our search for practical understanding about the role of coping in adaptation to the stresses of living. To make the study of coping as complete as it should be requires that we study the process in greater depth than we have to date, fleshing out its unconscious determinants, which the individual does not recognize (Lazarus, 1995). Coping often calls for instant decisions whose bases we cannot easily identify, but that give the process its organismic quality and ties to the individual's personal history.

Although it added greatly to our understanding, the *Ways of Coping Questionnaire,* and all other procedures like it, are incomplete as a portrait of the coping process. These questionnaires, including ours, barely scratch the surface of the rich coping process by separating coping from the personalities of the people being studied.

We need to seek the deep structures of the individual's makeup, to identify the essential coherence and consistency with which that individual confronts life and its demands and opportunities, and above all to examine the *relational meanings* that underlie an individual's coping strategies. Coping is too important in the overall psychological economy of the individual to leave its study to superficial measurement.

By saying this, I don't mean to trash the *Ways of Coping* approach to coping measurement or my research based on it. I think it is very useful for certain kinds of questions, and perhaps even more for the theory of coping that lies behind it. Questionnaires allow us to obtain large amounts of quantifiable data rapidly and economically (Lazarus, 1996). But an epidemiological style of research, using large samples and limited questionnaire approaches to stress and coping, does not reveal the meanings on which these threats depend. Therefore, we cannot truly understand why these individuals cope as they do.

Questionnaires do not provide a rich, or even adequate, portrait of an integrated person with distinctive goals and beliefs, struggling with diverse threats. They are, in a sense, reductive, in that no effort is ever made to put the person back together as a living, breathing, adapting human being. They give us lists of separate coping thoughts and actions, which are disconnected from the personality of the one who is doing the coping. They do not describe the complex, organized, time-bound efforts of a person to actualize his or her goals and beliefs in a particular environment from which important life meanings are derived.

Consider, for example, my own pattern of coping with prostate cancer when, a few years ago, this diagnosis was made. I shall try to describe it as best I can.

> Shocked by the unexpected news, I struggled to grasp what was involved, its implications for the closing years of my life—including how imminent the danger was of my dying of this cancer, and what might be done. Fearful, but determined to deal with the situation as effectively as I could, I fended off counterproductive ruminations, obtained information about my condition, read scientific treatises, saw several doctors, and tried to decide whether to accept surgery, radiation, or just wait and see.
>
> Since I was a good candidate for surgery, a major factor in my choice of a radical prostatectomy was my reluctance to live under a "sword of Damocles" in which I would never believe I was cured of the cancer, and would always be awaiting evidence that it had spread to my spinal bones. I do not like ambiguity, which would be greatest under a wait-and-see coping strategy, but high too under radiation treatment, which is not truly a cure. I wanted to take decisive action, if possible.

Once I chose surgery, the problem was to find the right surgeon, one who would employ the best modern techniques to reduce the bleeding and conserve the nerves needed to regain urinary continence and sexual potency. Although my first urologist had treated me well, I got the impression that he was not the best man for the job, and after much inquiry, I chose a doctor who had a very poor bedside manner, but who had an outstanding reputation for technical skill in prostate surgery. It is deep within my character to be not too trusting of those I must depend on, but I knew that in the end I had to trust someone. I fought against my suspicious tendencies and hoped I had made a good choice.

One mistake I made, happily a minor one, was to defer the surgery for 2 months in order to make a visit to Haifa University in Israel, where I was to receive an honorary degree. It was a mistake because it put off the surgery, and despite reassurances by my physicians, I was uneasy that the delay might worsen my chances for a complete cure. I slept badly, and felt impatient about everything.

During this period, I seemed to others to be highly controlled and even cheerful though, without realizing it, I was mobilizing much effort to deal with the problem and to stay in control of my anxious emotional state. Nevertheless, my mood rose and fell without seeming provocation, depending on whether I accepted what happened, resented it, or was frightened by it.

This coordinated pattern of coping—which is but a fraction of what I was doing and thinking, is partly, but not described thoroughly by a list of separate coping thoughts and actions. Above all, it was not a preformed cognitive construction, but a searching for the right way to see what was happening and to act appropriately—a way that was realistic and yet puts the most positive interpretation possible on the matter. My whole person was engaged in the struggle. Though others might share particular features of this coping process, the details and ways it was organized are unique to me and my history as an individual with a distinctive personality, integrated with my personal goals and beliefs, and the relational meanings that fueled my emotional experience.

EXPANDING STRESS TO THE EMOTIONS

The most recent phase of my scholarly research and writing involves a shift in emphasis from psychological stress to the emotions. This change of emphasis began slowly in the late 1960s (see Lazarus, 1968) and early 1970s (Lazarus, Averill, & Opton, 1970) with increasing attention on my part to the emotions. What provoked this transition was the conviction that stress is mainly treated as a continuum, a unidimensional variable that places people on a scale from a little stress to very much, or as young people say these days, to the point you are "stressed out." Even if we identify different kinds of stress, such as harm, threat, and challenge, the range of reactions we are talking about is still limited compared with the large number and variety of emotions that flow from stress. Each such emotion depicts a complex relational meaning that tells us much about what is going on in the individual's adaptational struggles in life.

There are at least 15 different emotions, however, and each one reveals a distinctive relational meaning. Anger tells us something very different about the significance of what is happening for a person's well-being than, say, anxiety, guilt, shame, envy, jealousy, disgust, relief, hope, sadness, happiness, pride, love, gratitude, and compassion. It is this large panoply of emotions that conveys the richness and complexity of the human mind and the continuing struggle to adapt.

So, as I approached my seventieth year and retirement from teaching at the university, I undertook and subsequently published a major monographic book on emotion and adaptation, which spelled out how the emotions worked from a cognitive–motivational–relational point of view (Lazarus, 1991 a, b, c, 1993).

I suggested that each emotion has a distinctive *core relational theme*—for example, a demeaning offense against me and mine for anger, an uncertain, existential threat for anxiety, and so on for each of the emotions. These relational themes are the result of a number of separate primary and secondary appraisals. The appraised elements are synthesized into core relational themes—in effect, meaning wholes or gestalts are constructed, which permit us to respond instantly to complex social transactions with one or another of the emotions. These themes define the essential relational meanings underlying each emotion (Lazarus, 1997).

Coping is also a crucial feature of the emotion process, because in negative or stress emotions one deals with the person–environment relationship that brought them about, as well as with their personal and social implications once they have been aroused. For reasons that are obscure, the coping process, recognized for several decades as an essential feature of psychological stress, has been underemphasized in emotion theory. In reality, coping is an integral feature of the emotion process, and cannot sensibly be separated from that process except in special psychological states, such as ego-defense, which are often tantamount to psychopathology.

Given its importance in human adaptation, it would be unfortunate if the work that was begun in the 1970s and proceeded through the

1980s, ours as well as that of others, is not followed up and advanced beyond where it has been taken in recent years. As I come to the close of my life and research career, I hope that interest in, and effective research on the coping process and human adaptation continues with vigor and dedication.

The Berkeley Stress and Coping Project having come to a close, we move next to chapter 10, which examines of one of the great privileges of academic life, the opportunity to travel around the world in the pursuit of knowledge and to disseminate one's own research and thought.

REFERENCES

Aldwin, C. M. (1994). *Stress, coping, and development: An integrative perspective.* New York: Guilford.

Averill, J. R., Malmstrom, E. J., Koriat, A., & Lazarus, R. S. (1972). Habituation to complex stimuli. *Journal of Abnormal Psychology, 80,* 20–28.

Bolger, N. (1990). Coping as a personality process: A prospective study. *Journal of Personality and Social Psychology, 59,* 525–537.

Bukowski, C. (1980). The shoelace. *Bukowski reads his poetry.* Takoma Records, Santa Monica, CA.

Carver, C. S. Foreword. In M. Zeidner & N. S. Endler (Eds.), *Handbook of coping: Theory, research, applications* (p. xi). New York: Wiley.

Coehlo, G. V., Hamburg, D. A., & Adams, J. F. *Coping and adaptation.* New York: Basic Books.

Cohen, F., & Lazarus, R. S. (1973). Active coping processes, coping dispositions, and recovery from surgery. *Psychosomatic Medicine, 41,* 109–118.

Costa, P. T., Jr., Somerfield, M. R., & McCrae, R. R. (1996). Personality and coping: A reconceptualization. In M. Zeidner & N. S. Endler (Eds.), *Handbook of coping: Theory, research, applications* (pp. 44–61). New York: Wiley.

DeLongis, A., Coyne, J. C., Dakof, G., Folkman, S., & Lazarus, R. S. (1982). Relationship of daily hassles, uplifts, and major life events to health status. *Health Psychology, 1,* 119–136.

DeLongis, A., Folkman, S., & Lazarus, R. S. (1988). Hassles, health, and mood: Psychological and social resources as mediators. *Journal of Personality and Social Psychology, 54,* 486–495.

Folkins, C. H., Lawson, K. D., Opton, E. M. Jr., & Lazarus, R. S. (1968). Desentization and the experimental reduction of threat. *Journal of Abnormal Psychology, 73,* 100–113.

Folkman, S. (1997). Introduction to the special section: Use of bereavement to predict well-being in gay men whose partners died of AIDS—Four theoretical perspectives. *Journal of Personality and Social Psychology, 72,* 851–854.

Folkman, S., Chesney, M. S., & Christopher-Richards, A. (1994). Stress and coping in caregiving partners of men with AIDS. *Psychiatric clinics of North America, 17,* 35–53.

Folkman, S., & Lazarus, R. S. (1980). An analysis of coping in a middle-aged community sample. *Journal of Health and Social Behavior, 21,* 219–239.

Folkman, S., & Lazarus, R. S. (1985). If it changes it must be a process: Study of emotion and coping during three stages of a college examination. *Journal of Personality and Social Psychology, 48,* 150–170.

Folkman, S., & Lazarus, R. S. (1988a). Coping as a mediator of emotion. *Journal of Personality and Social Psychology, 54,* 466–475.

Folkman, S., Lazarus, R. S., Dunkel-Schetter, C., DeLongis, A., & Gruen, R. (1986). The dynamics of a stressful encounter: Cognitive appraisal, coping, and encounter outcomes. *Journal of Personality and Social Psychology, 50,* 992–1003.

Folkman, S., Lazarus, R. S., Gruen, R., & DeLongis, A. (1986). Appraisal, coping, health status, and psychological symptoms. *Journal of Personality and Social Psychology, 50,* 572–579.

Gal, R., & Lazarus, R. S. (1975). The role of activity in anticipating and confronting stressful situations. *Journal of Human Stress, 1,* 20–28.

Gottlieb, B. H. (Ed.). (1997). *Coping with chronic stress.* New York: Plenum.

Gruen, R. J., Folkman, S., & Lazarus, R. S. (1989). Centrality and individual differences in the meaning of daily hassles. *Journal of Personality, 56,* 743–762.

Holmes, T. H., & Rahe, R. H. (1967). The social readjustment rating scale. *Journal of Psychosomatic Research, 11,* 213–218.

Kanner, A., Coyne, J. C., Schaefer, C., & Lazarus, R. S. (1981). Comparison of two modes of stress measurement: Daily hassles and uplifts versus major life events. *Journal of Behavioral Medicine, 4,* 1–39.

Koriat, A., Melkman, R., Averill, J. R., & Lazarus, R. S. (1972). The self-control of emotional reactions to a stressful film. *Journal of Personality, 40,* 601–619.

Krohne, H. W., Slangen, K., & Kleemann, P. P. (1996). Coping variables as predictors of perioperative emotional states and adjustment. *Psychology and Health, 11,* 315–330.

Lazarus, R. S. (1966). *Psychological stress and the coping process.* New York: McGraw-Hill.

Lazarus, R. S. (1968). Emotions and adaptation: conceptual and empirical relations. In W. J. Arnold (Ed.), *Nebraska Symposium on Motivation* (pp. 175–266). Lincoln, NE: University of Nebraska Press.

Lazarus, R. S. (1983). The costs and benefits of denial. In S. Breznitz (Ed.), *The denial of stress* (pp. 1–30). New York: International Universities Press.

Lazarus, R. S. (1984). Puzzles in the study of daily hassles. *Journal of Behavioral Medicine, 7,* 375–389.

Lazarus, R. S. (1985). The trivialization of distress. In J. C. Rosen & L. J. Solomon (Eds.), *Preventing health risk behaviors and promoting coping with illness. Vermont Conference on the Primary Prevention of Psychopathology* (Vol. 8, pp. 279–298). Hanover, NH: University Press of New England. Also printed in B. L. Hammonds & C. J. Scheirer (Eds.). (1984). Psychology and health (The Master Lecture Series, 1983, Vol. 3, pp. 121–144). Washington, DC: American Psychological Association.

Lazarus, R. S. (1991a). *Emotion and adaptation.* New York: Oxford University Press.

Lazarus, R. S. (1991b). Cognition and motivation in emotion. *American Psychologist, 46,* 352–367.

Lazarus, R. S. (1991c). Progress on a cognitive-motivational-relational theory of emotion. *American Psychologist, 46,* 819–834.

Lazarus, R. S. (1993a). From psychological stress to the emotions: A history of changing outlooks. In *Annual review of psychology* (pp. 1–21). Palo Alto, CA: Annual Reviews Inc.

Lazarus, R. S., Averill, J. R., & Opton, E. M., Jr. (1974). The psychological of coping: Issues of research and assessment. In G. V. Coelho, D. A. Hamburg, & J. F. Adams (Eds.), *Coping and adaptation* (pp. 249–315). New York: Basic Books.

Lazarus, R. S. (1995). With commentaries and author's response. Vexing research problems inherent in cognitive-mediational theories of emotion, and some solutions. *Psychological Inquiry, 6,* 183–265.

Lazarus, R. S. (1996). The role of coping in the emotions and how coping changes over the life course. In C. Malatesta-Magai & S. H. McFadden (Eds.), *Handbook of emotion, adult development and aging* (pp. 289–306). New York: Academic Press.

Lazarus, R. S. (1997). *Fifty years of the research and theory of R. S. Lazarus: Perennial psychological issues.* Mahwah, NJ: Erlbaum.

Lazarus, R. S., Averill, J. R., & Opton, E. M. Jr. (1970). Towards a cognitive theory of emotion. In M. Arnold (Ed.), *Feelings and emotions* (pp. 207–232). New York: Academic Press.

Lazarus, R. S., Averill, J. R., & Opton, E. M. Jr. (1974). The psychology of coping: Issues of research and assessment. In G. V. Coelho, D. A. Hamburg, & J. F. Adams (Eds.), *Coping and adaptation* (pp. 249–315). New York: Basic Books.

Lazarus, R. S., & Folkman, S. (1984). *Stress, appraisal, and coping.* New York: Springer.

Lazarus, R. S., & Folkman, S. (1987). Transactional theory and research on emotions and coping. *European Journal of Personality, 1,* 141–169.

Lazarus, R. S., Speisman, J. C., Mordkoff, A. M., & Davison, L. A. (1962). A laboratory study of psychological stress produced by a motion picture film. *Psychological Monographs, 76,* No. 34 (Whole No. 553).

Lazarus, R. S., Speisman, J. C., & Mordkoff, A. M. (1963). The relationships between autonomic indicators of psychological stress: Heart rate and skin conductance. *Psychosomatic Medicine, 25,* 19–21.

Mikulincer, M., & Florian, V. (1996–97). A cognitive-relational approach to emotions—the appraisal and coping components of sadness, shame, guilt, jealousy, and disgust. In K. S. People & J. L. Singer (Eds.), *Imagination, cognition, and personality: Consciousness in theory, research, clinical practice.* Amityville, NY: Baywood.

Monat, A., Averill, J. R., & Lazarus, R. S. (1973). Anticipatory stress and coping under various conditions of uncertainty. *Journal of Personality and Social Psychology, 24,* 237–253.

Monat, A., & Lazarus, R. S. (1991). *Stress and coping : An anthology* (3rd ed.). New York: Columbia University Press.

Nomikos, M., Opton, E. M. Jr., Averill, J. R., & Lazarus, R. S. (1968). Surprise versus suspense in the production of stress reaction. *Journal of Personality and Social Psychology, 8,* 204–208.

Oxford English Dictionary (1970), Vol. II, p. 969. London: Oxford University Press, 1970.

Speisman, J. C., Lazarus, R. S., Mordkoff, A. M., & Davison, L. A. (1964). The experimental reduction of stress based on ego-defense theory. *Journal of Abnormal and Social Psychology, 68,* 367–380.

Staudenmayer, H., Kinsman, R. S., Dirks, J. F., Spector, S. L., & Wangaard, C. (1979). Medical outcome in asthmatic patients: Effects of airways hyperactivity and symptom-focused anxiety. *Psychosomatic Medicine, 41,* 109–118.

Stein, N., Folkman, S., Trabasso, T., & Richards, T. A. (1997). Appraisal and goal processes as predictors of psychological well-being in bereaved caregivers. *Journal of Personality and Social Psychology, 72,* 872–884.

Zeidner, M., & Endler, N. S. (Eds.). (1996). *Handbook of coping: Theory, research, applications.* New York: Wiley.

Travels of an Academic

Travel is one of the most enriching and interesting features of an occupation that provides what are called sabbaticals. It gives a teacher the opportunity to step back from the daily educational grind, refresh one's outlook, think creatively without job pressures, carry one's intellectual product to others in the world, and have one's own knowledge and ideas enlarged by the ideas of those others. As I look back, I realize, especially when my wife and family could come along, we could never have financed these travels on our own.

In chapter 7, I described my family's fascinating year in Japan and the aftermath. Not counting tourist travel, as part of my work I have also visited Argentina, Australia, Canada, Denmark, England, France, Germany, India, Israel, Korea, The Netherlands, Norway, Puerto Rico, Scotland, Sweden, Switzerland, many of these countries more than once and some repeatedly, and in some cases for several months. My wife Bernice often accompanied me, and sometimes we could take advantage of the opportunity to go even further on our own—for example, to the Algarve in Portugal, Bangkok, Florence, Hong Kong, the Mediterranean, and Venice.

In this chapter, I have been very selective, choosing only some of my more interesting travel experiences abroad to hold down the length of this account. The trips I describe in this abbreviated account include, roughly in this order, a series of visits to Stockholm, Sweden; a series of visits to West Germany; Perth, Australia; Buenos Aires, Argentina; and a series of visits to Israel. To save space I have not included Bernice and my two visits to Denmark, though they were also notable.

STOCKHOLM, SWEDEN

From 1965 to 1976, I made seven trips to Stockholm, five of them to participate in a series of symposia, which were organized by Lennart Levi, the Director of the Laboratory for Clinical Stress Research, at

Stockholm's Karolinska Institute. The sponsors were the University of Uppsala and the World Health Organization, with funds supplied by the Trygg Insurance Group of Stockholm. I supply these details because I have never been more generously treated than I was there.

I first came to Stockholm in 1965 as the only foreign scholar at a scientific meeting at the Karolinska Institute. Just before having to travel to Stockholm, I had attended a conference at Vanderbilt University in Nashville, Tennessee, organized by Charles Spielberger. It led to the first of a series of books on anxiety (Spielberger, 1966) and boasted a distinguished group of research scholars that included R. R. Cattell, C. W. Eriksen, R. R. Grinker, C. Izard, R. B. Malmo, G. Mandler, O. H. Mowrer, E. M. Opton Jr. (the Ned Opton of my research project), S. B. Sarason, S. Schachter, J. T. Spence, K. W. Spence, S. Tomkins, D. L. Watson, and J. Wolpe.[1]

On the first of my seven visits to Stockholm, I decided to make an overnight stop in Oslo on my way home. I visited a psychologist by the name of Arvid Åas, who had published research on the subincision film. As is usual on a visit to any Scandinavian city, I was taken to the city hall, which was a beautiful building, as city halls in these countries usually are. I also stopped to look at the works of a sculptor, Gustav Vigeland, who was given a lifelong stipend by the city of Oslo to pursue his art.

While I was in Stockholm in 1965, Levi had talked about organizing a series of five major conferences, which later were held and published in five volumes entitled *Society, Stress and Disease* (Levi, 1971, 1975, 1976, 1981, 1987). This was long before health psychology became a distinctive field, drawing substantially on the stress concept, and eventually becoming a separate division of the American Psychological Association (APA).

The participants in these five conferences included distinguished Scandinavian, European, and American scholars and researchers in what, in those days, was called psychosomatic medicine. A few of them attended several or, as in my case, all of the conferences. For those who have never heard of many or most of these medical and psychological researchers, it was an extraordinary group of contributors to knowledge. For those who might be interested, I shall identify some of the best known individuals.

Well-known American participants included R. Bell (child development, NIMH), J. Birren (distinguished scholar of aging), R. Butler, prior

---

[1] There was to be an extended series of such books by Spielberger, and by Spielberger and Sarason, later on.

Director of the National Institute of Aging; G. Caplan (crisis management, psychiatry, Harvard); S. Cobb (pioneering work on social support); S. A. Corson (psychiatry, Ohio State U.); V. Dennenberg (behavioral sciences, Connecticut U.); R. Dubos (evolutionary biologist); C. Eisdorfer (psychiatry, Montefiore Hospital, NY); A. Etzioni (Center for Policy Research, NY); D. Freedman (Human Development, Chicago U.); J. French (person–environment fit); E. M. Gruenberg (epidemiologist, Johns Hopkins); D. A. Hamburg (psychiatry, Stanford U., and later the president of the prestigious Institute of Medicine); B. Hamburg (psychiatry, Harvard); J. Henry (physiology, USC, L.A.); S. Levine (psychiatry, Stanford U.); H. Levinson (motivation and work, Boston U.); M. Mead (renowned cultural anthropologist, Emeritus, American Museum of Natural History, NY); D. McK. Rioch (psychiatry, Walter Reed); A. McLean (triune brain, IBM, NY); J. Money (biological development of sex characteristics, Johns Hopkins); H. Persky (psychiatry, Pennsylvania U.); S. Wolf (protection against heart disease in Roseto, Italy); R. Rahe (Life events measure, Navy, San Diego), and others.

Because most of them publish abroad, non-Americans are not likely to be easily recognized by many people in the United States, but some whose names might have a cachet for some readers include Leo Eitinger (famous for research on Holocaust victims); Marianne Frankenhaeuser (well-known for research on stress and hormones, Stockholm U.); Bertil Gardell (work stress, Stockholm U.); Walter Fenz (stress and sports parachutists, Waterloo, Canada), Hans Selye (the undisputed dean of physiological stress research, Montreal U., Canada); and T. Theorell (Type A and heart disease, Stockholm).

The conferences took place from morning until evening, and on many occasions, after supper; European conferences are very hard-working. We sat around a huge rectangular table, a microphone and mineral water handy. I loved being at these conferences, but I must say frankly that there were too many participants to have really interesting or focused discussions. The problem with conferences like this is that they are designed to have an impressive and well-known list of specialists for later publications, rather than to be truly working sessions. Over many years, I have only attended a handful of really exciting conferences in which the organizers were less concerned with appearances and more with substance.

Still, for a young man, it was exciting to meet many of these well-known and knowledgeable people. One time I found myself sitting next to Margaret Mead (shown in Figure 10.1, at the table to my right; I'm the fellow with his hand over his mouth). I had never met her before. She was quite an old lady at this conference and seemed to spend

FIGURE 10.1   **Some participants of the Stockholm conference, 1977; one corner of the table.**

much of the time sleeping, or at least I thought so. However, just when she seemed to have been out like a light for awhile, she would suddenly open her eyes and say something sensible, as if she had been paying attention all along, then she would seem to turn off again. I don't remember whether we ever talked to each other beyond a greeting. I'm sure she didn't have any idea who I was, or cared.

Each conference covered a different topic, for example, psychosomatics, childhood and adolescence, gender issues, working life, and old age. My own presentations at these meetings varied greatly, depending on the central topic. They were about my current ideas and research on stress and coping, which, of course, changed over time. In some instances, I gave more than one presentation, as in the first conference in which I spoke of the concepts of stress and disease and the way environmental issues should be viewed from my subjective perspective. On one occasion, I didn't present a formal paper, and in still others I wrote about social unrest, adaptation, work stress, and the stresses of aging.

One of the delightful features of these conferences was that once or twice during each there would be very distinctive entertainment. On one occasion, we went on a cruise on the Stockholm Archipelago and we were served aquavit ad libitum and a varied smorgasbord buffet with many varieties of herring, warm and cold, and other dishes. We eventually arrived at what had once been the Swedish King's castle, which contained a private theater. I wish I could remember which opera was performed, but the opulent and beautiful setting made the whole affair an enormous treat. For a few hours we all felt like royalty.

The five conferences were always held in June during the longest days of the year, which was a very different experience from my first visit in January. Sweden is very far north and in summer it would stay light until after 10 PM; it never really got totally dark. You had to close the opaque window blinds at bedtime to shut out the light of dawn, which returned around 4 AM. I'm told Swedes lose about an hour of sleep a night during the summer. It was also balmy at this time of year, and I loved walking around the city with pleasant company in perfect safety. There was not much of a night life, but it was a very pleasant city to walk in, and I never found one better.

The early conferences had a special ambience that I thought was charming. The newspapers made much of them, and I have saved many clippings. In those days, rather than photographs, a newspaper artist would make portraits, actually caricatures of the participants. I was treated as a celebrity, and it was lots of fun.

I got to know many of the local Swedish scholars, and visited in their homes. Marianne Frankenhaeuser and her husband had me to a lovely family dinner in a suburb north of Stockholm. It was my first experience with venison, which I liked. I am forever grateful for their hospitality. Alcoholic drinks were usually served at parties, but each visiting couple would always agree on one person as the designated driver who was not permitted even one drink because the penalty for even a little alcohol in the blood while driving was severe.

One evening, my hosts, Professor Levi and his lovely wife, Isabella, took me to the Opera House in the city, where we watched Aida sung in Swedish. And on another occasion in his home, Levi and I listened to Russian songs recorded on his record albums; as a Russian Jew he had immigrated to Sweden many years earlier.

I had some fascinating conversations with my Swedish hosts. In one, for example, we talked about the body language of Americans, Swedes, Danes, and Norwegians. Americans are very outgoing in style, casual, with free and expansive body movements. Among the Scandinavian countries, the Danes are said to be the most similar to us. Swedes are much more reserved than Americans in manners and gestures.

Swedes are also slow and cautious in making friends, as well as being socially reserved. In some of my conversations, mild annoyance was expressed about Americans who, with their very open and friendly style, generated in them a false expectation that a permanent friendship had been struck. Then they would discover it was only skin deep, and would feel they had been sandbagged. There was some poignancy in what was said about this, but they were right. Americans are hail-fellow-well-met, and social relationships in the United States are apt to be superficial.

Lennart Levi visited us in Walnut Creek with his wife Isabella, and once after his wife died, when he was still crushed by the loss. We also saw him in Japan where we both talked about stress at the same meeting. He has invited me numerous times to speak at meetings he had helped organize, but I was always too busy with some new manuscript or book.

Lennart always chided me for my academic approach to stress and coping, and urged me to apply my concepts more to practical human welfare. His view was that people often must work under harsh, stressful conditions, and these conditions should be changed. He wanted me to be more of an activist in influencing social policy. Though I agree with condemning the work conditions he deplored over the world, I was more interested in the subtle conditions that produced work stress as a result of a person's makeup—that is, the person–environment relationship and the way people coped with it (Lazarus, 1991).

I view myself as a researcher and theoretician, and my approach to garden-variety as opposed to extreme work stress emphasizes individual differences and the relational meanings that underlie work. This position argues against an emphasis on making the same environmental change for all workers, except when it is abusive. Anyway, our contacts have faded, which I regret, though life is too complicated and short to have too many regrets.

These travel experiences to Stockholm had a profound influence on my sensibilities and outlook. I learned a great deal and gained confidence. I was treated as someone who had something valuable to say, which is a tonic for the spirit. It was especially supportive to be taken seriously abroad when at home I felt ignored or pressed to conform. I would come home from these trips exhilarated, though sometimes I felt depressed to return to the same old impersonal rat race with its dull routines. Over the years I learned that this is a common reaction, experienced by many professionals I know if they are candid enough to speak of it.

GERMANY

My flirtations with West German psychology actually began with a request from a young member of the German Defense Force, Erhard

Olbrich, who in 1968 or thereabouts was seeking to spend a year with the *Berkeley Stress and Coping Project.* He had good academic credentials and wrote me a letter saying he had funds for a year's stay. I discussed it at length with Ned Opton and Jim Averill and we agreed to invite him, though not without some ambivalence. For one thing, I was conscious of the awful history of Germany before and during World War II during the Holocaust, and the fact that he was part of the West German[2] military added to my uncertainty. But he was a member of a new generation of Germans and we couldn't really hold him responsible for what his parents might have done. So we invited him to come.

Olbrich turned out to be a very gentle, thoughtful, and spiritual young man—he had originally studied for the Catholic priesthood—who was about as far removed from German nazism and racism as could be imagined. He worked hard and published at least one study with us (Averill, Olbrich, & Lazarus, 1972).

The reason Erhard plays an important role in my visits to Germany is that many years later, he became a professor at the University of Erlangen-Nürnberg and in the summer of 1981, he arranged for me to give a lecture tour, support for which came from the Volkswagon Foundation and the West German government. As a result, Bernice and I spent 3 weeks in West Germany.

The visit began with our arrival at Giessen, which is near the Frankfurt airport, where we were hosted by Klaus Scherer, who has now settled at the University of Geneva and is a major figure in research and theory on the emotions. At lunch we were introduced to a number of talented German research psychologists whom we would meet again many times over the next years, including Lothar Laux from Bamberg University. Lothar also played an important role in our many later visits to Germany, and his to California when Bernice, he, and I went boating in the Delta one spring. We have many research interests in common, and we have had a warm friendship now for many years.

On our 1981 visit, Erhard Olbrich generously offered to lend us his Volkswagon Golf and we traveled for several days on our own to Rothenburg and Dinkelsbühl, which are interesting tourist towns on what is referred to as the Romantische Road, which winds through country roads in southern Germany. The countryside reminded us of parts of Pennsylvania and Maryland, rolling green hills and farm country.

---

[2] I use the designation West Germany throughout my account because the country was still divided into West and East, and the tearing down of the Berlin Wall did not happen until many years later.

We also stopped overnight in Würzburg, where we had dinner with an academic psychologist there, J. Wettkowski, with whom we discussed West German academic job problems. He was waiting, without much hope I sensed, for an opportunity to obtain a permanent university position, but this requires a relatively rare opening and the recommendation of a university-wide academic committee. He has given up on the prospects of an academic appointment.

All this was prelude to my participation in a 5-day conference on emotion at Bad Homburg, Germany, to which we drove after Würzburg. The conference had been organized by Paul Ekman and Klaus Scherer a few years earlier at a winter meeting a number of potential participants attended in Paris. The conference led to an important book of proceedings by Scherer and Ekman (1984). The distinguished group of international participants is shown in Figure 10.2.

When the conference ended, Bernice and I took a Rhineboat cruise from Mainz to Bonn where we were met by Erhard Olbrich, who drove us on a lecture tour around the Northwest part of West Germany. The tour included lectures at Aachen, Bonn, Cologne, and Trier, with sight-seeing stops at Limberg and Marburg, and later at Erlangen-Nürnberg, where Erhard was a professor. At Trier, the last of my lectures, I found myself exhausted, I assume from the constant pressure of lecturing and traveling, and maybe eating too much German food. I'm afraid my lecture was a poor one, which was too bad because several psychologists there, including Professor Sigrid Filippe, had been working closely with my ideas and procedures used in coping measurement. Some photos from some of our stops are shown in Figure 10.3.

When we left Trier, Erhard drove us to Hamburg, the last lap of this 3-week West German journey, to participate in the International Congress of Psychogeriatrics. I was scheduled to give an invited address on coping. I know it went well from the compliments I received but, of course, one can usually tell oneself. We remained in Hamburg about 3 days, ultimately leaving for San Francisco. It had been a demanding, though often gratifying and certainly stimulating first stay in West Germany. I learned, for example, that my work on stress and coping was well known, and taught in the graduate psychology programs. I had talked with a wide range of the most active West German research scholars and learned much about their work and ways of thinking. The groundwork had also been laid for some later visits.

The most difficult feature of this first visit to Germany was our internal emotional struggle to come to terms with Germans themselves. I found the young people open and engaging. We didn't talk much about the past, but when it came up it was clear that this generation did not

Top row: Colwyn Trevarthen, Randall Collins, Robert Levy, Theodore Kemper, Robert Zajonc, Peter Marler, me, Richard Davidson, Peter Whybrow, Robert Plutchik, Silvan Tomkins
Bottom row: Karl Pribram, Paul Ekman, Howard Leventhal, Klaus Scherer

FIGURE 10.2   Participants in Bad Homberg conference, summer, 1981.

want to have anything to do with its country's ugly past. When, however, I spoke to groups that included people of our own age, it was more difficult. Bernice and I could never get over the thought that most of them had accepted and contributed to the unbelievable evil, as ugly as has ever been directed toward people in history. They participated, either actively or passively, in attempted genocide against those whose only crimes were to be Jewish, homosexuals, or Gypsies. It was difficult to look them in the eye, lest resentment well up in us.

We tried to tell ourselves that throughout history ingroups have behaved badly toward outgroups they hated or regarded with contempt. In light of this history, one should be wary of feeling superior to others, even those who do evil. I have always thought that the worst feature of the human animal is the ease with which it manages to justify evil. Yet, on the other side of the ledger, we can find much decency and altruism, which often goes well beyond the call of duty and can therefore be called heroic. I suppose this is reason for hope against an otherwise bleak landscape of human cruelty and suffering. In any case,

A. Erhard Olbrich and I.

B. Walking and talking in Aachen.

C. The Hans Sachs caricature of a professor in Nürnberg.

FIGURE 10.3   A few highlights from my lecture tour with Erhard Olbrich.

despite the ambivalent beginnings, our relationships with many Germans have continued, often with considerable respect and warmth.

On a later trip, Bernice and I went to a World Health Organization (WHO) Symposium at Bad Honnef (near Bonn) on the Rhine in June 1987, where I spoke about stress and coping. The conference dealt with the problems posed by chronic, life-threatening, and terminal illness, mainly cancer. It was the strangest meeting I have ever attended.

There were two kinds of participants. One was the usual collection of scientists who wanted proof of the efficacy of treatment approaches. The other group were enthusiasts of alternative medicine, touting inspirational treatment programs, and a number of patient followers who gave testimonials. There was, as might be expected, little communication between the two groups. The conference struck me as a great waste of funds, which didn't add to my confidence in the work of the United Nations.

Then, in July 1988, we spent about 10 days in Mainz, where I had the great honor and pleasure of receiving an honorary degree from the Johannes Gutenberg University, where we were entertained by the University and by Werner Fröhlich, a psychologist and University Dean (see Figure 10.4). My good friend from Haifa University, Shlomo Breznitz, came without warning to Mainz for the ceremony, and we could spend a little time together. I was much moved by this warm gesture.

To receive an honorary degree requires that someone do a great deal of hard work seeking the support of the faculty and the university administration. Often other faculty and administrators make competing suggestions about who should be honored, which go along departmental or other local political lines. In Mainz, it was Werner Fröhlich, Dean of the faculty, who took the responsibility for pursuing the award and arranging the ceremony, during which I made a short speech. In Germany, where such things are taken quite seriously, I would be formally referred to as Professor Doctor Doctor, one for my acquired graduate degree, the other on the basis of *honoris causa,* or in English, "for the sake of honor."

After a second such degree from Haifa University quite a few years later in 1995, one must stutter out Prof. Dr. Dr. Dr. to address me accordingly. Unlike Europe, and especially Germany, Americans don't put this honor on our letterheads, and not many of my friends are aware that I have two such degrees and how they were attained.

I like to make fun of having an honorary degree from both Germany and Israel. Given recent world history, for a Jew to receive one from Germany requires that the scales be balanced with another from Israel. This is, of course, a joke, and all jokes contain a psychological

A. Bernice, Dick, and Werner Fröhlich.

B. Shlomo Breznity, Bernice, Dick, and Werner Fröhlich.

FIGURE 10.4 At my honorary degree ceremony, Johannes Gutenberg University.

226

bite. You see, even in the absence of strong religious conviction, it's hard for Jews to forget who they are in the world, such as it is. However, I am very proud that a German institution sought fit to honor this particular Jew, and equally proud that Haifa University in Israel made the same decision.

On the same trip, we also visited Klaus Scherer and his group in Fribourg, Switzerland and drove to Alsace, France with Werner Fröhlich and his young son. We then took the train to Bamberg where I gave a lecture, and we were again entertained by Lothar Laux and family.

Our longest stay in West Germany came as a 3-month appointment as a Visiting Professor in the Psychology Department of the University of Heidelberg, between May 20th and August 20th, 1989. Our host was Reiner Bastine, a clinical professor there. We lived in a government-supported pension, Gästehaus III. The building housed a varied group of technically trained foreigners from Europe and Asia (and one American couple from Kansas) studying the biochemistry of cancer. Our balcony looked out over a pleasant courtyard. We rented a Volkswagen Passat to get around locally, a MacIntosh word processor for me to write with, and a TV set. In addition to enjoying the local scene, we used Heidelberg as a central point in Europe to travel in all directions.

I gave lectures at many universities on these trips, which covered the costs of our travel; Bernice used to say I sang for my supper. My talks in Europe were all about the theoretical ideas I was struggling with, some of them controversial, about appraisal and coping for a book on emotion and adaptation. I had started on it a year or so before, and I was working on it while we lived in Heidelberg that summer. It was published in 1991 (Lazarus, 1991b).

I spoke at the Ist European International Congress of Psychology in Amsterdam in July and visited the Psychology Department at the University of Amsterdam. Nico Frijda arranged a delightful party at his home for us. On the next day we took a canal-boat ride, which explored a good part of this city of canals.

On the same trip, which was a month or 2 before the wall came down, we also visited Berlin. We were hosted by Ralf Schwarzer, Wolfgang Schönpflug, and Matthias Jerusalem, with whom we had dinner. We stayed in a lovely university house in a northern suburb from which we could go anywhere in the city conveniently by subway.

Ralf had been uncertain about the room to use for my lecture; the school session had already ended (it was July). But he began to get indications of great interest, and worried that the room he had first arranged for my talk was too small. So he finally chose a large auditorium that very easily accommodated the 500 or so people who attended.

Occasions like this have indicated that I am something of a celebrity abroad. People probably come to see what I look like or how I act, but I always hope some of them want to hear what I have to say. I don't think I can generate that kind of crowd in Berkeley.

I spoke for about 1½ hours, then responded to questions on my feet for another 1½ hours before the session broke up. The questions were tough and searching and I responded with candor. I relish extended interchanges of this kind even more than formal lecturing. It gives me a chance to candidly express my uncertainties about certain positions, and to clarify why I take them. I think they enjoyed it and so did I.

My hosts were surprised that the audience stayed so long, and I was too, because in Germany I had learned that if students don't much care for what they hear, they will leave without hesitation even in the middle of the talk. Stress, emotion, and coping were obviously appealing topics, and the excellent questions kept matters interesting and lively. The next day we enjoyed a sunny boat ride on the Wanssee, a local lake, with Ralf and Matthais.

We then flew from Amsterdam to Geneva where we were due the next day. There, I gave a lecture and participated for 2 days in a remarkable meeting, organized by Klaus Scherer and Meinrad Perrez for advanced postdoctoral students. Shlomo Breznitz and Nico Frijda also participated, making this quite a collection of emotion-theory mavens. I was hard pressed to justify one of my most controversial conceptions that the most common provocation to anger was being slighted or demeaned. The discussions were long and stimulating, and they influenced what I was writing. We ended the visit the next day with a delightful boat trip and lunch on Lake Geneva, in pleasantly warm weather.

We also spent quite a bit of time with Lothar Laux and his family, sometimes in Heidelberg and sometimes in Bamberg. Because we have been there often, and I have referred to it several times, I should say that Bamberg is a lovely German town southeast of Frankfurt, which, in turn, is a few hour's drive from Heidelberg. Bamberg, on the river Regnitz, was not seriously damaged during World War II, and is still serene and pleasing to the eye, a tourist town for Germans. Lothar drove us more than once to the lovely area south of Bamberg known as the Fränkische Schweiz (see Figure 10.5). On one such visit, we saw, of all things, an outdoor, slightly comical and colorful performance of Robin Hood and his merry band in Sherwood Forest, presented in German.

We also visited Wilhelm Janke, Professor of Psychology at Würzburg where I lectured about my research and ideas, adopting an epistemology that I knew deviated sharply from his views. But he has always been a gentlemen about our intellectual differences. This time he and his wife

FIGURE 10.5   A day's drive with some of the Lothar Lauxes.

had us to a very pleasing lunch in his home before we left for Heidelberg by train. Imagine my surprise, however, at meeting Nickolas Longo, a visiting psychology professor at Würzburg, with whom I had published some research while he was an undergraduate student at Johns Hopkins University about 40 years earlier (Lazarus & Longo, 1953).

Our last major trip that summer was to Munich. We were hosted by psychologist Michael Frese, whose book with Sabini (Frese & Sabini, 1985) contains a chapter of mine. Each time I speak about the emotions, it comes out differently, as I change and solidify my views and strategy of presentation.

While in Heidelberg we made many local sidetrips by car, usually with the other American professor and his wife from Kansas who were staying at the Gästehaus. Often in the evening, we would walk along the Neckar river, which runs through the city, sit on a bench, and watch people fishing, picnicking, and walking. Our last week in Heidelberg was climaxed by an evening visit to the castle (schloss) on a promontory overlooking the Neckar to see a production of *The Student Prince,* a romantic operetta by Sigmund Romberg.

As I think back on this series of visits to Germany, it is difficult to resist making some editorial comment about our experiences with people there. Living 3 months in Heidelberg gave us some insight into life in Germany. Germans struggle much more than Americans with the daily tasks of living. Even middle-class Germans had very small refrigerators, which hold so little food that they must shop every day. The same could be said for their other appliances.

One shopped separately for fresh bread, which was far better than we get back home. Fruit and vegetables too were outstanding in flavor, not picked long before ripening, as in the case of our tasteless tomatoes, a genetic product of modern corporate agribusiness. For us, the daily walk to the store for bread, pastry, fruit, herring, or whatnot was a pleasure, but it is hardly an efficient way to live if one had other tasks to perform. Labor in Germany is powerful and coddled, with many and long holidays. When Germans work they do a good job, but they do not work as much as Americans and Japanese. Even professors there seemed to be away on holidays a great deal.

We found run-of-the-mill Germans rather cold and distant in comparison with Swedes and Danes, whom we met when we spent a month in Aarhus, Denmark in 1990, and another 10 days in 1997. We remember that the Danes risked their lives to save many Jews from the Holocaust. In Aarhus, if we greeted someone we had seen in the neighborhood, even if they couldn't speak English, they would respond in a friendly way, using sign language to try to make themselves understood. But Germans who shared the same courtyard where we lived, or regularly sold us fresh bread and fruit every morning, would not interact more than necessary with foreigners, whom they seemed to distrust. If we spoke a greeting, such as "gutentag," our neighbors typically made no response. Of course, we couldn't tell what was really in their minds and hearts.

But here I find myself on the horns of the dilemma I touched on earlier, stereotyping a people without regard for individual differences. The professional people with whom we interacted were, in most cases, very warm. We feel very close to Lothar Laux, his wife Christa, and their children, two of whom (the older daughters) visited us in California. The same applies to Erhard Olbrich, Wilhelm Janke and his family, and many others with whom we have developed a friendly relationship. It's puzzling.

I also know from my conversations with Germans who have lived in other European countries, and from Northern Europeans and Scandinavians, that a considerable degree of hostility exists toward Germans living outside Germany, probably as a result of the long history of wars, especially World War II. Others have had much to fear from warlike Germany. One German who lived in Switzerland told us that he still feels the hostility keenly, which he believes is directed at him as a German, even more than 50 years after that War.

Besides, a given people can show different characteristics at different times in their history. To see this clearly, one need only think of the Danes, Swedes, and Norwegians during Viking times—that is, primitive, harsh, and violent—and then consider their modern highly civilized and socially concerned outlook and way of life. Japanese are ethnocentric too, but today they are generally courteous about it. Like Germans, they were also very harsh in the past as conquerors in China and Korea, and in their treatment of British and Americans in Southeast Asia, but seem to have changed in modern times. I've had the same experience of unfriendliness in France, which has also been a hotbed of anti-Semitism and acted badly toward victims of the Nazis.

Given these complexities and contradictions, we must resist at all costs the tendency to characterize a people as good or bad, whatever their national history, and take them as they come—that is, as individuals, because it is not easy to tell what lies in their hearts. Hatred gets perpetuated by stereotyping a people, and Jews, especially, have thousands of years of reasons to eschew stereotypical thinking about any group.

AUSTRALIA

In the late summer of 1984, I was invited to be a Misha Strassberg Visiting Research Professor at the University of Western Australia in Perth. The invitation was arranged by an old friend, Laksyri (Laki for short) Jayasuriya, Professor and Head of the Department of Social Work. He had been born in Sri Lanka, educated partly in London, and we met in Berkeley while he was a visitor.

The appointment fitted my needs wonderfully. I was due for a sabbatical leave of 4 months (one teaching quarter) and I wanted some time away from heavy obligations and pressures. Perth, a small, quiet, and pleasant city on the West coast of Australia, far from the madding crowd, seemed ideal. Bernice and I jumped at the chance. The appointment was arranged to run from September through December, which in the climate of the southern hemisphere, has weather like our March through June.

Perth is a long way from San Francisco, so we planned to get there by easy stages to avoid being bothered too much by jet lag. We flew New Zealand Airways and our first stop was Fiji, where we stayed at a beach resort in the warm sunshine and took the 3-day Blue Lagoon cruise on a small ship that was comfortable but not luxurious. It stopped at some of the most spectacular island bays, with water as sparkling clear and blue green as I have ever seen. Marvelous swimming and snorkeling. There were only about 40 passengers and we all had an informal and very jolly time drinking and eating good food.

When, a few months later we returned to Sidney, we visited a couple we met in Fiji who lived in a high-rise condominium on the fourteenth floor overlooking Sydney Harbor. They had a deck that allowed a 360° view of the hills, bays, and ocean. It was truly spectacular, at least as impressive as the views from the hills and high rises of San Francisco.

After 2 nights in Sydney, we proceeded to Perth, which is on the western coast of the Australian continent about 3000 miles away. Luckily, Laki had helped arrange a small house for us near the beach in a pleasant northwestern suburb of Perth. The house was owned by a member of his department who was also on sabbatical, Rae Lindsay, on whose published dissertation I had written a foreword some years before. She allowed us to use her car as part of the arrangement. It was a perfect situation. Living there for 3 months we would rise early, as we always did at home, have our breakfast in the warming spring sun, either outside on the patio or inside next to it.

During the day, when not teaching or exploring locally, I worked on a major theoretical article. Before I left for Perth, I had submitted a paper on my approach to emotion to a journal named *Brain and the Behavioral Sciences* (BBS), which presented a target article or two each issue and a series of commentaries from other professionals. The journal had first encouraged resubmission after some favorable editorial reviews, and I brought the article with me to Australia with the intent of revising it.

The reason I mention it here is that I worked on it while in Perth, resubmitted it, only to learn later that it was rejected by BBS. I felt sandbagged after the initial encouragement. This journal has a pretty narrow focus, strongly experimental and physiological, and probably for that reason, a comparable social science version later came into being—namely, *Psychological Inquiry,* which has published a number of my target articles.

In any event, this failure led me to consider expanding that article into a book, which became the 1991 monograph (Lazarus, 1991b), *Emotion and Adaptation,* the one I was working on in Heidelberg. In retrospect, I can see that the rejected article tried to do more than it should have in the limited space of a single article. It had good ideas, but they were not as effectively presented as they might have been because of the pressure of space. I began to think that a full monograph could do a much more effective job of treating the complexities of emotion. So, in a sense, that monograph had its origins in my writing efforts in Australia in 1984, and later in Heidelberg in 1989.

Jayasuriya's relationship with Australia and its government is interesting and worth a comment. He is very black as people of Indian ancestry often are, and his wife and two sons are also. Though his credentials and scholarship are excellent, it is remarkable that he became chairperson of an academic department. Until 1973, the country had a firm White Australia policy, refusing immigration to most people of color, though Laki had gotten in.

Laki was an activist in writing and speaking against this policy, and against racism. The first racial problem of the country was the existence of the natives of the outback, the Aboriginals as they were called—a people analogous to our Native Americans (once mistakenly called Indians). Surprisingly, he had gained the favorable attention of many in the government with his outspoken criticisms. He was a first-rate scholar, had excellent communication skills, and had been honored both in England and in Australia, and was appointed to a number of panels of experts to formulate relevant social policies. Quite a remarkable history.

One of the nicest features of staying in Australia for three months is that we lived somewhat like natives. Because the language is English— well, Australian (pronounced Awstrilian), which takes some getting used to, both in vocabulary and accent—we read the local paper every morning and we kept up with the Australian scene. After a time, we became familiar with the Australian accent and terminology.

During our entire stay in Australia, we never once heard the word "bloody," but we often heard "mate," "bloke," and "bastard." of which there are many kinds. We have an Australian audiotape on which there is an account of all the kinds of bastards there are. Surprisingly, you can call someone this or that kind of bastard with impunity, but there are a few kinds that constitute a serious insult. That year, the Australians were having a presidential election between two men with bird-like names, one candidate named Peacock (a conservative), the other Hawke (a liberal). We discovered that Australian politics is very emotional. One day Bob Hawke broke down and cried about the drug addiction of his daughter, and everyone speculated about whether this would turn off Australian macho men so that he would lose the election. It was reminiscent of Muskie's (the U. S. Senator from Maine) ill-fated presidential campaign in which a bad public reaction to his tears for a different reason forced him to end his campaign. In Australia, however, Hawke won by a landslide, and was reelected several times thereafter. Predicting political fallout, like the weather and psychology, is hardly an exact science.

Every week I went into the Uni, as the university is called, to teach a seminar for the Psychology Department, to pick up mail from the Berkeley Stress and Coping Project, and to visit with students and faculty. The seminar was a weekly affair extending over most of the period of my stay. The students I taught were at the graduate level, mostly clinical, and focused on their dissertations. I also spent 1 day a week in my office in the Social Work Department seeing any student who wanted to talk. I tried to advise them about their research. And I gave some lectures to different groups, some of them at other local universities.

On one occasion, I gave a well-advertised free public lecture, entitled *Stress, Coping and Health Outcomes: Basic Issues.* It was given in a huge auditorium at 4:30 in the afternoon, which was packed with people, mostly well dressed as if for a formal affair. All our neighbors were there, a large group of faculty, students, and some of the Perth public attended. I don't remember much about it except that it went well, and people seemed attentive. Afterward, we had dinner at a local restaurant with our suburban neighbors.

Our first really big excitement in Australia came when we decided to take a trip East to Adelaide, Melbourne, Canberra (the capitol), and Sidney. We would fly to Adelaide and then return on one of the great train rides of the world, from Sidney to Perth on The Australian National Railway. All told, the planned trip would take 18 days.

The reason for the stop at Adelaide was that Roger and Kay Russell had a ranch there. He was now a professor of Psychology at Flinders University, and had served as Chancellor of the university. You may remember that Roger was the Chairperson of my dissertation committee in Pittsburgh (see Figure 10.6). We were keen to visit them. Roger was 70 at that time and Kay 73. It was a very sentimental visit for Bernice and me. When we got there, we found them in more or less good health, older but still lively and involved.

The day after we arrived I gave a talk at Flinders, which Roger had arranged, met Leon Mann, the collaborator of Irving Janis on the important 1977 book, *Decision Making,* and Norm Feather, a pioneer in the value-expectancy approach to motivation and emotion, whom I had met in the States.

On our last night, the Russells had a large party for friends, and we were up until very late despite the fact that we were due to travel by bus the next morning to Melbourne. The visit was a very sentimental one for us, and had us reminiscing about graduate school and thinking about life in general.

Aside from the several lectures I gave at La Trobe University, hosted by George Singer, Melbourne was notable for our visit to the Art

FIGURE 10.6   Roger Russell and I.

Center. One evening we saw a play there, Shaw's *Candida,* which we had seen many years before, but enjoyed again far from home.

In Canberra, to which we also traveled from Melbourne by a sight-seeing bus, we were met by Bill Scott, an expatriot American serving as head of the Psychology Department at Canberra University. Canberra is a totally planned city, quite beautiful. Its property, like our District of Columbia, is not owned by any of the Australian states, which was a solution to the hopeless deadlock that Sidney and Melbourne got into from both wanting to be the capital of the country.

Canberra has rolling hills and is in one of the few fertile areas of Australia, the others also being in the eastern part of the Great Dividing Range, which includes Sidney, Melbourne, and Adelaide, or west along the North Coast. We saw kangaroos in the wild, Emus that we could feed, and impressively colored birds. We stayed in a modern motel with a bathtub for the first time on the trip, and had air conditioning. A good low-key stop for refueling and cleaning.

After picking us up Bill Scott toured us around until mid-afternoon, and in return I agreed to a chat (rather than give a lecture—I was getting tired of lecturing) with about 25 to 30 graduate students. The Scotts had come 10 years earlier from Colorado University, for reasons I am not sure I understand exactly. He was an experimental social psychologist who had been one of the *Journal of Personality and Abnormal Psychology* (JPAP) editors, before it changed to the *Journal of Personality and Social Psychology* (JPSP). They spoke very warmly about their decision to come, but one never knows about such matters, because one often feels it is necessary to justify such an unusual decision.

The next day we took a tour bus to Sydney, with the expectation of visiting Ian Waterhouse, who had published some well-known papers with Irwin Child in 1954 on frustration. As we came through the west end of Sydney, it looked like a sleazy, sprawling, industrial Los Angeles, a congested city, which reinforced our good feeling about the choice of Perth to live in.

However, we were to stay in the high-rise Harborside Apartments on the fourteenth floor with a bedroom, large sitting room, dinette, kitchen and bath, right on the water. For the next 2 days, Waterhouse had organized a program with faculty and students from MacQuarrie, Sidney, and New South Wales Universities. Bernice went to town with the woman we had met in Fiji, while I listened, interacted, and gave two talks, one on hassles and the problem of confounding, the other on coping.

The one bad lecture I gave in Sydney was at the Medical School Hospital in an after-lunch meeting. From what I heard before I was to speak, it seemed advisable to change my plans for my talk, but that turned out to be a mistake because I didn't have time to put together a better one. As a result of my reputation, most of the people had come to hear me, and I fear I disappointed them. I don't know exactly what went wrong, but I couldn't get my head together.

That night, glad to be out of the lecture circuit, Bernice and I saw a play at the Sydney Opera House, you know, that impressive silhouette that has become a logo for Sydney. The play was strictly Australian and unusual, entitled *The Blind Giant is Dancing.* It was substantially anti-American, our country being the blind giant, a graphical portrayal of the foolish use of power. But what made the play unusual is that it was strictly Australian left wing, a dead ringer for the Marxist and socialist plays we saw on Broadway during the Great Depression, only this was the 1980s, and the message was, unlike the 1930s, cynical rather than hopeful and uplifting.

The story was all about political power, which had warped the labor movement and was corrupting. The hero was a decent left-winger with his heart in the right place, in contrast to his father who was a conservative. Ultimately the hero takes over, and when he does he makes it clear that he is only interested in power, not in ameliorating the problems of the working poor. The private lives of his family members provide an intimate portrait of the economic and political struggle, reflected in marriage and in the relationship with the parents. Unlike the American socialist plays of the Great Depression, this one was nihilistic, with a palpable sense of social doom. It provides a deft portrait of the ambivalence of Australians, only a little over 14 million strong, about the traditional liberal, labor-centered and conservative, industry-centered split.

On the one hand, there was a strong labor movement, which resisted big business; on the other hand, there was the tradition of the pioneer, as in the American legends of the Wild West, the entrepreneur who would make it on his own. Service by working people was poor in Australia and it is said that this weakens the competitive economic position of the country. And there was the gradual dawning, despite the British–European background, of what Australia's future was as part of the Pacific Rim. The problem of Australian identity was not resolved at the time, and I don't know whether it has been yet.

When we were there, Australia was having economic troubles, and was also resentful about having first blindly followed the British into the Turkish peninsula of Galipoli, the entrance to the Dardanelles, and then having followed the United States into Vietnam. Both were useless disasters, with great losses of life. A sad and angry Australian song, "And the Band Played Waltzing Matilda," is about the tragedy of Galipoli when crippled men returned only to find no respect, no thanks, and no help (as in the case of our own Vietnam veterans). All they got was the playing of "Waltzing Matilda," a song that had become emblematic, at least to foreigners, of the Aussie fighting man, but which expressed only their sorrow.

That song, incidentally, which Americans like and associate with Aussies, is not about a woman who danced but a minor tragedy about a small-time thief who traveled with a pack bouncing on his back (called a waltzing mathilda). He is caught at a billabong, a small pond, and is ultimately dispatched.

I have one more brief story to tell about this trip. On the way back from Sydney, we took the Australian National Railway trip across the country to Perth. The train trip costs much more than flying. The train was packed—it holds a maximum of 150 people. It is difficult to get tickets for it. We had a bedroom and bathroom, so it was reasonably comfortable, and interesting too except for the third day, which began to get boring. Food and service were poor, consistent with what I said previously about Australian labor.

The people on the train were very friendly, mostly working stiffs, not well educated, but cheerful, talkative, and good to be with, at least in the short run. There was a parlor car with a piano where we met lots of Aussies and listened to their songs. The last lap of the train trip, on the third day, is the longest stretch of straight track in the world, over what is called the "nullarbor," meaning from the Latin, no trees. That was pretty tiresome and we were glad to see civilization once again.

When we left, we headed for a 2-week tour of New Zealand, then from Christ Church, where we spent the last night, we flew to Auckland, thence to Los Angeles (12 hours in the air), and finally San Francisco. The scenery on the tour was beautiful, but we were ready to get home. After three planes, and the long flight to LA, that last lap of 1 hour to the city, and then the hour by limousine home, seemed to take forever. And then we were home again.

ARGENTINA

Our 10-day visit to Buenos Aries in May 1987 was, in my mind, one of the most unique trips we ever made. I was invited by a Foundation for the Study of Stress to an international conference there. It is affiliated with the Argentine Medical Association (of which I am now an honorary member) and with the University of Argentina Medical School in Buenos Aires, which trains all the physicians in the country. Because almost none of the people organizing the conference could speak English (they speak Spanish), I was contacted first by a member of the Board of Directors, Dr. Abe Peña, a bilingual psychiatrist living in Miami.

Dr. Peña explained to me that this period in Argentina was a very heady time. For the first time in its history, there was a democratic government, its first elected president being Raoul Alphonsin. Democracy had come after a terrible and violent period of right-wing military dictatorship in which anyone suspected of political opposition, or left-wing sympathies, was secretly abducted, tortured, drugged, and dropped into the sea from an airplane. Fifty-five thousand people are said to have disappeared this way in 2 days during what is called the "Dirty War," which took place between 1976 and 1983. The total death count has been estimated at 30, 000 people, and Argentina is still haunted by these terrible times.

With democratic elections in 1983, it was hoped that the country would now emerge from these dark days of dictatorship and extensive corruption. Throughout its history, the wealth of Argentina had been siphoned off by corrupt governments, yet in terms of its resources, it is potentially the wealthiest country in South America.

Because Argentineans looked toward Europe for its origins and identity, and because so many years had passed without significant scholarship, professionals now wanted to make contact with Europeans and North American scholars to help it catch up intellectually with the developed Western world. The conference was intended to be a step in that direction. The Foundation had first thought of inviting someone from Spain, but when they learned that my work on stress and coping was highly influential (my 1984 book with Folkman had been translated into Spanish), they invited me and my wife to travel there first class.

About 4 days before we were to travel, I developed a severe sciatic attack and was in great pain. I called Dr. Peña and reluctantly told him I couldn't come, and he reacted with some panic. I then discovered that the conference, which, I had assumed, was international, with me as a major participant, was not that at all. It had been built entirely around me as the *only* foreign scholar. The other participants would be Argentine doctors who would speak about their research on stress and psychosomatic diseases.

My decision not to come was viewed as a potential disaster. I began to feel guilty about the lateness of my decision. I spoke to my orthopedist, who said it would probably not do significant physical harm to make the trip, and that I could go pretty well doped up with all sorts of pain killers and tranquilizers.

So we decided to go after all, and as it turned out, we had a ball. Because I was heavily drugged throughout the visit, I hope my lectures made sense, though I'm not sure anyone would have noticed if they were poorly constructed. I came off the plane in a wheelchair and saw the jaws of those who met us drop. I quickly explained that my condition was not as bad as it looked, but used a wheelchair to save me from having to lift and carry our bags. We were quartered very comfortably in a Sheraton high rise.

Bernice and I were both featured several times on TV. She was interviewed on one occasion without me, and asked how it was to live with a famous expert on psychological stress. She said it was wonderful; I was her stress reducer and she mine. They loved it. I gave some formal lectures on the basics of a subjective, appraisal-centered approach to stress and coping, and some interviews.

We were entertained by the president of the university, who revealed to me candidly that things had so deteriorated under the military dictatorship that educational standards for physicians had become a social disaster, and many badly trained doctors were practicing in the countryside. There was open enrollment and no standards restricting admission to medical school. She was, however, optimistic about reinstating a sound medical education. This was to be a time of rebirth for the whole country. And in a public ceremony, I was presented with a certificate of membership in the Argentine Medical Society (see Figure 10.7)

On one occasion, we were taken on a lengthy ride to San Ignacio Mission, the site of the American movie, *The Mission,* which was playing in theaters in the United States about this time. This was where a Catholic group of priests resisted Spain's religious hierarchy and were ultimately attacked by the Spanish cardinal and killed. The rebellion and the struggle it generated is the theme of the movie. We saw how they lived and carried out their ultimately failed resistance.

Even more interesting to me was a lengthy conversation we had with the driver of the van in which we traveled. He had been a dedicated Peronista, and his description of what was happening in his country was far more negative than we had heard until then. In his view, the economy was still poor and corrupt, though admittedly safer, especially for the middle class and the rich. President Alphonsin was portrayed as well meaning, but inept, and as representing the well-to-do not the working poor. The driver showed none of the optimism about the future that the medical group had shown. It is sobering to remember that Juan Peron and his wife Eva (called Evita in the stage play and movie), were power-hungry tyrants who stole from the state and the people at the same time they were being lionized by much of the public for their humanity.

One of the main highlights of our visit was a 2-day side trip on Argentine Airlines to the Iguasu Falls, which lie on the border of Argentina and Brazil. We had never seen anything so spectacular, and it puts Niagara Falls to shame. I used up enormous amounts of film as we walked along the edge of the falls on the Argentine side, through thick, jungle-like foliage.

We were then driven to the Brazilian side to see even more spectacular views, but not having visas made us uneasy as we were, in effect, illegals. All went well, however. We lunched while listening to Brazilian Indian and Portuguese music, and were returned without incident to the hotel in Argentina.

In Buenos Aires proper, we had two other fascinating experiences. One was a visit to La Cabaña with the governing board of the Foundation and their wives for an Argentine steak dinner. The steaks were huge, very different in flavor from North American beef, but very tasty. There was plenty of scotch to help wash it down. The other was the evening we spent at the Elviejo Almacén, a Tango theater. Plenty of scotch there too. Argentineans love the tango and feel ecstatic, almost mystical, about it.

FIGURE 10.7   Dr. Alberto Guedikian (left) presents to me, for the Foundation, a Certificate of Membership in the medical association, while Dr. Peña looks on.

We had been to a tango performance in San Francisco and liked it. The imported show wasn't anything like the real thing, however, which was intensely emotional, the music as well as the acting. It combined singing, comedy, fiery dancing by groups and individual dancers, wonderful to watch, and performed with a verve and style that would be hard to match. Argentine men comport themselves physically in a distinctive, seemingly affected way unlike anything we had ever seen, conveying the impression of extreme machismo. This is not just true when they tango; they move that way constantly and relate to women with an exaggerated air of masculinity. And the women respond in kind.

We had a truly marvelous time in Argentina despite my sciatica, but there is a tragic quality to what happened afterward. I had accepted the task of providing source material about psychological stress and the coping process, which I started to do after we got home. Several factors were to undermine this effort. First, the indigenous corruption made it difficult to mail things back and forth, especially presents we sent people we had met in appreciation for their generous hospitality. They never received them because presents, and books too, were simply stolen. One women sent Bernice lovely stories and poems she had written asking for her reactions and advice about a possible publisher.

Bernice responded appropriately and encouragingly, but nothing came of it. Ultimately, the contacts became more infrequent and all but disappeared.

Second, and perhaps more important, there was the major language barrier. I have never been to a country in which so little English was spoken, even by the educated class. Perhaps they should have invited a Spaniard after all, rather than a North American who couldn't speak Spanish.

Third, after awhile the country seemed to degenerate again politically. Futile struggles about what to do about punishing the perpetrators of the crimes during the military dictatorship added to the malaise. Argentina has a new, Peronist-oriented president Carlos Menem, who was elected in 1989, but the intrinsic corruption has never been overcome, and there continues to be much poverty and unemployment. I can't make any fact-based diagnosis about why the professional relationship that had begun so hopefully died. In the absence of any feedback, I soon got involved in other matters.

I fear things are not good there. Bernice and I have a strong ambivalence about our brief connection with Argentina, which we remember fondly, but feel uneasy about the fate of the people we got to know so briefly. I presume I am still an honorary member of the Argentine Medical Society, and a member of the Board of Governors of the Foundation, but neither role has been functional.

ISRAEL

Although there are American Jews who are anti-Zionist, most of us feel a close identity with the fate of Israel and its people, and many have visited there. I have been to Israel five times over the years, and Bernice three times. I was first invited in 1975 by Norman Milgram, of Tel Aviv University, right after the Yom Kippur War, which, after the euphoria of the 6-day war in which the Arab coalition was swiftly defeated, left Israelis more sober about the dangers of being overwhelmed and defeated.

Professor Milgram had organized a large meeting in Tel Aviv with the ungainly title of *First International Conference on Psychological Stress and Adjustment in Time of War and Peace*. When I arrived at the hotel where the meeting was held, there was a large banner proclaiming this title across the entire hotel front. Israel being a small country, its people were deeply concerned with the issues of this conference. There were to be two later comparable meetings, one in 1978 in

Jerusalem, which I attended, and one in 1983 in Tel Aviv, which I did not because I was participating in a conference on denial in Haifa. One of the photos from that conference is shown in Figure 10.8.

My paper at the 1975 meeting, which was published later (Lazarus, 1985) addressed the difference in outlook between Jews in the Diaspora (the dispersion of Jews over the world following the Babylonian exile) and Jews in Israel. Israelis had become farmers and soldiers who apologize to no one.

Most Diaspora Jews, in contrast, had lived in European ghettos, in Shtetls as social outcasts, and being relatively powerless, they offered no consistent opposition to existing political regimes. In effect, given the realities of their existence, they manifested a kind of passive coping, employing a self-deprecatory humor and turned hostility on themselves. They kept their counsel peacefully and managed as well as they could under restricted conditions of living. In effect, ghetto Jews depended heavily on the sufferance of others, whereas Israeli Jews thought of themselves as masters of their own fate.

In my paper, I drew on some survey data that showed that the Yom Kippur War had greatly shocked Israelis and suggested to them that they were more vulnerable than they had thought. I also suggested that the prolonged political and military struggle had made of Israel a "great natural laboratory" for the study of stress and coping.

American magazines, such as *Time* and *Newsweek,* reported what I said, emphasizing far more than I had the downside of Israeli morale. This produced a strong protest in Israel from psychologists who felt that no attention had been given to their claims that Israeli morale was high, and that the American media wanted to create an image of Israel as distressed and unstable. *Newsweek,* for example, spoke of 3,000 psychologists and psychiatrists at the conference having placed Israel on the psychoanalytic couch.[3] In my view of this, some Israeli psychologists didn't want to condone an image abroad of morale problems, which the evidence suggested was present, albeit without any sense of desperation.

I was unhappy about the outcome of what I said, but in the long run I seem to have weathered the storm, partly because the Israelis didn't blame me as much as the media, and partly because most Israelis saw the truth of what was happening. Most important, however, they knew also that my concerns about Israel were sincere. Israeli psychologists, who are well trained and deeply involved in the fate of their people,

---

[3] This was reported in Hebrew in the Israeli publication *Ma'Ariv,* January 30, 1975, p. 7.

FIGURE 10.8   At the podium (left to right): Rollo May, Avner Ziv, myself, Abba Eban, and Norman Milgram.

have done enormous amounts of stress research and have drawn heavily on my ideas. They have also recognized the validity of the idea that Israel was, without wanting it, a natural stress laboratory.

My lecture in Tel Aviv in 1975 implied the possibility of a major difference in preferred styles of coping between Israeli Jews and Jews in the diaspora. The self-image of Israeli Jews is said to be deliberately, and counterphobically quite different from that of the Diaspora Jew. Instead of coping by philosophical acceptance of a bad lot, with their backs to the wall, they had became fighters, refusing to accommodate easily. They emphasized active coping rather than passive. Israelis react badly to feeling helpless. They would rather act than do nothing, sometimes even when doing nothing would be more adaptive. They owe nothing to anyone except their community, and give equal aggression back.

As a result of this outlook, Israelis reacted painfully to the insistence of the United States during the Gulf War that Israeli planes not attack missile sites in Iraq lest such action destroy the fragile military alliance of Arabs, Europeans, and Americans against Iraq. They suffered greatly in having to shut themselves up passively in close quarters while awaiting Scud missile attacks. It was painful for them to see American pilots hunt for missile sights when they believed that they, Israeli fighter pilots, could do it more effectively.

I am not confident about how accurate this view of Israeli coping is, or of the coping of Jews in diaspora—that is, whether or not it is correct, an exaggeration, or Zionistic rhetoric. Often too much uniformity is relegated to culture when there is actually great diversity among individuals and subgroups in any given culture. However, I think it is an interesting and important question. The answer to whether or not there are cultural differences in coping remains obscure because of an absence of good, in-depth, cross-cultural studies. Regardless of how this question is ultimately answered, in light of the Israeli experience with recurrent warfare against bitterly hostile Arab neighbors, issues of stress and coping remain a major preoccupation of Israeli psychologists, whose research is at the forefront worldwide in this field.

These visits to Israel had actually been preceded by a growing educational relationship in the 1960s and 1970s between me and Israeli graduate students in psychology at Berkeley (and with other faculty members too). Despite the distance from home, Israeli students liked to come to Berkeley, partly because of the quality of the department and the university, and partly because of the compatible climate, which was similar to the Mediterranean. Most completed their doctorates and took positions in Israeli universities or did research in other settings.

My closest friendships with Israelis have been with Shlomo Breznitz, of Haifa University and his wife Tzvia, whose two children, Narit and Ruth, are now grown up, and Reuven Gal and his wife Ivria, whose three children, Danny, Shahar, and Jonathan, are also now adults. My connection with Shlomo began when he spent a year in Berkeley as a visitor. After that we had many occasions to meet in the United States and in Europe, and we have corresponded over the years, and remained warm friends. You may remember that he visited me in Mainz, West Germany when I received my honorary degree at Johannes Gutenberg University.

We also participated together in a lively meeting in Washington, DC, in 1985, sponsored by the National Institute of Mental Health Center for Prevention Research (CPR). We jokingly called it the Great Debate, which was presided over by Norman Garmezy (University of Minnesota). Shlomo and I had an extended but friendly argument about whether stress should be considered as an objective environmental stimulus or was best viewed as dependent on an individual's perceptions and appraisals. The reader should have no trouble guessing which side each of us argued.

Everyone had a good time especially the CCNY boys, who are pictured in the photo in Figure 10.9, from left to right Donald Meichenbaum (University of Waterloo, Canada), Edward Katkin (State University of New York at Buffalo), myself, and Norm Garmezy (University of Minnesota), all of whom had graduated from the City College of New York.

Reuven Gal came to Berkeley in 1972 as a graduate student intending to work with me on stress. At the time he was the Chief Psychologist of the Israeli Navy. He did his dissertation with me, and we published a paper together on the role of active efforts to cope, just doing something even if it was unproductive, in lowering physiological stress levels (Gal & Lazarus, 1975). When he finished his dissertation, he went back to Israel to become the Chief Psychologist of the Israeli Armed Forces. We have remained warm friends ever since. Reuven and Ivria have visited us in California, and we stayed in their home in Israel. We also spent a day on our boat together in the California Delta.

After the conference in Tel Aviv, Bernice and I traveled on our own to Jerusalem—how can one go to Israel without seeing Jerusalem?—where we stayed as tourists, seeing the city and exploring the history of three of the worlds major religions, Judaism, Christianity, and Moslem. When the tour bus stopped for a brief look from the bus at Lazarus's tomb, I stood up—I should probably say that, like the biblical Lazarus, I rose. We also visited the Dead Sea, Jericho, and Masada, a settlement on top of a steep mountain, the site of the last stand of a rebellion against the Romans, which ended in the death of all.

In June of 1979, I participated in the conference I mentioned above on the *Denial of Stress,* which was organized by Shlomo Breznitz at Haifa University. In addition to his professorship in Psychology, Shlomo is Director of the Ray D. Wolfe Centre for the Study of Psychological Stress. It was a most interesting meeting, truly a working conference in which people from diverse fields talked about denial as a process of coping, and had valuable debates about it.

My paper, *The Costs and Benefits of Denial* (Lazarus, 1983) is, as I said in chapter 9, one of my favorite think pieces (Bernice's too) in which I examined the contradiction between important writers and the tradition of clinical psychologists and psychiatrists. A major theme of great writers is that life is intolerable without illusion, whereas for psychologists and psychiatrists, one cannot have mental health without a tight grip on reality. My effort at resolution was to suggest that denial is harmful when it prevents people from doing what needs to be done to preserve health and well-being, otherwise it can help morale. In the article, I also reviewed research that identified some of the conditions under which denial is either harmful or helpful.

FIGURE 10.9   The CCNY boys. From left to right Donald Merchenbaum, Edward Katkin, myself, and Norman Garmezy.

During the conference, we lived in the Beit Oran Kibbutz on a mountaintop. We went swimming in the Mediterranean Sea with the other conference participants and visited Cesarea, an old Roman port. Then, with Reuven and Ivria, we made an extended tour of Northern Israel, which included the artist colony in picturesque Safed, saw an ancient Roman temple, a new kibbutz, the Jordan river, the Golan Heights where we found some broken-down Syrian tanks, and made a stop at an army base where we had lunch and talked with Israeli soldiers, finally returning after a few days to the Tel Aviv area where we spent the night with the Gals before departing for California.

In 1993 I was invited by the Israeli Psychological Association to give an invited address at their annual meeting at Bar Ilan University. When I arrived, I was met by Reuven and Ivria at the hotel in Tel Aviv, where we had drinks together and a dish of Israeli olives, which I love. On the day after of my arrival, I did a 4-hour workshop for Reuven's research group, the Israeli Institute for Military Studies, which he directs. I was driven back to my hotel on the beach at Tel Aviv by Yahava Solomon, a Ph. D. who is also a Colonel in the Israeli Armed Forces. Her books on the reactions to war make important additions to the stress and coping literature. I wrote a foreword for one of them.

The next day I gave another 4-hour workshop to about 30 members of the Israeli Psychological Association who applied on the basis of their familiarity with my work and paid a fee to help defray the expense of my trip. After a brief introduction in which I noted some of my current concerns about stress, coping, and the emotions, we had a lively discussion. I love the give and take of such extended discussions, and as in Europe, I welcome tough, searching questions because they allow me candidly to elaborate my own ambivalences and concerns about where psychology has been going. It allows me to clarify the ambiguities and misunderstandings that are always present in a changing body of work. I enjoyed this morning at the workshop more than any other part of my visit.

When I gave my formal lecture, there was a tremendous turnout and the room was overflowing. The University President had toured me earlier, and I met and chatted with the faculty in a holding room before the address. We talked about Bar Ilan, which is the only university in Israel with the mission of educating students in the concepts of Jewish religious life.

To accommodate everyone, a huge hall was provided, which unfortunately was not air-conditioned. Members of the Psychology Faculty were on the platform with me. Because of my fear of becoming aphasic while suffering from jet lag, and because it was a complex theoretical message about the emotions, I read my paper. I'm afraid it was not a scintillating performance. I do better when I talk from notes.

The next few days before leaving for home, I swam at the beach, attended some of the meetings, and participated in some of the discussions, talked with young faculty and some students about their research, and had a pleasant and relaxed time. One evening was spent at dinner with two of the outstanding psychology research faculty at Bar Ilan, Victor Florian and Mario Mikulincer (an Argentinean Jew who immigrated to Israel). Another evening was spent at dinner at the Giora and Nira Keinan, with other guests, such as Michael Rosenbaum and Stevan Hobfoll.

My last visit to Israel, which came a year later in June 1995, was the most emotional, because I received my second honorary doctorate from Haifa University. This time it was Shlomo Breznitz who arranged the award and the visit, and Bernice came with me. The only other academic to be given an honorary degree was Professor David Ayalon of Haifa University, a noted orientalist and expert in Arabic studies.

This, of course, is par for the course. Most honorary degrees every-where are given to public celebrities. They honor wealthy donors to the university, and it is rare for professors to be given such an honor, which always requires the approval of the professorate. Universities use the honorary degree as the payback for something. So I was very proud.

During this visit, I lectured to one of Shlomo's classes, and some of the psychology faculty came. Bernice and I went to a number of lunch-es, dinners, and other celebrations, which were part of an international fund-raising effort that lasted several days. The University was gener-ous in providing me with a photo album of the ceremonies one of which is shown in Figure 10.10.

I made a short speech of thanks, honoring my wife for her steadfast support and patience about my work, suggesting that she was entitled to at least half of the diploma. Then, as we filed out of the auditorium, I ceremoniously handed it to her where she was sitting. The women loved it. Then it was all over, and we embarked on the long trip home, with a brief stop in Bamberg, Germany, which is not far from Frankfurt where the plane stops on the way to San Francisco.

The only important negative feature of this trip was that a few months earlier I had learned I had prostate cancer, and had agreed to a radical prostatectomy in seeking a cure. The surgical date was post-poned 2 months so I could receive the honorary degree and provide

FIGURE 10.10 My brief speech at the honary degree ceremony at Haifa University.

time for my immune system to fully recovery from the trip. The period in Israel was, therefore, also marked by a degree of anxiety. I, for one, was concerned that I might have increased the risks of metastasis by the delay of surgery. However, the operation was a complete success and there is no evidence of spread of cancer cells. It now appears that I am entirely free of the cancer, and fully recovered.

Before closing this personal account, given what has been happening with the Palestinians at this writing, I must add the briefest of comments addressed to my friends in Israel. Though the matter of peace and war could change quickly, the effort to assure peace seems currently in a very fragile condition, with the Israeli mood being one of "It can't go on like this." Without offering an analysis, and concerned as I am about the fate of Israel—not only with respect to war and peace but also the quality of its life and institutions—permit me to express by guarded hope that it will all work out positively. And I hope that the struggle between the orthodox rabbis of Israel does not poison the ties that have existed between Israeli and American Jews.

REFERENCES

Averill, J. R., Olbrich, E., & Lazarus, R. S. (1972). Personality correlates of differential responsiveness to direct and vicarious threat: A failure to replicate previous findings. *Journal of Personality and Social Psychology, 21,* 25–29.

Folkman, S., & Lazarus, R. S. (1988). *Manual for the Ways of Coping Questionnaire.* Palo Alto, CA: Consulting Psychologists Press (Later changed to MIND GARDEN, same address.)

Frese, M., & Sabini, J. (Eds.). (1985). *Goal directed behavior: The concept of action in psychology.* Hillsdale, NJ: Erlbaum.

Gal, R., & Lazarus, R. S. (1975). The role of activity in anticipating and confronting stressful situations. *Journal of Human Stress, 1,* 4–20.

Janis, I. L., & Mann, L. (1977). *Decision making: A psychological analysis of conflict, choice, and commitment.* New York: The Free Press.

Lazarus, R. S. (1983). The costs and benefits of denial. In S. Breznitz (Ed.), *The denial of stress* (pp. 10–30). New York: International Universities Press.

Lazarus, R. S. (1985). The psychology of stress and coping. In C. D. Spielberger & I. G. Sarason (Eds.), *Stress and anxiety* (Vol. 10, pp. 399–418). Washington, DC: Hemisphere.

Lazarus, R. S. (1991a). Psychological stress in the workplace. In P. L.

Perrewé (Ed.), Handbook of job stress (Special Issue), *Journal of Social Behavior and Personality, 6,* 1–13.

Lazarus, R. S. (1991b). *Emotion and Adaptation.* New York: Oxford University Press.

Lazarus, R. S., & Longo, N. (1953). The consistency of psychological defenses against threat. *Journal of Abnormal and Social Psychology, 48,* 495–499.

Levi, L. (Ed.), 1971). *Society, stress, and disease.* London: Oxford University Press. Also see Levi, 1975, 1978, 1981, and 1987, for the remainder of the series.

Scherer, K. R., & Ekman, P. (1984). *Approaches to emotion.* Hillsdale, NJ: Erlbaum.

Teaching, Family Life, and Struggles with the University

I return now to the 26-year period from the mid-1960s to retirement in 1991 to provide a picture of other aspects of my life, aside from research and theory-building. The topics to be covered are teaching, family life, and troubles with the university.

TEACHING

Because a college professor's life is built substantially on teaching, let me sketch very briefly my teaching role. The brevity stems from my sense that the details, which are not in any way remarkable, change from time to time with revisions in the organization of the department and are not very interesting.

I have already said I felt alienated from the educational program and research of the personality program, and this led me to pursue my own teaching interests. When I began at Berkeley, I taught courses primarily in accordance with the stated needs of the department. By the time I returned from Japan and completed my first major monograph on stress and coping, the educational program had gotten rather narrowly separated into subfields, which were combined into three large groups, as I noted in chapter 6.

Few of us at Berkeley realized at the time that this fractionation of the discipline was a trend at most universities in the United States. Though I taught within the personality group, I also had an affiliation with clinical psychology, often attending the clinical case conferences and working with clinical students who were interested in research issues of stress and coping.

Because these topics had become more popular, my courses, both lecture and seminar, were increasingly centered on this subject. It was also my way of promoting the subject even before it was well established in the psychology curriculum. For quite a few years, for example, I taught a large undergraduate lecture course on this subject, identified as stress and adjustment. Not a required course—my subject never achieved required status—but it still enrolled about 300 to 400 students.

I also gave an upper-division lecture course on this subject for many years, which was also well attended. After my book with Folkman, *Stress, Appraisal, and Coping* appeared in 1984, I used it as the text for this course (Lazarus & Folkman, 1984). Because it was intended as a monograph rather than a textbook, it was challenging to undergraduates, but it was clearly written and richer than most of the potboilers written on the subject, the better students felt they learned much from it.

Berkeley has always had the honorable tradition of dividing each faculty member's courses into half undergraduate and half graduate. Although sometimes honored in the breach, this division of undergraduate and graduate teaching applied even to the most distinguished faculty members, many of whom did a stint teaching introductory-level courses. Added to this were special study courses in which one worked with a number of individual students taking honors, directed study in some given area, or dissertation studies.

How Professors Spend Their Work Time

According to surveys, faculty members at Berkeley work at their jobs for over 65 hours a week. For those not intimately familiar with university life, let me say something about how a diligent faculty member's time is typically spent. Teaching in a university goes on in dozens of different ways, not just in the lecture hall, and much of it is invisible to the outsider. In addition to formal class teaching, special exams are given to doctoral candidates at different stages of their education, including ultimately a several-hour oral, during which five faculty members of the department and one professor from an outside department question the candidate's knowledge.

Many faculty members spend quite a bit of time over many months rehearsing a graduate student facing an oral exam; the student is often quite anxious about the upcoming exam, and such rehearsals can help both in preparing for it and in reducing the level of anxiety. If the student passes, a major piece of research called the dissertation must then be undertaken, which requires another committee's approval at a several-hour meeting, and then close supervision of the research and its write-up by the chairperson, who is often the student's mentor.

To be effective at the job, responsible professors also must disengage from teaching and student contacts to pursue their scholarship by reading scientific journals and books, manage their research, and meet national professional obligations, such as reviewing research submitted to journals or research proposals for the National Science Foundation (NSF), the National Institutes of Health (NIH), and other organizations that distribute funds for research. They also serve locally on many committees that deal with educational issues and policies, some at the university-wide level and others within the department.

Professors also spend much time during the academic year going to research meetings within the country and abroad where they listen to and discuss the research of others and present their own work. If professors want funds for research, they must also write research grant applications, and revise them in response to criticisms from the granting agency, a process that takes a tremendous amount of time, both for the applicant and for the research scholars on the review committee. Finally, they write large numbers of letters of recommendation for their students and colleagues seeking promotion, and serve on committees to evaluate others who are being considered for appointment or promotion.

As is the case almost everywhere, the most demanding academic teaching is done with individual students, both graduate and undergraduate. Because I had major research programs ongoing throughout almost all of my academic career, students were interested in working with me. A group of students, postdoctorals, and faculty working on the Berkeley Stress and Coping Project, would meet regularly, usually once a week to discuss particular studies, issues, and plans.

As our research program became well known, we would have visitors from other universities in the United States and abroad, and postdoctorals who spent a semester or year as visitors, who lectured to our group and participated in our discussions. Such a program was not only stimulating and instructive for us all, but it also gave students an opportunity to publish and explore issues in depth. Some, for example, obtained research assistantships, which provided them with financial support.

Perhaps of greater interest than these routine details, which are typical at first-rate institutions, are my attitudes toward teaching. Basically a shy man, I was always anxious before each new lecture course as a new semester or quarter began. I enjoyed the give and take of small seminars better than large classes. But I would quickly come to enjoy the lecturing as the weeks passed and I became comfortable with the class.

Like most good lecturers—I think I am generally effective and received good evaluations from my classes—I have a lot of ham in me, and I tackled my lectures with enthusiasm. I enjoy turning people on, explaining difficult matters clearly, and hearing from them about their reactions. One never reaches everyone in a large class—if a teacher is lucky, he or she connects well with a quarter to a third of the class—and even at Berkeley, the level of interest can be spotty.

As you already know, I have also had some bad moments lecturing. I often said this to students, but sensed they didn't believe me. They assumed I was just trying to encourage them, which is partly true. In addition to the occasion in Sydney, Australia, which I mentioned in chapter 10, I also remember an uncomfortable lecture in western Canada. For reasons that are obscure, the audience seemed cold and unresponsive, and I began to experience that bane of all performers, thoughts about failure that get in the way of what I was trying to say. I sweated throughout the hour lecture without ever achieving mastery.

To speculate about why, I was giving a public lecture, and the audience consisted of professionals in my field and others, educated people but not aficionados of my subject. The problem was to decide what to talk about and at what level. I was being well paid for my travel and lecture, which added to the pressure. You want to give your money's worth and live up to your reputation.

Before I started to talk, I began to think I had misjudged the situation and my talk was going to be too simplistic for the caliber of the audience. My host had indicated that a high proportion of professors there had come to hear me, but I had prepared for a lay audience, which would know nothing of my findings and thoughts about stress and coping. I guess that intimidated me; I was under stress and found I couldn't cope with it effectively.

When I started to talk, I tried first to make a joke that fell flat. The audience, well-dressed and austere, gave no evidence of any emotion, seeming to stare at me dourly. Actually, audiences usually want to like you, want you to be good, and usually forgive your gaffs. They are made uncomfortable if you are obviously uncomfortable.

In this situation, whatever I did seemed to fall flat, and I found myself in a vicious circle. Perhaps I should have realized that Anglophile Canadians are not very demonstrative. I was visibly uncomfortable and the audience got that way too, which made my problem worse. Though I got through the talk, I never completely recovered my aplomb. On the way home on the plane, I reassured myself that I was probably my own severest critic. Although my performance might not have been scintillating, it was probably not as bad as I had thought. Since then I have learned all sorts of ways of handling such situations and most of the time they seem to work. I usually enjoy speaking to audiences, large and small, and it is a special pleasure when the situation makes feedback and interaction possible.

Performers wither when their audience is cold, but expand to the point of joy when their audience is warm and responsive, which draws out the best in them. I always thought Richard Nixon did poorly when he thought the audience didn't like him, but John Kennedy was a natural; he could remain charming and seemingly at ease regardless of how he was received. We do not know what is in the mind of performers unless they tell us, however, though we can make educated guesses.

There can be a wonderful symbiosis between performers and their audiences. Professional performers, such as comedians, are sustained by evidence they are loved; not to be loved is to be rejected. I have an appreciation for their need for evidence of an audience's enjoyment of their humor. They probably are attracted to what they do by this need, but performing is also a drug; exhilarating when it works, a bad trip when it fails. I am not aware of any research studies on the developmental factors that push people into careers of this type, but it seems to be an interesting question.

I have known graduate students who were petrified to give a lecture, say, to undergraduate students, and as part of their training they need to have opportunities to do this. For some, being chronically anxious and inhibited generates doubts about their aspiration to be a university professor. In seminars many students fear to speak up lest they reveal their ignorance. Yet, if they don't speak, they cannot test what they know and rehearse their communication skills, and so will not learn as much. Most important of all is to discover that others too, prominent people included, may have the same anxieties.

I talk about this because my own anxieties are real, and I would like to encourage young people with self-doubts to get them to recognize that many others have the same problem. Usually this anxiety can be ameliorated if not totally overcome. I have always felt good when students came by years later, some of them having gone on to graduate work or even became college professors, and spoke warmly about their educational experience with me.

But to return to my university teaching, stress and coping are lively topics for students because they relate to their lives, which made my courses relatively popular. On the other hand, I was always an academic through and through, rather than a popularizer, so I gave less emphasis to the dramatic side of the subject matter, explored important issues in depth, and tried to engage students' critical faculties about popular but erroneous ways of thinking. Nevertheless, I was not above telling a lively story dramatizing my research and graphically describing stressful movies and our findings about how we raised or lowered stress levels with sound tracks, as described in chapters 7 and 8.

I also had a tendency to give Talmudic-like lectures, which is odd given my lack of enthusiasm for organized religion. I'm not really sure how this tendency developed. I was not a student of the Talmud, which analyzes the perplexing problems of human existence with different rabbis debating some of the biblical issues in great detail.

The Jewish religion is not very authoritarian, and we can even debate with God, as Tevye does in the musical drama, *Fiddler on the Roof,* imagining in song what it would be like to be a wealthy man. Seeing both sides of issues and disputation came naturally to me. I have published numerous times in journals such as *Psychological Inquiry,* in which a number of colleagues give critiques of what is said, and the author, in this case I, responds to their critiques (see, e.g., Lazarus, 1990, 1993, 1995).

Anyway, when I lecture I often state a position then criticize it, extending the line of thought to the implications of the position for other issues and, in doing so, I sometimes digress extensively. This kind of lecturing can easily get confusing, and is not liked by the student who wants mainly to get the material into his notes for the purpose of studying for exams. But it is appreciated by many students, especially those with lively minds and a genuine interest in the subject matter. The field of education has not been much interested in the match between the cognitive style of the learner and the teacher, but it seems to me to be an interesting problem.

The pressures of academic life can be intense and endless. My sense is that these pressures have gotten worse over the last few decades of academic life. To survive academically, it is necessary to be very hardnosed about saying no, which includes not getting caught up in too many writing opportunities, so that everything needs to be done hastily and at a high cost to quality. There is a great amount of moralizing in university life about all this, and hypocrisy too. Constant vigilance is needed to avoid being swamped. One must set priorities and stick to them as much as possible. I have found this the most demanding requirement of an occupation with great autonomy, which is very open-ended and ill defined. And, surprisingly, knowing when and how to say no remains the most important consideration for my retirement years too.

It is this autonomy, however, that provides the unique challenges and opportunities for creativity in academic life and makes it possible for one's work to bear one's own distinctive stamp. Professors at distinguished universities are apt to be intellectual entrepreneurs. As I said in chapter 1, a professor professes (the Latin word "docere" for doctor actually means to teach) rather than merely being only a borrower of the work of others. I have never regretted my choice of occupation, and despite plenty of hassles, conflict, and disappointment, I am still unable to imagine another way of life that would be more to my liking.

TEACHING BY WRITING TEXTBOOKS

While I am on undergraduate teaching, this is a good moment to speak of textbooks I have written. I have already mentioned the book I wrote with Shaffer at Johns Hopkins which, given my age and limited academic experience, could be considered an exercise in chutzpah (Shaffer & Lazarus, 1952). I initiated the project wrote significantly more than he, so I assumed I would be the first author. But Shaffer insisted he should be first because he was very senior to me. I protested mildly, and he suggested that when I eventually became senior, I would also have that privilege. All I could do was make the best of it, and learn to discuss such touchy subjects before embarking on collaboration. Later on, I never pulled rank with anyone else, but I tried accurately to reflect what was done by each contributor, and give younger people a chance to become visible by being first author.

The truth is that I asked him to join me long after I had done most of my chapters because I felt a bit uncertain about whether I could handle the therapy chapters about which Shaffer knew much more than I. It was a foolish mistake—I didn't need a collaborator—and I never made that mistake again. The book did okay, but never became *the* basic text for clinical psychology. Unlike other subfields in psychology, clinical training never depended much on textbooks for the educational program.

I published a text on adjustment that did quite well (Lazarus, 1961). It was not a potboiler, or a touchy-feely book, which was characteristic of most of its competitors, but a serious effort to treat the subject matter of adjustment as academically substantial. The substance of the field is largely about personality dynamics and it draws heavily on the psychology of stress and coping. I later wrote an extensive revision (Lazarus, 1969) in the second edition, and a third edition followed in 1976 (Lazarus, 1976), which outdid earlier versions and is still in print today.

In 1963, I began an unusual publishing venture with a different publisher, Prentice-Hall, which consisted of a series of 14 brief (about 125 pages) paperback books designed to teach each of the subfields of psychology. I was the editor of the series and wrote one of the books. The idea was that these small paperbacks could be used as supplements in courses, or combined to comprise the textbook of the course. Each was written by a leading authority in his or her subfield of psychology.

The authors and fields of what was called *The Foundations of Modern Psychology* included Jack Bardon and Virginia Bennett (school psychology), John Carroll (language and thought), Sheldon Cashdan (abnormal), Julian Hochberg (perception), Ray Hyman (the nature of psychological inquiry), William and Wallace Lambert (social), myself (personality and adjustment), Sarnoff Mednick (learning), Conrad Mueller (sensory), Edward Murray (motivation and emotion), Paul Mussen (developmental), Julian Rotter (clinical), John Shaffer (humanistic), Edgar Schein (organizational psychology), Philip Teitelbaum (physiological), and Leona Tyler (tests and measurements).

Editing a series with a number of temperamental authors is not the most trouble-free undertaking. You must choose authors who will do an effective job in the time allotted, and who will have some cachet with instructors who might adopt the volume. Most of those I chose were an editor's delight, some requiring almost no editing or second-guessing about coverage or approach. In one case, when I would inquire how he was doing, and when a draft would be available, the designated author kept saying he was making good progress and would have a manuscript soon. As deadlines came and went, the story was the same, and I didn't see any copy. Finally, after consulting with the publisher, and having the strong impression he had not written anything, I voided the contract and sought another author. An editor's lot is (sometimes) not a happy one.

The series was wildly successful, with many of the books going into second and third editions in which the length was considerably expanded. Some of the books still sell today, the outstanding example of which is organizational psychology by Schein. The series was eventually translated into 14 languages, though I can't remember all of them. At the very least they included Danish, Dutch, Finish, Hebrew, Japanese, Norwegian, Polish, Portuguese, Spanish, and Swedish.

An unsuccessful attempt in 1974 to change the way introductory psychology is taught and the books used to do so is one of my most interesting textbook ventures. It was entitled *The Riddle of Man* (Lazarus, 1974). Even today, introductory psychology is a great hodgepodge of seemingly unrelated topics, with a focus on research and so-called facts, without any coherent or comprehensive way to think about mind and behavior.

My book went about presenting the subject in a way quite different from the usual pattern. Instead of making psychology the figure, with applications to human problems as the background, it centered on classic human problems, with psychology taught as the background because it offered some of the answers. The problems included the environment—for example, the crisis of overpopulation in the world; the psychology of aggression and violence; prejudice; the problem of adaptation and its failures (e.g., emotional dysfunction and mental illness), psychotherapy as a way of dealing with adaptational failures; the quest of the good life, which has to do with mental health, physical well-being, and utopian fantasies.

The book achieved some critical praise and sold modestly, but was essentially a failure. The publisher believed in the idea, and did the best job possible, turning out a handsomely illustrated volume. An editor worked hard to help make things lively and find good illustrations. But it didn't work well enough to justify the effort. I believe one reason for the failure was that most teachers of introductory psychology were conservative, experimental psychologists, who were only marginally sympathetic with a radical teaching outlook. Even if they were sympathetic, instead of assigning it, they constructed some of their lectures from it, using the traditional type of book for the course text.

I suppose it was a fantasy to think that this kind of approach would attain enough adherents to make for substantial sales. Psychology has always been a fractionated discipline, without a coherent philosophy and system of thought, and it follows the fashion of the times. To this day I remain proud of this venture, convinced that I wrote an interesting book that deserved more than cursory attention. If I pick it up and read parts of it today, I still believe I gave a good account of human problems and the psychological principles that lie behind them. Few today have ever seen the book.

Given the expansion of interest in stress and coping, in 1977 Alan Monat and I edited a successful reader in this field (Monat & Lazarus, 1977), which has gone into second and third editions. Bernice and I also published a lay-oriented book on the emotions (Lazarus & Lazarus, 1994), which had a good sale in trade outlets and is now being used in undergraduate course in many colleges and universities. This doesn't exhaust my textbook writing, which I consider part of my teaching life, since what I wrote is read by many more students than I can reach in the college classroom.

FAMILY LIFE

Inasmuch as this is, in large measure, an intellectual autobiography, I have not said very much about my family life, fearing it might be boring and self-indulgent. To some, a family narrative is not important or interesting, whereas to others it is of central importance for obtaining an understanding of a life. My family has been of major importance to me, though I have not been the most dedicated father, certainly not as much as my son and my son-in-law have been to their children, which I think reflects the social attitudes of our respective times. Fortunately, I have escaped the most serious family crises, and we have not had tragedies, such as those that befall so many others.

You already know the way Bernice and I met and married. Although I am reluctant to enthuse about such matters because it can be seen as self-serving, our relationship has been too good to ignore. At the century's end in 2000, we will have been married 55 years. Considering the widespread rate of divorce, we have been very lucky, with each of us giving love and support to the other, and being compatible in a variety of ways, including physically and intellectually. We still spend a great deal of time together, work together, and enjoy being with each other. What more could one ask of a marital relationship. Our photograph albums offer a rich panorama of shared experiences, and I'm embarrassed to say, the photos make it look like we have been on a perpetual vacation.

Allow me also say something about my two children. Though very different in personality, outlook, and life style, David and Nancy get along very well, not just in a pro-forma sense, but they seek each other out for enjoyment. I believe they like each other. This is a great source of satisfaction for any parent. Married with two children each, by the year 2000, David and Mary will have been together for 28 years, Nancy and Rick for 27. Both families live only 20 minutes drive from us.

David's wife, Mary Lazarus (maiden name Panacci), was raised as a Catholic from Italian and Episcopal parents, with four siblings and their families living in the Bay Area. In the year 2000, David's daughter Jessica will be 24, and his son Adam 21; Nancy's daughter Maiya McKenzie Holliday will be 18, and Ava Rose Holliday, 15. Like their parents, our four grandchildren enjoy being with each other despite the large age differences.

David is a Field Marketing Manager with a company called *Steam On Wheels,* which does industrial surface cleaning. The company uses high-pressure steam and chemical methods to clean city buildings, mostly in northern California, using a fleet of trucks and mobile aerial booms. Mary teaches third grade in a local public school, having obtained her credentials after she was wed and her children were born.

Nancy obtained her Bachelor of Arts degree at the University of California at Berkeley, and a master's degree in exercise physiology, a field in which she worked for a time. She now runs her own business, *Design Mesh,* in which she creates design plans and does model houses for builders in the Bay Area. When they married, Rick Holliday was also a student at Berkeley where he obtained his master's degree in city planning and environmental design. Nancy's marriage is also religiously mixed, Rick being an Episcopalian.

Rick later became a well-known, innovative developer, distinguished for his skill in combining public and private funding for modest-cost housing projects. He pioneered the process of renovating older buildings for live-and-work housing complexes in the South of Market Street (SOMA) section of San Francisco, similar to what was done in the gentrification programs of rundown neighborhoods in Manhattan (SOHO), New York City. Early on, Nancy worked with Rick on his housing-unit designs before she developed the work into her own independent design business. I am proud to say the artwork of the cover of this book is hers as her signature attests.

Like many families today, David and Nancy and their spouses work hard meeting the requirements of their jobs and at the same time remain effective and supportive parents. All four wanted to have time to raise their children with care and attention while not foreclosing their working life.

You might wonder about the religiously mixed pattern of both my children. Neither Bernice's parents nor mine were ever really religious Jews. You might remember too that my mother was a Christian Science Practitioner, which helped to complicate my religious identity.

We sent our children regularly to Sunday School at the local temple in the city of Lafayette in hopes they would learn something of the Jewish outlook and ways. We also had Passover parties (as distinguished from a formal Passover Seder, which is a religious as well as educational exercise) at which the meaning of the holiday was discussed. But we ourselves never go to temple or synagogue, even during the High Holy days when secular Jews often crowd the pews, which are normally pretty empty on Friday-night or Saturday-morning services. Consider also the comparable phenomenon of "Christmas Christians," who are never in church except during the Christmas holiday, and pose a problem for the ministers because they overload the available space at the expense of regular churchgoers.

We have always felt a strong commitment to our Jewish heritage without religion being its basis, a state of mind that is quite common among Jews, even—or perhaps I should say, especially—in Israel, but that is hardly different from the way most nonpracticing Christians, Moslems, and so forth, are.

Given what I have just said, you might ask how we felt and what we did when first David, then Nancy, chose religiously mixed marriages, David when he was 21 and Nancy when she was 20. I can't deny that we would have preferred them to marry within the faith, so to speak, though clearly faith is the wrong word. Given our lack of religious involvement, it is hard to justify such a preference. Our instincts in the matter had to do with protecting the kids, and I suppose ourselves too, from what are often contentious social and life-style religious distinctions.

As members of a despised religious minority, we had the impression that life is made unnecessarily complex and difficult with the crossing of religious ties. It has always been my conviction that religions contribute to human hatreds by the conviction, especially on the part of dedicated zealots, that they have the only valid way of thinking about life and how to live it.

The harm is compounded by those, and there are many, who believe that anyone outside the true faith cannot attain heaven or the comfort of God, or live a highly moral life, and are doomed to the eternal fires of hell. I don't believe in a heaven or hell, but this is one of the most offensive positions that can be taken about other people who have different views.

The Catholic religion, for example, is severely strained these days by conflict over this issue. Rome has disciplined and even ex-communicated a number of priests who reject Rome's standard conservative position on many issues. Such in-group, out-group thinking has long sustained prejudice and discrimination, and much worse over human history. And now the Baptists are trying to proselytize Jews with the insensitive and disingenuous message that they are only interested in saving our souls. What chutzpah!

But when one is not truly religious, as in our case, the moral and logical grounds for objecting to mixed marriages in one's children are thoroughly undermined. Only those who are themselves dedicated religionists and set an example of faithfulness, have the right to push their children to "keep the faith." Only if our children were to marry a true religious bigot would such a mixture of religions truly carry a major threat.

I note too that, although in the Eastern and Midwestern part of the United States Jews tend to be ghettoized—that is, they live in almost completely Jewish communities apart from other groups—in California, and the West in general, they are scattered throughout the community. Being such a small minority in a largely Christian world, I sympathize with Jewish children who feel they have a very restricted choice of a spouse, which is at least one reason why perhaps 50% of Jews today intermarry. (The exact figure is contested.)

When David and Mary decided to marry, it soon became apparent that they were fully cognizant of the problem and determined to resist any effort by either set of parents to control what they did. It also quickly became evident that Mary's parents would not challenge the children's autonomy by insisting on religious domination. A warm and accepting relationship between our two families developed. Year after year we would celebrate our Jewish holidays, such as Passover, by having the Panaccis to our secular version of the holiday—that is, a Passover party not a religious Seder—and they would have us to their Christmas-day family dinners. David and Mary's children—that is, our grandchildren—have been brought up in an easy-going fashion to recognize both religious identities, and they will do as they wish as adults and with their own children.

Nancy and Rick knew each other through the high-school years. Rick's father is a retired Professor of Medicine at the University of California in San Francisco, having specialized in pediatrics. At 20 the two kids were deeply enmeshed in their relationship. We knew that the evidence on early marriages was not encouraging; young people continue to change over the next years, often growing in different directions. It is risky to marry too early. What should be done?

We were influenced partly by the fact that we liked Rick, and thought he was a decent and sound young man, and partly by the fact that Nancy was a strong-minded young woman who might well do what she wanted anyway. Three outcomes of their relationship seemed possible: First, if we objected to the relationship, we might succeed only in encouraging a defensive counterreaction. Second, they might break up, which might not be the best answer. Third, they might get married, and our only real objection to this was that they might be too young to make it work.

Imagine our surprise when 1 day, at our poolside, Rick literally asked my permission for them to marry and gave a graceful and thoughtful justification of the decision. This was so out of character for children of the 1960s that it was almost camp. However, the issue had to be confronted seriously, and seeking permission was an obvious attempt to make allies of us, hardly a foolish ploy. Caught by surprise, what could I do but agree after consulting with Bernice? The decision obviously was a good one. Our relationship with Rick's parents and family has been cordial, but not as close as it has been with the Panaccis.

The effects of the decision to intermarry by many modern Jews living in the diaspora (not having a separate country, such as Israel) are difficult to evaluate. It can be looked at in two quite distinctive ways—namely, psychologically, and with respect to the survival of Jewish culture.

Psychologically speaking, it seemed to have worked out well for our children, but it is too early to know about this for our grandchildren. I believe adults should choose for themselves, and one may do this at any time in life. For those concerned about the survival of Judaism, which rabbis are wont to be, the results are obscure. On the one hand, intermarriage could expand the numbers of people with Jewish sensibilities, but the religious commitment and deep knowledge of the cultural values may well be diluted. I am not familiar with any actual studies on this.

All my life I have heard rabbis offer dour predictions about the end of Jewry if we assimilated and didn't commit ourselves to conservative religious tenets. It is almost as though they believe persecution is a good thing, as it kept Jews together as believers, at least until the Holocaust when many began to doubt what they had been taught about good and evil, and about an omnipotent and benevolent God.

I believe that in this view rabbis are self-serving and wrong. What drives secular Jews away from their identity is the very insistence that they are not Jews if they do not adopt a strict religious orthodoxy. At this writing, a battle is going on about who should be considered a Jew. In Israel, Orthodox rabbis control this definition. Instead of seeking to hold Jews together on the basis of a common history and outlook, they risk driving secular Jews, who are the overwhelming majority, away from the fold, which will result in the end of Jewry far sooner than religious irreverence or disinterest.

I also believe that Pope Paul in Rome does much to drive Catholics away from their religion by a disproportionate focus, spawned in the Middle Ages by Augustine, who was probably a sexual neurotic, on the details of what happens in the bedroom. Among other things, there is the catch-22 of making abortion a sin but refusing to sanction birth control, and the doctrine that women cannot be priests. Jews, Catholics, and Moslems need to move away from some of their medieval customs, and to recognize that these customs are not necessarily sanctioned by God, but by the people who claim to represent God.

Given my view of the damaging role of religion on social suspicions and hatreds, I'm not at all sure that the loosening of religious ties is such a bad thing. Opinions undoubtedly vary depending on one's own personal view of religion, its place in one's life, and in the society. But if the preservation of world Jewry is of major concern, then the solution is to strengthen the ties among Jews, not prosetylizing about who are the true members of the faith. We will survive better if we try to be inclusive rather than exclusive, and if we pull together and worry less about religious practices.

Returning to our family, I am tempted to say that parents like to take credit for the good things that happen to their offspring, and to evade responsibility for the bad. I know better than to attach myself to either of these positions. At the very least, however, we seem to have been lucky. We think our children are fine people, regardless of the positions they take on all sorts of things, which is, after all, their business.

TROUBLES WITH THE UNIVERSITY

By all academic criteria, the University of California, and especially the Berkeley campus, is, without argument, one of the great institutions of learning and research scholarship in the world. Yet such an institution is capable of petty, destructive, and dishonest policies toward the very people on whom this greatness depends, its distinguished faculty.

I shall discuss two instances that should be embarrassing to Berkeley, among many others that are not as personally compelling. The first deals with an altercation over the privilege of members of the Berkeley faculty to apply for federally supported research scientist awards. The second concerns the effort that began in 1991 to push early retirement.

THE RESEARCH SCIENTIST AWARDS DEBACLE

As I tell the story, which is known to many of my immediate colleagues and a few professional associates outside of the University of California at Berkeley, I must make an effort to avoid reactivating the resentment I originally felt, though I'm not sure I can avoid this. I tell it in part because many people think I have had a storybook career, everything positive, lacking in major frustration and disappointment. Surface and substance are often quite different. What happened, however, was one of the major downsides of my career, and I want to portray some of the realities of academic life, rather than sugarcoat it.

One of the major honors that an academic research psychologist can receive is a Research Scientist Award (RSA) from the National Institute of Mental Health (NIMH). For those unfamiliar with it, allow me to explain. The award provides the university at which the professor is employed with a very ample sum of money each year of the appointment to make it possible to reduce the awardee's teaching load. In addition to the honor, there are a number of very practical advantages of the award for the pursuit of knowledge and fame, which also redounds to the advantage of the institution.

The main advantage is that it frees an enormous amount of time for research, including that needed to compete for research grant funds. The intent, of course, is to aid the most creative and productive research scholars to advance our knowledge about mental health and illness, which would benefit the public good. Such awards also add to the prestige of the individual and institution.

There are also junior awards for beginners, but as the awardee is generally a senior scholar with a higher than average salary—that is, a full professor or top associate—the financial gift to the university is usually enough to hire one or two beginning assistant professors to make up for any loss of teaching. Looked at objectively, there is mostly gain for the institution—namely, at my salary level two teachers instead of one, and the awardee continues to be active in graduate teaching, even more so than before. No wonder most universities regard such awards as a great asset and encourage their faculty to apply for them.

The RSA was originally created for medical schools, but its use was later extended to any type of campus. All the campuses of the University of California, both medical and nonmedical, *the one and only exception being Berkeley,* take advantage of this opportunity because they consider it advantageous to the institution. In the early days, some of the awards were even given for one's entire professional life, career awards as they were called, but this was eliminated later with the rule that an awardee must reapply every 5 years to have the appointment renewed.

The initial refusal of Berkeley to allow its faculty to apply for RSAs led some of its top faculty to take academic jobs elsewhere. In the late 1970s, however, the Berkeley campus began to reconsider its position and decided that if a department were willing, this option could be opened to its faculty. As a test case, the Psychology Department ultimately voted two to one in favor, and three faculty members from the department applied, all excellent candidates with a good chance to win the award because of their distinguished reputations and continued leadership in research. The three were Jack Block, Irving Zucker, and myself, all senior professors. We submitted our applications in the fall of 1979 through the Campus Research Office, with the appropriate signatures of approval from the appropriate university official.

After the academic year ended, Bernice and I went to Maui, Hawaii for a vacation. Just before leaving, I learned that the RSA applications had been summarily, and without consultation with us, withdrawn from the NIMH by Provost Robert Middlekauff, who evidently decided belatedly that the policy that had been approved was wrong. And so our applications were never reviewed by the NIMH. I have no idea of what brought him to this position or whom he might have consulted. Later on I could see that most of the top administrators supported him in this negative judgment.

We were notified by a brief note, which stated that the financial arrangements were unsatisfactory to the university, and implied that it was inappropriate for faculty members to evade their teaching obligations by means of such an award. This implication was baldy stated to me orally when I managed to speak to him, and far more insultingly than in his letter. Administrators are always protecting their asses by avoiding tipping their hands too openly on paper. So my documentation, which I kept in my files, leaves out some of the more juicy expressions of the administration's negative and mistrustful attitude toward faculty.

You should also understand that completing an RSA application was itself an enormous task, and if we were not to be evaluated as candidates by NIMH, we never should have spent the many months of intense work to prepare the applications in the first place. We had to summarize all the scholarly research we had already done and specify in detail the program of research we planned to pursue for the next 5 years if we won the award. Such an application was comparable to a modest-sized book, taking up hundreds of pages and requiring a prodigious commitment of time and resources.

It is interesting to contemplate the psychologists who have held RSAs throughout the country at among the most distinguished universities. To name some of the most visible, my partial list includes Robert Ader (Rochester), Jack Barchas (Stanford), William Dement (Stanford), Bruce Dohrenwend (Columbia), Paul Ekman (UCSF), Robert Emde (Colorado), Charles Eriksen (Illinois), Frances Graham (Wisconsin), Myron Hofer (Albert Einstein), Robert Holt (NYU), Norman Garmezy (Minnesota), Mort Lieberman (Chicago, now UCSF), Seymour Levine (Stanford), Lester Luborsky (Penn), Melvin Marx (Missouri), John Mason (Yale), Karl Pribram (Stanford), and George Valliant (Harvard). Six of these were lifetime awards, which are no longer given.

To withdraw the applications summarily on what I believe to be a bureaucratic whim dealt a severe blow to all three of us. Most of what was said and written after this was, in my view, pure double-talk, which always suggested speciously that these awards would harm the university. Middlekauff provoked righteous and extended anger and resentment toward the university administration in three of the Psychology Department's most productive faculty members.

The irony here is that, of the entire period I taught at Berkeley, I failed to obtain large research grants for only six years out of 34, and the cumulated overhead to the campus from them—even allowing for the half that goes to the state treasury—greatly exceeds my cumulated Berkeley salary. I have never forgiven the institution for what was, in addition to folly, essentially a form of administrative arbitrariness, always self-serving but expressed as if it were for the good of the university. So much for the myth of faculty governance and democracy.

One has to speculate what thoughts might have been in the mind of the administrator who belatedly took this course of action. I have often been asked about this, and those who ask assume that we were given credible reasons other than a polite but brusque note. No such thing. Nor did any other administrator. Therefore, those who were not party to the process can only speculate.

In my opinion, aside from the possibility of envy, the basic threat was to lose control over a faculty member by an appointment that would be almost as much regulated by the federal government as by the local administration. To tolerate this loss of control for 1 year was no serious problem; such brief academic leaves are given readily. Just as the policy of Berkeley was at one time against endowed chairs, however, 5 years of support with the opportunity to reapply regularly was another matter. Power over programs and people is undoubtedly one of the primary motivations for becoming an administrator in the first place and, in fact, is one of my reasons for rejecting this kind of role. I don't like exercising power over others, but I am even more resistive to arbitrary power over me.

In any event, the official action of the Berkeley administration succeeded in adding to the already substantial cynicism of working professors about self-serving politicians who run universities and claim, often with a considerable measure of self-deception and arrogance, that the interests of the institution are their only guide. It is clear to me that the Berkeley administration does not really respect its faculty and offers little support for efforts to compete with their counterparts at other institutions.

Other lesser administrators, such as chairpersons and deans, might also have contributed behind the scenes to undermining the RSA program, including members of the Psychology Department who were in a position discretely to stab us in the back. Remember that one third of our departmental colleagues had voted in secret ballot against the privilege of applying. I have no credible evidence of such a base motivation, however, and did see evidence of emphathic efforts to help by the Chairperson.

If I sound paranoid in this, please remember that often a paranoid sentiment is quite realistic rather than screwy, given the hostile and competitive culture in which we live. After all these years, I am pleased to unmask the way things work in places like Berkeley, and I suppose it might have been dangerous to do this when I was still in thrall to the institution.

Why would one's colleagues try to thwart a good deal for a faculty member and the department? The cynical, but not entirely unwarranted answer, given the standard professorial outlook, is that what is good for one faculty members is bad for the rest. The award would provide an advantage to those receiving it, because research productivity and excellence is the coin of the realm of academic advancement.

University life is commonly conceived of as a zero-sum game. As in college grading on the curve, what is good for one is bad for another. If one student gets an A, there is less room for this grade for anyone else. The same competitive principle underlies much of the sense of isolation and distrust in academic life. Like the board rooms of major corporations, the distrust is rarely overt, but operates silently when nasty motives are made less visible by means of superficial civilities. I am not saying that all competition is bad, but much of it is often counterproductive and at any rate, one must come to terms with it if one wishes to be a professor in an institution of high repute, or to get anywhere in our society.

For the first 4 or 5 days in Hawaii, after I learned of the decision, I was relaxed, at least so I thought, as if I had put the RSA debacle behind me. Then suddenly I began waking in the middle of the night and rehearsing unpleasant conversations with Provost Middlekauff and anyone else in the administration I might consult with to overturn the negative decision. The late-night rumination went on throughout the remainder of the vacation. I tried to put what happened out of my mind, to no avail. I had passed the stage of denial-avoidance and reached the stage of intrusive thinking, to draw on Mardi Horowitz's (1976, 1988) well-known analysis of the stages of coping with trauma.

It was the worst time I ever had in Hawaii. I vowed I would never do anything I didn't have to for the Berkeley campus from that day on. I explored opportunities at other universities. When I became an emeritus, I even left my university affiliation off my stationery so the institution would not benefit from my continuing efforts. All this ideation was very foolish for many reasons. The reality was that we couldn't leave Berkeley, because our whole family was here. I also knew that the grass is not always greener in other pastures. And my affiliation was known to most colleagues and students anyway. I was merely flailing about fruitlessly.

In 1981, Professor Glickman, then the Psychology Chairperson, formed a departmental committee to meet and discuss the matter with Dean Keppel. A number of stipulations were made that weakened the RSA privilege, but to which the affected faculty members agreed. For example, we agreed to make the one course we would teach our primary undergraduate lecture course in alternative years. We would be expected to serve on departmental search committees for new faculty, and participate in departmental meetings about curriculum. The department would appoint replacement faculty on a yearly basis. It was all petty and in my eyes adds to the further shame of the university. This too was all a monumental waste of time and negative emotion. The administration would not budge from its negative stance.

The distress of the three applicants continued long after the initial action by the provost, in fact, for years. Speaking for myself, until 1986 I was still trying to overturn the decision. I wrote letters to a later provost, Leonard Kuhi; the Dean of the Graduate Division; Joseph Cerny; Edwin M. Epstein, the Chair of the Committee On Priviledge and Tenure; and even to the Chairperson of the Board of Regents, Vilma S. Martinez, to no avail.

Professor Epstein of the Committee on Priviledge and Tenure finally wrote after much delay that the committee believed the university had the legal right to make this decision, even if it might be unwise. In some cases, I never received an answer. It was most insulting. Recently, along with the rest of my papers, I sent this voluminous correspondence, which I think is instructive about academic life, to The Archives of the History of American Psychology at Akron University in Ohio.

Nevertheless, the complicated truth is that Berkeley *is* a remarkable institution in very important ways, mostly because of its outstanding faculty—not because but *in spite of* its hostile administration, which, as is the case at most universities, consists of professional politicians who seem to want to run things. Most of them went into the administration to advance themselves, often when they had lost the drive and credibility to make distinctive contributions to their own field. In effect, I am accusing them of too often being either failed academic scholars or worn out ones who are seeking another role and who, despite their protestations, have little intrinsic interest in improving the institution.

Berkeley could be far more remarkable than it is, but then I suppose, given the realities of such institutions, we are talking about utopia. Oddly enough, I don't regret coming here—I knew what I was getting into—but I have for some time recognized that I paid a steep personal price.

A RETIREMENT OFFER I COULDN'T REFUSE

In 1991 the scanty funding of the university by the state of California, and its meager budget for higher education, which had once been the envy of the country and the world, came to a head, and someone had the "bright" idea that the retirement fund had more money than was needed. Therefore, if the older faculty members, who were also among the highest paid, could be induced to retire, the budget pressures on the university and the state would be reduced. Her retirement budget was plush.

To encourage people who are doing their work well to leave because they have at long last earned top salaries—that is, simply to save money, not because they are less productive than might be wished—is offensive and short-sighted. There is substantial doubt that this legerdemain really helps the state or the university financially, given the costs, many of them hidden. But no matter, it was done, as it has been elsewhere too, a monument to bureaucratic folly.

The details here are not particularly important. One need only understand that a plan was worked out to bribe faculty and nonacademic staff to accept early retirement with an attractive financial package. The main qualifications had to do with one's age and number of years service. In addition to a cash bonus for leaving, each retiree would be granted 5 years of extra service, thereby increasing retirement pay if it weren't already at maximum.

It was emphasized by the administration that these benefits were part of a *"one time only" offer.* I emphasize this phrase because of what happened in the next several years. We had to sign papers in the spring indicating our willingness to leave at the end of the 1991 academic year. In other words, we thought we had signed a binding contract, that this would be our only opportunity to obtain an attractive retirement package.

I was to turn 70 in March of 1992. At that time, it was presumably necessary to retire because of a policy exempting universities from antiageist rules forcing older people to retire against their wills. I did not want to retire just yet, and believed that retirement at 70 could not really be enforced, though it might lead to a lengthy and personally counterproductive legal battle.

Along with many others in my circumstances, however, an offer had been made that I couldn't refuse. If I stayed on, it would take 5 more years to equal the retirement pay that the bonus of service credit would now produce. If I stayed 1 more year, even with a few thousand dollars of salary added by an additional advance in rank I had earned, then retired, I would have gained 1 year but lost 4 in service credits. It was a catch-22 situation. Unless you believed you would live vigorously forever, you had to be out of your mind to stay at the job regardless of how dedicated you were.

The result of this program was the sudden retirement of large numbers of senior faculty, many of them among the most productive in the institution. Five retired from psychology that year, a department of 43 full-time faculty. It was, I believe, a phoney deal for the people of the state, a form of financial legerdemain that would be fiscally counterproductive in the long run.

Anyway, morale suffered, and work loads increased, because there was a moratorium on hiring, so those who left were not replaced. But the numbers of students kept increasing, and over the next years, tuition and fees kept increasing too, though faculty salary levels did not. Merit increases were also unfairly suspended for one cohort of faculty, leading to a court action that the university lost.

As if there were no financial doldrums, the public was regaled with newspaper accounts of unconscionable increases for high-placed administrators, such as university presidents, chancellors, vice-chancellors, the university president, as well as outrageous golden parachutes for those who resigned. These have been a constant embarrassment to the claim that the state and the university were responding to a financial emergency with these early retirement machinations.

The duplicity of the University became evident when 2 years later, it was decided to repeat the "one-time only" inducement to retire. And, believe it or not, a third "one-time only" early retirement program followed in 1994–1995, when four members of the Psychology Department resigned, making nine in all, leaving a remainder of 34. In effect, our signed contract had been entirely one-sided, with the university failing to live up to its part. Roughly one quarter of the senior faculty of the great University of California—one out of four—left in consequence of this retirement policy, and finally 6 years later a slow hiring of replacements has been instituted.

What can one say, but to express disappointment with the governance of a great institution of learning, which is not capable of setting an example of probity and wisdom for the rest of our society, especially our children, but plays political games with the lives of its personnel and students. It may be that the initial offering was sincere in the statement that it would be a one-time only arrangement. But there was no excuse for breaking this pact only 2 years later, and then again for a third time. The sky wouldn't have fallen had the powers that be inhibited the impulse to again push more senior faculty out the door.

And in the spring of 1997, we learned what many of us had long suspected, that nine students had been admitted to Berkeley who would not normally have been as a result of the pressure from wealthy donors to the campus (*San Francisco Chronicle,* Friday, May 16, p. 1 and A 17). What is outrageous about this is that Berkeley is a public institution; moreover, a committee of the Regents of the University killed a proposal that would have said that "fund-raising objectives may play no role in determining whether an applicant is admitted." Imagine that! According to the *Chronicle* article, eight regents refused to consider it, a policy also favored by the nine campus chancellors.

Look how corruption eats away at our democracy and honor, when elected regents who govern the university and its top administrators fail to see that allowing people to buy their way into the university is a breech of faith and morality. They have adopted the sleaziest mores of our society—admittedly, business as usual—and what is even more remarkable, they did so without showing any evidence of recognizing how dishonorable their actions were.

Lest the reader think I am making too much out of too little—after all, so what else is new these days?—let me quote from an article by Jeff Stryker (1996) in the *New York Times,* December 29 (p. E10), entitled "Lies, Justice, the "American Way." It addresses the issue of governmental hypocrisy and lying at a time when the public has become cynical about politics:

> Many philosophical and religious traditions condemn all lies and deceit. Perhaps the best-known recent exposition of this sentiment is "Lying: Moral Choice in Public and Private Life" (Vintage Books, 1989) by Sissela Bok, the philosopher. After exploring the many ways people deceive one another and themselves—from puffery in letters of recommendation to placebos to unmarked police cars—she decides lies are seldom worth the social cost. As lies spread, she writes, "Trust is damaged." She describes trust as a "social good to be protected just as much as the air we breathe or the water we drink."

And a little later in the same article, Stryker continues:

> Lying, for all its potential social value, is almost never called by its real name. Public officials rarely admit, "I lied," even if they believe in the cause they lied for. Instead euphemisms bloom. The passive tense is used to distance the liar from the lie ('mistakes were made'). Broken promises are not lies but unfulfilled hopes. Even though Oliver L. North has been convicted of lying to Congress during the Iran-contra hearings, he prefers to say that

Congress was misled. When Newt Gingrich, the House Speaker, was confronted last week with having lied to the House Ethics Committee about whether he used taxpayer money to set up a college course he taught, he said he had submitted "inaccurate, incomplete and unreliable" information.

To some it may seem terribly naive not to see that the kind of corruption I am offended by is a daily occurrence in our society, and far worse in much of the rest of the world. But I know this only too well. There may also be generational differences in the way I am reacting compared, say, with today's young people. I don't know about that, though I suspect many long for a society with better standards. Lewis H. Lapham (August,1997), Editor of Harpers magazine, has recently documented the low status of ethical concern in our society, dominated by the marketplace, suggesting that we are in limbo between one set of values and whatever set is coming to replace it. He quotes Will and Ariel Durant, who said "Caught in the relaxing interval between one moral code and the next, an unmoored generation surrenders itself to luxury, corruption, and a restless disorder of family and morals." (p. 35).

Many my age remember fondly some of the Frank Capra movies, such as *Meet John Doe, Mr. Smith goes to Washington,* and *It's a Wonderful Life,* whose stories express disdain for political and social corruption and present an idealist hero—acted by Jimmy Stewart or Gary Cooper—who somehow manages to help purify everything.

Simplistic? Yes. Unrealistic. Yes. But in an ever-acquisitive value system, which justifies greed as in our best societal interests, and where personal integrity is difficult to find, what do we have instead today to offer those of us who wish for social decency, justice, and harmony if we cannot express our best aspirations, as these movies did for the children of the Great Depression? Is idealism groundless? Is it naive? Should it be denigrated as self-righteous or viewed as camp? I hope not.

Ironically, I personally gained greatly from what happened. It was a good financial deal for me, though I believe short-sighted for the university and the state. Retiring when I did was a boon to my health and well-being, and has increased my opportunities to think, write about my ideas, and explore difficult issues with colleagues and students. My regret is only for the loss to education and the potential damage to a worthy institution.

REFERENCES

Bok, S. (1989). *Lying: moral choice in public and private life.* New York: Vintage Books.

Horowitz, M. J. (1976). *Stress response syndromes.* New York: Jason Aronson.

Horowitz, M. J. (1988). *Introduction to psychodynamics.* New York: Basic Books.

Lapham, L. H. (Essay, August, 1997). In the garden of tabloid delight: notes on sex, Americans, scandal, and morality. (pp. 35–43). New York: *Harpers Magazine.*

Lazarus, R. S. (1961). *Adjustment and personality.* New York: McGraw-Hill.

Lazarus, R. S. (1969). *Patterns of adjustment and human effectiveness* (2nd edition). New York: McGraw-Hill.

Lazarus, R. S. (1976). *Patterns of adjustment* (3rd edition). New York: McGraw-Hill.

Lazarus, R. S. (1974). *The Riddle of Man.* Englewood Cliffs, NJ: Prentice-Hall.

Lazarus, R. S. (1990). Theory-based stress measurement with Authors response to commentators. *Psychological Inquiry, 1,* 3–51.

Lazarus, R. S. (1993). Book review essays about Emotion and Adaptation by R. A. Shweder; T. Trabasso and N. Stein; and J. Panksepp; and Author's response. *Psychological Inquiry, 4,* 322–342.

Lazarus, R. S. (1995). Vexing research problems inherent in cognitive-mediational theories of emotion, and some solutions, with Author's response to commentators. *Psychological Inquiry, 6,* 183–265.

Lazarus, R. S., & Folkman, S. (1984). *Stress, appraisal, and coping.* New York: Springer.

Lazarus, R. S., & Lazarus, B. N. (1994). *Passion and reason: Making sense of our emotions.* New York: Oxford University Press.

Monat, A., & Lazarus, R. S. (1977). *Stress and coping: An anthology.* New York: Columbia University Press. (The second edition was in 1885, the third edition in 1991.)

Shaffer, G. W., & Lazarus, R. S. (1952). *Fundamental concepts in clinical psychology.* New York: McGraw-Hill.

Stryker, J. (1996). Lies, Justice, the "American Way." *New York Times,* Dec. 29, 1996.

CHAPTER TWELVE

Retirement Years: Musings About Life and Death

T his chapter is about arriving at that time of life when one knows life is almost over. Most people get there, but for the major portion of their lives they are not yet fully able to appreciate what this means.

Allow me to begin with mention of Bernice and my 50th wedding anniversary on September 2, 1995, which was celebrated at a party given by our family in the home of our Daughter, Nancy and her husband Rick in Orinda, California. Three photos are shown in Figure 12.1. One was taken at the anniversary party, a second on a cruise ship that took us through the Panama Canal, and a third is a recent semi-formal portrait of our nuclear family, taken in August 1997. You can see what we all look like at this stage of our lives, which is a fitting accompaniment to this last chapter of my autobiography.

Not everyone reflects on the significance of death, but as an introspective man I occasionally do. This chapter, in addition to examining my life in retirement, discusses my thoughts about living and dying. I do so partly for the benefit of readers who might be interested in my musings, and partly to put my views into bold relief for myself as I contemplate the closing of my autobiography, and of the book of my life too. Because I feel in command of my mind, and am still energetically engaged in life and professional work, it is truly the best time publicly to reflect on such matters.

I am keenly aware that many once-vigorous people experience a catastrophic loss of resources and increasing infirmity as they approach their 80's. These losses can lead to depression, perhaps especially in those who have been productive and sanguine most of their lives (Shneidman, 1989). Thus far, my losses seem modest, though I have

279

A. Celebrating 50 years together.

B. On a cruise through the Panama Canal

C. Top row: Mary, David, Jessica, Adam, Nancy, Rick
Bottom row: Maiya, Bernice, Dick, Ava Rose

FIGURE 12.1   Bernice, I, and our nuclear family as of August 1997.

the usual problems of aging, including the struggle to retrieve words and ideas, which is so common at this stage of life. I am not certain how I will cope with the inevitable final chapter of my life when the time comes, but I hope with wisdom and fortitude.

I first take up a few crucial issues of aging, such as health, the social life, and interests that sustain me. Then I turn to existential issues, and end with an off-beat vision for psychology in the future.

HEALTH

My elderly comrades and I recognize that the most important asset in our lives now is good health, and when we make a toast, it is often to health and life (*L'chaim* among Jews). The reader already knows enough about my state of mind and morale, so I will say nothing further about my emotional health, which has always been reasonably sound. I should also resist making a joke here about the wisdom of judging one's own mental health.

I come from long-lived parents, my father having died of prostate cancer at 85 and my mother of leukemia at 87. Their longevity bodes well for me, at least statistically. But I am not a stranger to serious illness, as the reader knows. The most serious have included the bout with scarlet fever when there were no antibiotics (chapter 1), which kept me out of gradeschool for 6 months, my back injury in the army (chapter 2), the insulin-secreting tumor of the eyelet cells of my pancreas (chapter 6), recent arthroscopic knee surgery (I will need a new knee fairly soon), and the recent prostate cancer in 1995 (chapter 10), the latter four ailments having been treated successfully by surgery.

In 1994, I had a salivary gland removed from my neck because of a suspicious growth that could not readily be studied by a biopsy, but it proved to be benign. In 1997, I had a growth removed from my bladder, a first-stage cancer which is not especially dangerous if not allowed to grow to third or fourth stage. Because there is a good chance it will grow back, it must be reexamined every three months, but if diligently monitored, is not life threatening. I note these medical efforts to keep me alive because they are a common, natural feature of elderly life, and most of my contemporaries, if they have lived this long or longer, commonly experience these sorts of medical problems, or worse.

Modern medicine deals more effectively with acute than with chronic ailments. Some months after my prostate surgery, I developed symptoms of cardiac arrhythmia. The disorder is referred to in cardiology by the terrible sounding name "sick sinus syndrome, with an AV block." It is possible (my cardiologist thinks it likely) that at some point in the future I will need a pacemaker and medication to avoid a more serious condition that would be life-threatening.

I show no signs of coronary artery blockage, have no chest pain, generally feel well, have considerable stamina and the capacity to handle stress, and I can outdo most people my age. Despite the arrhrythmia, I can climb the steep hill where I live faster and with less strain on my breathing than most of the physicians I go to for medical care and advice, and my hunch is that I will outlive them. Only a problem knee holds me back from walking rapidly, or being as fluid at table tennis as I would like, but I have been among the top players (maybe number three in rank) in the Rossmoor Table Tennis club.

I think I should stay away from physicians, many of whom seem keen to find something to treat and uniformly manage to make me feel less than healthy. One of my biggest complaints about growing old is the amount of time that must be spent ministering to my body, waiting in and being treated in doctor's and dentist's offices, skin doctors who burn off keratoses from sun damage, and regular diagnostic tests, such as electrocardiograms, colonoscopies, blood assays, and other procedures, all of which are intended to spot serious ailments that can be treated before they do me in. I have other, better things to do, but prudence and fear keep me checking out my health regularly.

HOME, FRIENDS, AND NEIGHBORS

We lived in Lafayette, California in a lovely but unpretentious home for 32 years where we raised our two children. In April 1989, we moved to Rossmoor in the city of Walnut Creek, which is a well-managed city a bit east of Lafayette. Rossmoor is considered to be one of the better adult communities in the country. Never using a euphemism where a harsh reality is more accurate, Bernice and I jokingly refer to it as the old-age home. It is restricted to people over 55 years of age, but the average age of the residents is 77, placing Bernice and me close to it. There are also 900 people or so over 90, many more women than men.

Rossmoor is a gated community and seems quite secure. For many it is a haven away from the turbulence of modern urban life. It is nestled in a lovely coastal valley, due east of San Francisco, Oakland, and Berkeley. We own a nearly 1,700 square foot condominium near the top of a modest-sized coast range hill, which overlooks the valley and most of Rossmoor. Facing east, we have a magnificent view of Mount Diablo, the tallest mountain in the immediate vicinity, about 3,700 feet.

At one time I assumed we would remain in our Lafayette home until we died. One reason we moved to Rossmoor is that taking care of the pool and grounds resulted in recurrent attacks of sciatica as residuals of my Army surgery. At Rossmoor, we no longer need to do heavy labor, which is a major advantage of our current life style.

We have never regretted our decision to come here. It is a pleasant place that meets most of our needs. If anything our social life is a bit too full, with friendly neighbors with whom we chat occasionally, have cocktails and snacks, go together to theater locally and in the city with a group by a bus that picks us up at Rossmoor and brings us back in the evening, or we play bridge and table tennis. Once a week I have lunch locally with two or three of my table tennis partners after a competitive workout of an hour or so.

My three main complaints about Rossmoor describe mainly modest sources of frustration. One is that most of our neighbors are aging, and some have had serious heart attacks, whereas others are being treated for inoperable cancers, so illness and death are never far away. When we hear a siren, we know it is the "Rossmoor bus," our euphemism for an ambulance or fire truck with a respirator for someone having a medical crisis.

As I write this, our next door neighbor's wife has suffered her third heart attack, and there is uncertainty about her future. Another next door neighbor has recently died of cancer after a shockingly brief illness. Fortunately, most of us avoid talking too much about our ailments, and I have vowed not to attend funerals lest I spend too much of my time being reminded of our closeness to death. This is not an unusual way of coping here.

A second complaint flows from the first, which is that most social relationships are superficial; and although many residents are remarkably active for their ages, their physical and social resources are also limited. Rossmoor mostly closes down by 9 o'clock in the evening, and there is a kind of unspoken understanding that parties will end by 8:00 or 8:30, except on rare occasions, or a regular evening of bridge.

A third complaint is that traffic is heavy, as it is all over the Bay Area, and many old people drive very slowly, although the main roads on the "reservation" or "campus" (as we sometimes jokingly refer to the community) are very safe—in fact, some are basically like four-lane highways with both directions separated by greenery—but the speed limit is 25 miles an hour and Bernice and I tend to be among the hot rods, going at the dizzying speed of 35 to 40 mph, as long as a police car is not in sight.

Many old folks are crotchety and complain constantly about speed, despite the lack of accidents. These same drivers, however, weave around and over the road lane lines as they drive, fail to give signals for a turn, and make their turns to the right by moving all the way to the left, and vice-versa. Even on the roads off the reservation, we get stuck behind people driving 10 miles an hour below the speed limit on two-lane roads where passing is not possible. Rossmoor is a place at which it is best to be relaxed and easy-going. We are trying, but so far unsuccessfully, I guess because we still seem to be in a hurry, classic type-As.

PERSONALITY CHANGE FROM YOUTH TO OLD AGE

There is a widespread notion that when people age they get mellow, which usually means that they lose their fire and become relaxed and easy-going. There are, of course, many varieties of response to retirement and aging, and I was always struck by the evidence, weak though it is, that in institutions for the aged, mellow old people who accept their plight pleasantly, die sooner than those who are aggressive and complain.

I see few signs that my male friends and associates, or for that matter, the women in Rossmoor, most of them well over 70 and many in their 80's, have abandoned their competitiveness in the process of losing their earlier identity. Some, of course, were always mild and noncompetitive, but others want you to know they know what they are talking about, have substantial expertise, and can even be snide in putting you down if they think you are patronizing them. One's ego-identity, a lifetime of knowledge, and sometimes wisdom, all cultivated over the whole of life, don't easily get transformed, even by old age.

I suspect, and Bernice confirms, that I am just as competitive as I have always been, whether it's in pressing my point in a conversation or argument, or in driving. Maybe at 76, which is the age I'll be when this book appears, I am not yet old enough to withdraw from the fray, but my guess is that I will never be what is called mellow; worn out maybe, but not mellow, if by that one means bland. Except for the fact that they no longer work for a living, my elderly buddies are no different in spirit and outlook than my young ones. There seem to be many myths about us geezers, most of them inaccurate.

Allow me to make one more observation, which may sound like a complaint but is more a wistful thought about aging. When an old person like me gives a major talk or keynote address, he is apt to be appreciated more for what he has done in the past than for what he is doing now, or for just being alive and still active. We have little time left, so we are not going to be on the cutting edge much longer, and have little power to make much of a difference in the world. It's nice to be addressed with respect and regard, but there is often something subtly patronizing in it, which we must learn to understand and accept.

I began this account of my life with the theme, stated in the foreword, of a youthful conflict within myself between having abundant self-doubts and an opposing belief in my competence and future potential, even superiority. I also experienced a conflict between feeling I was an alien in the world, especially in the gentile community—but even among religious Jews whose zealotry I never trusted—and an opposing sanguinity that arose from my ambition and hope for the perfectibility of the human condition based on knowledge and reason. I wanted to be a great man and was inspired by examples of those I thought had achieved greatness.

What has happened to this conflict over the years? It is still there, though muted somewhat by age and experience. I never achieved greatness—I really didn't expect to—but I can certainly not complain about my status in my field. I have come to believe that the yearning to belong and be a part of the community endangers our distinctive identities. On the other hand, if we are self-serving and favor our own specialness, we also remain alien. This conflict is, I think, universal—that is, from babyhood we must all reconcile our distinctive identities and the contrary pressures to conform to society. Each of us tries to resolve this conflict in our own way.

I am reminded here of the views of Otto Rank, Erik Fromm, Karen Horney, and other neo-Freudian writers who recognized and elaborated on this type of conflict. In choosing to emphasize one side of it, we sacrifice something of the other. My own distinctive identity remains very important to me, making some degree of alienation inevitable.

I am aware of the fashionable distinction made these days between individualistic and collective societies. I think it is overdrawn in a period of politically correct multiculturalsm. Many in American society, however, long for more connection and community, and there are plenty of variations in so-called individualistic societies such as Japan. The cultural difference is probably more a matter of stated values than internalized outlooks by varying individuals; maybe also more a matter of degree than kind in the either-or sense (in support of this position, see Kim et al., 1994).

In any case, my solution to this inevitable conflict of accepting some degree of alienation, makes it easier for me to be critical of the human condition. I constantly ask how we can accept with equanimity the cruelty and indifference to the fate of others that is endemic in the world, and allow society to avoid responsibility. How can we accept the hatred of one group by another? And how can we serve only our own interests without also serving those of the community? I regard these questions as largely rhetorical, as my answer is that we cannot and still remain civilized.

The sense of alienation I felt keenly when I was in my late teens and as a young adult has abated somewhat, and my fervor to see things changed has cooled, though it has not disappeared. I am still offended by the ugliness of much of what I see in my species and the social conditions under which so large a proportion of humanity lives. And I still get much too riled up about this from time to time. But I know this sad condition of human life will not disappear in the remainder of my lifetime, and I have no sensible choice except to let it be, while holding to my personal standards as best I can. I can find no other sensible way.

HOW I OFFICIALLY RETIRED WITHOUT REALLY RETIRING

The problems of men and women in retirement overlap but are not necessarily the same. I speak here as a male, but as I am lucky to be a partner in an intact marriage after 53 years, let me first say something about our version of retirement.

We typically have lunch in local restaurants about 4 days a week. For me, it is a good break from reading and writing, and a chance to enjoy good company. Each week Bernice has lunch with friends, or sees our children and grandchildren and often shops with them. I too see our children and grandchildren fairly often, and from time to time we all go away together. Bernice often plays bridge with female friends, and has done volunteer work at the local hospital. Some years ago she taught math to returning women at the local community college.

We no longer go regularly to San Francisco to theater, but subscribe to the local theater and see the musicals and operas that come to Walnut Creek. We prefer plays, but they are now so poor that we prefer to miss most of them. We have the feeling that we have seen just about everything. These days what is available is apt to be repeats, whether in theater or TV, and there is very little worthwhile in entertainment for us any more. We both remember the halcyon days of Broadway in New York City, and for awhile in San Francisco when we first came here.

From time to time, for example, at Passover or Thanksgiving we make a big dinner for the family. In the spring of 1997, however, the

Passover party so exhausted Bernice, she has finally decided to give up on this tradition, which I have been urging her to do for some time. We go to our Delta home from time to time to boat, typically staying over Thursday and Friday nights, but increasingly this has become so physically taxing, and the community out there has become so crime ridden, that we have been reducing the frequency of these outings. I suppose we will sell the condo and boat one of these days.

One of our major problems is that Bernice has had a very serious auto-immune disease for about 15 years called Myasthenia Gravis, which is Latin meaning severe muscle weakness. This was another reason for our move to Rossmoor, perhaps the most important one. The disease actually breaks the connection at the synapse between her voluntary nerve impulses and the muscle. This saps her strength, makes it impossible for her to rise from sitting on the floor or a low sofa without pulling herself up by her arms. To compensate for this weakness, she must take a drug called mestinon, which helps for a few hours, but it is tricky; if it gets into her bloodstream too fast, for example, if she does not take it with food, her whole body cramps severely.

In recent months, she has gone downhill, with growing trouble breathing and swallowing. This poses the risk that food or saliva will enter her trachea and make her vulnerable to pneumonia. She also gets double vision, and has trouble talking when she needs a mestinon pill. These problems are expectable for this disease, and for a long time she has managed well despite it. We can both recognize the symptoms. Every 3 months now, she must spend 4 days as a hospital outpatient to obtain an intravenous infusion of a globulin type chemical, which seems to help for awhile.

She has had a wonderful attitude toward all this, determined to live until she dies, trying to do as much as she can. I worry about her more than she does, I think, especially when I know she is driving and is late to arrive home. At this writing, in the fall of 1997, we have just returned from an 18-day trip to Aarhus, Denmark, where I gave a number of lectures, and in Bamberg, Germany, where I addressed 150 European personality psychologists. When I saw her increasing physical problems, I tried to talk her out of the trip—I won't travel long distances without her any more—but I am convinced she truly wanted to go and would not hear of our cancelling the trip. She managed well. But I worry.

Bernice still does all the shopping, cooking, manages the household, and on Sunday she usually makes a dinner for the two of us, which I still enjoy immensely. Her major function, however, is still to be chancellor of the exchequer, paying bills, making deposits, and handling investment and tax issues. She reads most of what I write—for example, this autobiography, catching typos, confused sentences, checking out family facts, and advising me on sticky issues she has spotted. And she reads other books for her own pleasure. There is no one I love and trust more. And the thought that she might no longer be with me is a terrible one, which I try as much as possible to push into the background.

Mainly there are two kinds of men who retire at Rossmoor, whether or not the decision is voluntary. The first kind is tired of working and glad to have reached a point in life where working is no longer financially necessary. Many have socked away enough and invested it, or, like me, have an adequate pension. Their problems as retirees are to avoid being shunted off to a nonfunctional status in the world, and even more important, to avoid boredom.

They do a variety of things with their time. Living as I do in a community of the elderly, my impression is that many play golf or engage in other sports (the oldest lawn bowl, which makes limited physical demands). The golfers ride around the course in electric carts and get only limited exercise. Some walk regularly and briskly; not many run. Others swim. The tennis players and those who choose table tennis, as I do (at Rossmoor the tradition before I came was to call it table tennis rather than ping pong), get a good physical workout.

Others play bridge, take up elective managerial positions on Rossmoor boards, often doing for free what they did when they were employed, engage in volunteer teaching, provide hospital care for patients, cultivate various arts (one man in my building, who had been an architect, discovered he had a great talent for sculpting ceramic animals), or they take up other hobbies to keep busy. Most have families they visit, or that visit them. I often think many of the residents are, in a sense, waiting for death, though they are usually not in a hurry for it to come nor do they necessarily have an unpleasant time in the interim.

The second kind, and I fall within this group, are pleased to give up the most onerous features of their jobs, but remain active in their professions. Having spent my life cultivating and disseminating knowledge, and a way of thinking in my field, it seems unwise if not impossible, to turn off this commitment. I don't think I could find satisfaction in golf, table tennis, bridge, or boating in the Delta. They don't have enough substance to fulfill me or sustain my interest.

I need some relatively long-term project to engage me, and writing books and articles is my main solution. I work at writing 7 days a week, and am as productive in this as ever, maybe more. I find this a common pattern among my academic friends who have retired. The day I wrote this I picked up a fortune cookie at a Chinese restaurant that said "Idleness is the holiday of fools." What I like about this message is that it condemns idleness, not on the basis of moral values, but rather as a practical no-no.

I always wanted to write a play, but am skeptical that I could write a good one without a great deal of trial and error. I don't think I have enough time left to learn to do it well. I have always been thrilled by some of Arthur Miller's plays, especially *Death of a Salesman.* But the standard he sets is too high for me seriously to aspire to being a playwright at this late stage of my life. Shoemaker stick to your last; I'd rather do what I'm good at. Still, I have not completely abandoned the idea.

Years ago I painted and did pastel landscapes, some of which hang in our Rossmoor and Delta homes, and people wonder why I didn't go back to it. They seem to like what I painted, but in my opinion, this is not an area in which I have really significant talent, any more than I had the aptitude for piano, for which I took lessons, and found out I was pretty tone deaf. I would have to say, though, that play writing is an unfulfilled wish, but I assume everyone has such wishes. Bernice and I tried a novel, but failed to pull it off successfully. Who knows, maybe we'll try again.

I am often invited to go abroad to participate in conferences, and to give lectures and workshops in Europe, Asia, South America, or North Africa (mainly Israel), and although long trips are getting more and more difficult, they can still be a kick. We try to keep long-distance travel to once a year, and only if we can go together in business class to decrease the discomfort. We enjoy doing this, not because we are dedicated sightseers—we've travelled enough to have the feeling that most places are vaguely beginning to look alike—but to Bernice and me, people are more interesting than places.

We are up at 6 every morning, have breakfast, read the paper, walk the dog, and are at work by about 8. One day a week, I go to my office, give some work to a secretary, talk with students and faculty, have lunch with a colleague, then get back to my word processor to work on some book or other.

Every year since my retirement, a Berkeley colleague, Joe Campos, and I have held a series of colloquies with graduate students, visitors, and faculty members at the university, meeting for 2 hours every other week during the academic year. We chose the word colloquy to indicate a gathering for talk. We all read a chapter or a few articles and then discuss them in a freewheeling 2-hour session. Then Campos and I have a Chinese lunch of steamed fish.

Participants receive no academic credit, but the absence of a didactic commitment, and the opportunity for freewheeling discussion on interesting topics, seems to sustain considerable interest. One of the ironies is that, unfortunately, university life is not normally like this, with the exploration of ideas being rewarding intrinsically rather than extrinsically as a means to an end.

In 1988, two years before I retired, Paul Ekman and I applied to the NIMH for support for a postdoctoral training program in emotion, which had emerged as a hot field. Our objective was to facilitate the education of interested young psychologists about emotion in hopes they would begin to staff psychology departments throughout the country, in keeping with the new status of emotion. Paul did the yeoman's job putting the application together, and I contributed substantially to the application, particularly in planning the weekly seminar that was one of the educational foundations of the program.

The grant provided stipends for six postdocs and travel funds for 10 faculty of diverse outlooks. Each was to come to Berkeley from all over the country for a week to present their work and ideas and meet with the trainees. The program was funded and began in the late summerfall of 1989. Later incarnations of the program involved faculty changes, though a basic core remained.

No salaries were provided for the faculty, but the intellectual excitement attendant on the program and its educational challenges were sufficient reward. Quite a few other graduate students of the department were also allowed to participate in the weekly 2-hour seminar, which I led in the first year, and these meetings were attended regularly by several Berkeley faculty members.

The total program lasted for 3 years. After the first year, trainees chose one of the faculty members to work with in his or her own laboratory for the next 2 years. A second 3-year program was approved in 1992, still housed at Berkeley, the year after my retirement. I continued to participate because it stimulated me and allowed me to continue to relate to the issues of my field. The third round later moved from Berkeley to Madison, Wisconsin.

A new professional activity in which I have sometimes engaged during my retirement is to serve as a consultant or expert witness in litigation that involves issues of stress and emotion. This had actually begun many years before in connection with the My Lai massacre in 1969 during the Vietnam War. As an expert in stress, I was asked by the attorney appointed to defend the enlisted men who participated in the killings for advice about the handling of the upcoming trial. An officer, Lieutenant Calley, had already been tried and sentenced to prison, but he never served much time. The enlisted men's trial was abandoned by the government, probably because they appeared to be too much like victims themselves, given the conditions of combat they had to face, and it might have been viewed as shameful to try soldiers drafted to fight in a bad war.

Some of the other cases on which I have given opinions more recently include a court action defended by the State Bar of Texas to adjudicate a constitutional issue. A recent state law had made it illegal to approach an accident victim for 30 days on the grounds that they would be emotionally unable to make a considered judgment. This law was being fought by some lawyers, medical doctors, and chiropractors whose rights, they argued, were being abridged. I testified in the hearing in Houston, but the judge ruled the law unconstitutional in Texas, though it has been upheld in other states.

I was later hired as an expert witness in a case of plagiarism in which the plaintiff complained his ideas had been stolen illegally by another professional whose book was based heavily on my client's original writings, without credit being given. It was an egregious case of plagiarism without any effort to conceal it. I gave my analysis to the attorney involved and the case was settled out of court.

A more recent case involved a suit against someone whose late-night intrusion on Halloween onto the plaintiff's property frightened the plaintiff badly, or so he claimed. The intrusion led to a self-inflicted accident and the plaintiff sought damages for no longer being able to perform his job properly. I consulted for the defense. That case too was settled out of court. I find these cases interesting from a psychological standpoint, and I am also very well paid for the time I spend.

Since retirement, I have published 5 books and 14 other pieces, mostly book chapters, theoretical or meta-theoretical journal articles, a few empirical articles, and several critical reviews of the work of others. Over the years since 1948 when I obtained my first academic job, I published nearly 19 books (some edited), over 200 articles of all kinds, 8 of which are reviews, 5 encyclopedia articles, and 2 test manuals. Most have already been mentioned in earlier chapters. Two additional articles, one dealing with coping with aging that was given as a lecture in Aarhus, Denmark (Lazarus, in press a), the other a treatment of coping from the perspective of personality that was given as a lecture in Bamberg, Germany (Lazarus, in press b), are being readied for publication.

One of my recent books (Lazarus, 1991a) is a substantial monograph on the emotions. A second, which Bernice and I wrote together (Lazarus & Lazarus, 1994), is a trade book on emotion, designed for nonprofessionals, which is also used as an undergraduate text. A third is a selective anthology of reprinted articles over my 50 years of research and writing (Lazarus, 1978). It contains freshly written interstitial material discussing where the research issues came from, how the work was received, what happened during the intervening years, and how the field and my own views evolved and changed. This book is a kind of history lesson, built around the topics on which I have done research. A fourth book since retirement is this autobiography. The fifth is a sequel to the 1984 book I published with Folkman, which will probably take another year to be completed. It has the working title *The Stress Emotions: From the Standpoint of Appraisal and Coping Theory.*

EXISTENTIAL ISSUES

Not long ago, I had an unusual conversation with Ira Reiss, my wife's cousin, who is a recently retired sociology professor from the University of Minnesota. Every year, he and his wife Harriet come here as a kind of summer vacation in the winter to escape the Minneapolis deep freeze. We talked about how we intended to live our last years. Ira knows that I believe there is no life after death—in my view, life ends with oblivion—and so he raised the searching question of why it should still be important for me at this stage of life to continue to influence psychological thought. According to his challenge, if I am not going to be around to see how it is responded to, and because I'll be unable to care about anything after I'm dead, what then is the purpose of all this dedicated work?

It's an interesting and challenging question. Without much hesitation I responded more or less as follows: Since I am still alive, I still care, though it obviously won't matter to me when I'm dead. My commitment to certain ideas and values is strong and I want to leave them for posterity. For better or worse, its my mark on the future, which still matters while I am alive, even if I won't be around to see how it all works out. Maybe that's just as well.

It's as if someone were to ask me whether or not I care about my children's and grandchildren's futures. I won't be here to see what happens to them, but while I'm alive I care deeply that they will have a good life. I'd love to be aware of what they are doing, but that's impossible. So whether or not I'm around to see it is neither here nor there.

But there is another very important reason for working hard so close to the end of my life, and it is the most important of all. The satisfaction derived from work lies mainly in the *process of doing it* rather than the outcome. It's true that the motivation for such work would be muted by the belief that my work would be negatively evaluated, or even worse, ignored, so its outcome is not entirely irrelevant. To be fully motivated, I need to believe my work might have value—but this is not the main reason for my continuing effort. Being engaged in work now—in effect, doing it—is the essential reason.

On the other hand, if the books on which I am now working are published in the near future, and my health remains okay, the work will appear while I'm still able to appreciate what happens to it. I take this to be a good reason to progress with reasonable speed so I will still be around to enjoy the fruits of what I do. The income earned no longer means much to me, but I still negotiate the best contract I can get so my children and grandchildren might enjoy some of it too.

The essential point I am making is that the here and now, and the immediate future, are what counts in our lives, not so much the past. If there is no future to look forward to, even a short one, there is little basis for any excitement in living. One cannot live on past glories. I enjoyed the honors I received for awhile, but this enjoyment soon dissipates. Allow me to elaborate on this theme a bit further.

In addition to the two honorary degrees I mentioned in chapter 10, an example of what I have just said is an honor I received in 1989 with the following awkward phraseology: *Distinguished Scientific Contribution Award* of the American Psychological Association (APA).

I think of this as one of the highest honors the APA gives. In the main, only three psychologists have received it each year since 1956 and their names provide a who's who of modern psychology, and I'm thrilled to be in their company. I studied the works of many of these psychologists as a graduate student. Typically, one of the three awards is given to a physiological psychologist, another to a hard scientist type, say, in cognition or developmental psychology, or a related subfield, and a third is in personality, social, or basic clinical research. My presence on the list makes me feel proud, especially in light of the fact that the psychologists on the softer side of the field outnumber the hard-science types, so the competition I had to face was greater. Before I won the APA award, Donald Meichenbaum had nominated me for the Gold Medal for scientific achievement of the American Psychological Foundation (APF). Arranging for a nomination is quite a bit of work, because it requires many enthusiastic recommendations by eminent research psychologists. Nothing came of this effort, except that Don later sent me the letters with the kind thought that reading them would be reward in itself, which it was.

The Distinguished Scientific Contribution Award also requires that one be nominated, and in 1988 a committee of several members of my Department took on this task. It included Al Riley, then the departmental

Chair, Gerry Mendelsohn, and my junior research colleague Susan Folkman, who did most of the work of putting the nomination letter together. Most psychologists are not aware of how the award process works. A standing committee of the APA reviews these nominations and obtains letters of those qualified to make an evaluation.

I should say here that this action by my department greatly mitigated some of the negative feelings I have expressed in earlier chapters. I might add the fact that, as an emeritus professor, I receive a number of benefits from the Psychology Department, which I truly appreciate, though they are also a quid pro quo in that my continuing scholarly efforts also add to the department's luster. The benefits include the privilege, especially in a time of scarce resources, of continuing to occupy my office, some secretarial help when I need it—in short supply for everyone, including those still teaching—office supplies, and the good cheer of a pleasant greeting when I make my weekly visits. And if I apply for it, I can receive a modest research grant of up to $1,000 a year for nonequipment expenses attendant on my scholarly efforts. All this helps to create a favorable retirement situation.

I'm afraid, however, that with space at a premium, I may have to give up my office, or share it with someone else (which would not be so bad), but I must accept the reality of growing old in a society that has no place for anyone who is not young and up-and-coming. I remember being the promising young man, but suddenly, without warning, I became an older one that had to give way to the next generation. And given the widespread condition of urban centers, the commute to Berkeley from Walnut Creek has become daunting.

To return to the APA award, however, the personnel of the awards committee changes periodically and, as I understand it, one of its members must offer detailed and enthusiastic support for a nominee to help convince the others of his or her merit. I am not purview to the actual process in my case, or who my competitors were, but I got the award, and I'm very pleased to have it.

Word that I had been given the award arrived while Bernice and I were in Heidelberg, Germany. My obligations there made it impossible for me to return to the United States to accept it formally at the APA meeting in 1989. As was the normal custom, however, I gave the formal award address at the APA meeting in Boston a year later in 1990. I was introduced by my Berkeley faculty colleague, Mark Rosenzweig, who had been a prior winner. The address I gave orally was published the next year in the *American Psychologist* (Lazarus, 1991b). Some of the graduate students of the Berkeley Stress and Coping Project were there and we celebrated it afterward with a lunch at the headquarter's hotel.

But now here is the point of this illustration. It was a touching moment for me. At this lunch, students asked me how I felt about it, and I gave them my standard answer, which is that I was initially thrilled, though I empathized with all the other psychologists who deserved it (perhaps even more than I), but didn't receive it. But it had been a year since I first got the news, and though I basked in the satisfaction it generated for a few months, I told them it had receded into the background of my life and no longer could sustain me in the present. I needed to remain committed to current concerns, and I wanted an encore in the form of new work that I could be proud of. This is still true.

Despite my emphasis on present and future, I look back on my life with a good feeling. I am pleased, in the main, that what I've done has integrity and appears valuable to others. The qualifying phrase, "in the main," is simply an acknowledgment that we often have to make compromises with the realities of our lives and times. The proud claim "I did it my way" inevitably contains some denial. I'm satisfied I tried the best I could to achieve excellence, and was well rewarded. But it is not enough to live in the past.

What happens now? The candid truth is that I fear death, or I should say, I fear the end of "me." This fear is not mitigated by the thought I might be remembered. For me, being remembered doesn't solve the problem of dying. I don't share the conviction that my soul, which I take to mean my distinctive identity, knowledge, awareness, and products, will survive. That conviction, born of one of several forms of religious mythology, which people construct as an antidote to the dread of dying, cannot reassure me, though I would have liked to believe in such a reassurance. I also have no truck with the snide idea that there are no atheists in the foxhole where men are facing death; this is a naked and false put-down of those who do not accept the standard religious wisdom.

I know too that even believers commonly experience considerable doubt about what will happen after death. Nor can I look deep into their hearts and minds to know how much genuine confidence that consciousness does not end forever with death, which some gain from these beliefs. For whatever reasons—the main one being the human capacity to conceive of a self that has a past, present, and future, and to reflect on life—all humanity has always had to deal with the temporary nature of existence.

I suppose that people who believe in a hereafter experience considerable fear about going to hell or purgatory. When I lived in the deep South, I remember hearing Baptist ministers on the radio who waxed very eloquent about what would happen to their listeners if they sinned and were unrepentant. The preachers sought to frighten people about the terrible consequences of hell. But I don't believe in hell, though I can certainly imagine it in this life.

I also hear people speak about being "God-fearing Christians" in a world of sinners. I guess they fear the wrath of God, which has no meaning for me except as a reflection of childhood monsters, a fear suitable for nightmares rather than waking life. And I have always enjoyed the sardonic ditty "Oh he goes to church on Sunday, so they call him an honest man." I mean no disrespect by this to those with sincere religious beliefs; my barbs, as were those of Jesus, are meant for religious hypocrites, and they are legion.

I have often run into the notion that as one ages one should prepare oneself for death. I disagree. I have come to believe that avoidance—but not denial—is the best solution, at least for me. I have not been able to find any serviceable way to prepare, except not to think too much about it, and when I do, as now, it is in a psychologically dis-tanced way. I have not been able to find any utility in being preoccu-pied with death. Though I am not happy about it, I acknowledge my ultimate fate, so what I am saying is not a denial. I may or may not be taken by surprise when my time comes, but maybe surprise is better than just waiting.

There is a current psychological theory, called *terror management* (TMT) (Pyszczynski, Greenberg, & Solomon, 1997), the main theme of which is that coping with the terror of death is the master motive. Terror is really not the right word for the dread of death, however, as it is usually limited to rare moments in which one senses the immi-nence of one's demise—for example, when the airplane on which one is traveling is on fire or dives suddenly out of control. In my view, *exis-tential anxiety* (a highly redundant phrase that could, I think, be reduced to anxiety alone) is an older and more reasonable term. A full treatment of this emotion must include existential considerations. But whether this is *the* basic emotional motive, it is, without a doubt, a ter-ribly important and pervasive one.

What is particularly interesting about this theory is the effort to bring the issue of death, which plays such an important role in human existence, to the forefront of attention and discussion in psychology. It is remarkable that in most of academic psychology there is so little ref-erence to how people deal with the awareness of their mortality. An exception is Becker's (1973) Pulitzer-prize-winning book on the denial of death. The denial is accomplished by means of efforts to construct monuments or works of all kinds, which might serve as transcendent markers of our brief moment on earth. And as Mikulincer and Florian

(1997) note in a critique of TMT, there are other exceptions to the common failure to give a central role to death anxiety in our lives, such as the writings of Carl Jung (1933), and of existentialists like Frankl (1959) and Heidegger (1962).

Mikulincer and Florian make the very important point that denial is not the only way people deal with death. Individual differences in the personal meaning of death abound, and in how people cope with it. The awareness of the inevitability of death can have positive effects on the way people live their lives and may increase their appreciation of their existence. It can also have the opposite effect, as illustrated by the Theater of the Absurd, in which life is viewed as a meaningless absurdity, a sardonic joke. Some notable examples are the writings of Samuel Beckett, author of *Waiting For Godot,* and Eugene Ionesco, author of *Rhinoceros.*

Mikulincer and Florian (1997, p. 35) also point out that coping strategies depend on whether: "One's thoughts and acts throughout life will be punished or rewarded in the hereafter [as in Christianity], but they probably lose their validity in those religions (e.g., Judaism) that see behavioral and moral obligations in life as the main goal for human beings and not necessarily as a means for death transcendence."

The question of how people view their mortality and cope with it reminds me of an appearance I made some years ago, when I was still relatively young, on the public television program, "Over Easy," which was hosted by Hugh Downs. This program was devoted to the problems of aging and old age, and I was asked to talk about the coping process.

What I had long noticed about this program, however, is that it never presented aging and its problems in realistic terms, but always talked about it in an upbeat fashion, as if most old people really wanted to see only examples of the exceptional aged who seemed happy, heroic, or were portrayed as having transcended the physical and psychological losses that result from old age.

When I talked with one of the program directors, I told her I was not sanguine about the constant upbeat emphasis of the series. I suspected that many old people with a dour sense of their own infirmities and future prospects felt even more depressed about the conditions of their lives after watching the show. For many old people, to constantly see others who seem to have wonderful lives, while their's are so negative, is a downer, the wrong message to give on every program.

I'm sure many in the audience would have preferred to view things as they are, or at least see a realistically balanced picture of both the good and the bad, rather than to have their own suffering repeatedly trivialized. Although I urged her to consider an approach that was less centered on denial and more on the realities of aging and the options for managing its problems, and she seemed responsive, the policy was never changed. The program ultimately disappeared from television though, of course, I am not suggesting it was for this reason.

MY VISION FOR PSYCHOLOGY

I have been critical of psychology as a discipline in this book, and it seems to me that the best way to end this chapter would be to sum up how I think psychology could and should change in the future. I would be happy if it showed real signs of changing in my lifetime, but given the stakes that so many establishment people have in the system as it is, I consider this almost out of the question. In basic accord with the epistemological points made by Jessor (1996), which I cited in chapter 4, but putting my own spin on them, and at the risk of repeating myself, here is my *wish list* for a psychology of the future. Most of it has been said by others at one time or another, but seldom heeded.

1. First and foremost, a modern psychology must cease being so reluctant to think in terms of human *subjectivity*. We should be less afraid of concepts like intention and purpose, as much of what we think, feel, and do is impelled, not from the past, but by a sense of the future. This applies whether the source of data is what a person reports or arises as inferences drawn from multiple kinds of data—for example, the way an environmental condition is being responded to, observable actions, physiological changes, or introspective reports.

I acknowledge that what people say about themselves and why they behave as the do is subject to all kinds of distortion, but the problems of interpretation are just as great with other data sources. No single type of data represents a methodological gold standard, though combining them is important. Be that as it may, it is the personal meaning of what is happening that drives how we think, feel, and act, and this meaning depends on both the external conditions being faced and properties of the person, especially established goals and beliefs and situational intentions. Instead of constantly beating our breasts about the limitations of self-report, we should try to improve our use of it and, for that matter, any other data source we have available.

2. As psychologists, and social scientists in general, we must tone down our penchant for normative research and thought, which has dominated our field. Too much of psychology is about *people in general*, and too little about *individual and group variation*. Most of our

research has been directed to large, representative samples, thereby forcing psychology to fit itself into the reasoning of epidemiology, which is an important field, but if followed slavishly, distorts what psychology should be about.

The consequence of this pattern is we have lost a sense of the whole person with an individual history and life trajectory. We seldom study individuals in depth programmatically. Instead we have made psychology into a weak imitation of the physical sciences, having fallen in love with causal variables, which is an outlook that makes it difficult to view persons as complex and integrated beings, operating within larger systems.

3. By constructing a psychology of variables, we have forgotten the most important theme in psychology, that an individual's thoughts, feelings, and actions derive from ongoing relationships with a physical and social environment. We need a *language of relationships,* more than one of causal variables. We need to move from a psychology of interaction to a psychology of transaction or *relational meaning,* which I believe should be the most important construct of psychological analysis. Psychologists must come to see that science is defined not only by reductive causal analysis but also by efforts to resynthesize mind into holistic units, which operate at a higher level of abstraction and correspond more to the phenomena of life as these are observed. As John Dewey (e.g., Dewey & Bentley, 1949) argued, and I have too in the Dewey tradition (Lazarus, 1997), a full understanding requires both analysis *and* synthesis. One supplements the other.

4. In keeping with the outlook I am proposing, psychology should also give up its obsession with the laboratory experiment, and the large-sample survey, and give equal or more attention to field research under natural conditions. We should be more skeptical of the validity of what is found in experiments with confederates, which typically use deception and fail to convince participating subjects that they are in a scientific alliance with the experimenter in a search for knowledge. At the very least, we should be more open to a variety of methods, and wary of a single method variance.

Because of limitations and lack of detail in our theories, we are not in a good position to deduct precisely what should be observed in our research. Therefore, it is an affectation to speak of hypothetico-deductive research that is said to prove or disprove this or that idea. We are kidding ourselves if we are confident that such research reliably confirms or disconfirms what we learn about mind and behavior, or that we ever prove or disprove anything in our laboratories, especially when it comes to psycho- and sociodynamic issues. We should approach our observations more in the spirit of discovery than proof.

5. With respect to a renewed focus on individual differences, too much of psychology research today is without context. We must, in the future, soft-pedal our excessive emphasis on universal mechanisms, an outlook derived from the physical sciences where they apply better, and take more account of the particular settings in which the processes occur.

6. Many of the truly important issues we need to be concerned about have to do with the long-term patterns of development and change, and the trajectories we display as persons over a lifetime. This means doing more longitudinal research and biographical or narrative studies of individual persons and types, which an increasing number of psychologists have been calling for in recent years.

7. If psychology's original interest in longitudinal methods, which permit the study of stability and change, is renewed, researchers should give more attention to *process* and change than to *structure* and stability, which our field has generally favored. Psychometrics must be tailored to the idea that what we think, feel, and do is responsive to different contexts and temporal progression, and our research designs and measurements should be capable of reflecting this. This is particularly true within the subjects of stress, emotion, and coping—in effect, when adaptation is our concern, these subjects imply the need to change a condition that is either unsatisfactory or dysfunctional.

8. In addition to longitudinal research, which can cover large extensions of time and have a broad scope, we should also be looking at phenomena of the mind in depth. We need to be open to and allow for the operation of unconscious processes, especially the dynamic unconscious, which depends on ego-defense processes. That they are out of vogue in social and personality psychology is unfortunate. Unconscious processes—that bugaboo of behaviorism—are too important to be allowed to languish, despite the methodological problems they pose. Awkward though unconscious processes are for our theories, no psychology of mind and behavior can be complete without taking them into account.

With respect to the dynamics of stress and the emotions, I would like to suggest that there should also be short-term longitudinal studies in which emotional encounters are looked at closely, microgenetically, which is apt to be the best way to examine how emotions are aroused and changed. Couples having an argument, transactions between mothers and their children, and other charged encounters might be photographed and played back in an effort to explore exactly what happened and what was in the mind of the persons who are interacting. The clinical method is especially well suited for this kind of research approach.

Long-term longitudinal studies are probably better for other types of questions. They are needed especially when we want to know how prolonged stress might affect health, such as cancer and heart disease, which are slow to develop. Because these effects depend on sustained or recurrent stress emotions, rather than on brief emotional episodes, as in emergencies, which we are biologically capable of weathering without bodily harm, this kind of research undoubtedly needs to span many years.

9. We also need to be open to diverse models of mind and behavior, without fear or favor. We spend too much time in either-or testing whether this or that single explanation best explains the data. What we think, feel, and do is usually overdetermined, and more than one process or set of variables contributes to what we observe. The same thought, feeling, or action has multiple functions, each contributing a piece of the action. The same act serves different needs. Without a great deal more precision in our theories, either-or thinking is not likely to be the most fruitful way of trying to understand mind and behavior.

The gatekeepers of our field, journal reviewers and editors, need to be statespersons and more even handed and friendly to different methods and approaches. They should cease pressing researchers to rewrite their articles to fit the editors' or reviewers' dogmas about good science. By all means, help authors, but if they have done sound work, they alone should be responsible for interpreting what they found and for what they write.

It would be a mistake to think from what I am saying that I am advocating careless or sloppy observation or methods of analysis. The quality of our observations, as well as the reasoning that lies behind it, are crucial to valid understanding. But measurement needs vary with the phenomena and meta-theoretical outlook being employed, and the development of the best procedures of measurement should be progressive rather than static.

10. We should expect researchers in psychology to replicate their findings, and approach issues programmatically rather than seeking quick publication. We are now inundated by too much in the way of findings that fail to build on past work. Few of us are capable of assimilating the huge volume of what is today being published and, no doubt, much of it will disappear in a pile of rubbish, without having advanced our understanding of the human psyche.

At this stage of my professional life, I am struggling with a radically different way of studying the human emotions, an approach that has been proposed in recent years by a number of others (e.g., Bruner,

1990; Gergen, & Gergen, 1986; Josselson & Lieblich, 1993; McAdams, 1996; Sarbin, 1986; Schafer, 1981; & Spence, 1982). This is an outlook that has become increasingly popular in recent years. Consistent with my emphasis on the core relational themes that distinguish different emotions, I am increasingly convinced that a scientifically viable and productive way to do research on the emotions would be to examine the prototypical versions of emotions, such as anger, and its variants—for example, righteous anger, disdain or contempt, gloating, pouting, and so on. These variants should be indicative of antecedent person and environmental variables that transform protopical emotions into a variant, or into a totally different emotion, such as anxiety, guilt, shame, or relief.

A fortune cookie in a Chinese restaurant at which I recently ate wisely stated that "Discontent is the first step in the progress of a man or a nation." I am tempted to rephrase this to say that discontent is badly needed in a field that is suffering from arrogance, stultification, and ossification. The future well-being of the human species is tied to the way psychology understands and addresses what must be done to improve its lot, which seems to be in a sorry shape. The world has never had a greater need for a vital and effective discipline of psychology. We need to do better.

As a last word in this personal and professional story, I would love to have the opportunity to return in a hundred years to see what psychology has become, but it might be depressing to do so, because we may continue to travel down the same unproductive path. Lest this sound too pessimistic, I am mildly encouraged to find more voices in the social sciences than ever before that are critical of the way our field is progressing, and that advocate variants of the points suggested here and throughout this book.

Psychology is too important to leave to narrow-minded people without imagination, or those who evade the most important questions about mind and behavior because they are methodologically difficult to address. Despite my criticism of its present condition, as a field of inquiry psychology it is still for me the richest and most challenging intellectual arena, and the one with the greatest potential application to human well-being.

REFERENCES

Becker, E. (1973). *The denial of death.* New York: Free Press.
Beckett, S. (1954). *Waiting for Godot.* New York: Grove Press.

Bruner, J. S. (1990). *Acts of meaning.* Cambridge, MA: Harvard University Press.

Dewey, J., & Bentley, A. E. (1949). *Knowing an the known.* Boston: Beacon Press.

Frankl, V. (1959). *Man's search for meaning.* Boston: Beacon.

Gergen, K. J., & Gergen, M. M. (1986). Narrative form and the construction of psychological science. In T. R. Sarbin (Ed.), *Narrative psychology: The storied nature of human conduct* (pp. 22–44). New York: Praeger.

Heidegger, M. *Being and time.* (Translated by J. Macquarrie and E. Robinson). New York: Harper & Row.

Ionesco, E. (1960). *Rhinoceros* (2nd ed.). (R. Y. Ellison & S. Goding). New York: Holt, Rinehart, & Winston.

Jessor, R. (1996). Ethnographic methods in contemporary perspective. In R. Jessor, A. Colby, & R. A. Shweder (Eds.), *Ethnography and human development: Context and meaning in social inquiry* (pp. 3–14). Chicago: University of Chicago Press.

Josselson, R., & Lieblich, A. (Eds.). (1993). *The narrative study of lives.* Newbury Park, CA: Sage.

Jung, C. G. (1933). *Modern man in search of a soul.* New York: Harcourt, Brace, & World.

Kim, U., Triandis, H. C., Kâgitçibasi, C., Choi, S-C., Yoon, G. (Eds.), *Individualism and collectivism: Theory, method, and applications.* Thousand Oaks, CA: Sage.

Lazarus, R. S. (1991a). *Emotion and adaptation.* New York: Oxford University Press.

Lazarus, R. S. (1991b). Cognition and motivation in emotion. *American Psychologist, 46,* 352–367.

Lazarus, R. S. (1997). *Fifty years of the research and theory of R. S. Lazarus: Perennial historical issues.* Mahwah, NJ: Erlbaum.

Lazarus, R. S. (in press a). Coping with aging: A problem of misdirected research. In I. H. Nordhus, G. Vandenbos, S. Berg, and P. Fromholt, Eds.). *Clinical Geropsychology.*

Lazarus, R. S. (in press b). Coping from the perspective of personality. *Zeitschrift für Differentielle und Diagnostische Psycholgie.*

Lazarus, R. S., & Folkman, S. (1984). *Stress, appraisal, and coping.* New York: Springer.

Lazarus, R. S., & Lazarus, B. N. (1994). *Passion and reason: Making sense of our emotions.* New York: Oxford.

McAdams, D. P. (1996). Personality, modernity, and the storied self: A contemporary framework for studying persons. *Psychological Inquiry, 7,* 295–321.

Mikulincer, M., & Florian, V. (1997). Do we really know what we need? A commentary on Pyszczynski, Greenberg, and Solomon. *Psychological Inquiry, 8,* 33–36.

Pyszczyski, T., Greenberg, J., & Solomon, S. (1997). Why do we need what we need? A terror management perspective on the rots of human social motivation. *Psychological Inquiry, 8,* 1–71.

Sarbin, T. (Ed.). (1986). *Narrative psychology: The storied nature of human conduct.* New York: Praeger.

Schafer, R. (1981). Narration in the psychoanalytic dialogue. In W. J. J. Mitchell (Ed.). *On narrative* (pp. 25–49). Chicago: University of Chicago Press.

Shneidman, E. (1989). The Indian Summer of life: A preliminary study of septuagenarians. *American Psychologist, 44,* 684–694.

Spence, D. (1982). *Narrative truth and historical truth.* New York: Norton.

Name Index

Subject Index